SOUTHERN COUNTRY
HOME PLANS

300 PLANS

Historic Colonials to Contemporary Favorites

HOME PLANNERS, LLC
Wholly owned by Hanley-Wood, LLC
Tucson, Arizona
www.eplans.com

SOUTHERN COUNTRY HOME PLANS

Published by Home Planners, LLC
Wholly owned by Hanley-Wood, LLC
3275 W. Ina Road, Suite 110
Tucson, Arizona 85741

Distribution Center:
29333 Lorie Lane
Wixom, Michigan 48393

President—Jayne Fenton
Vice President, Group Content—Jennifer Pearce
Editor in Chief—Jan Prideaux
Managing Editor—Vicki Frank
Editor—Morenci Wodraska
Plans Editor—Nick Nieskes
Graphic Designer—Paul Fitzgerald
Graphic Production Artist—Teralyn Morriss
Senior Production Manager—Sara Lisa
Production Manager—Brenda McClary

Photo Credits
Front Cover: Design HPT750005 by Stephen Fuller, Inc., for details see page 9.
Photo by Visual Solutions, photography courtesy of Stephen Fuller, Inc.

Back Cover: Design HPT750004 by Donald A. Gardner Architects, Inc.,
for details see page 8. ©1997 Donald A. Gardner Architects, Inc.,
Photography courtesy of Donald A. Gardner Architects, Inc.

©2002 First Printing

10 9 8 7 6 5 4 3 2 1

Printed in the United States of America

Library of Congress Catalog Card Number: 2002102762
ISBN softcover: 1-931131-06-6

TABLE OF CONTENTS

ABOUT THE DESIGNERS

Andy McDonald Design Group

Andy McDonald, CPBD, is a residential designer whose scrupulous regard for scale, balance and historical detailing has earned him a stellar reputation. His classic designs have won many awards and are a rapidly rising force in the home design industry. Andy McDonald is located in Madisonville, Louisiana, a stimulating milieu for his historically significant architecture.

Archival Designs

David Marc Loftus of Archival Designs, Inc. has celebrated fifteen years in the residential design business. His firm has been growing at an accelerated rate because his designs reflect the collective wisdom of the past. His award-winning style is called "Classic Traditional."

Authentic Historical Designs, Inc.

Authentic Historical Designs was begun by two partners with a long history of creating stock house plans for the Victorian housing market, Cecilia Reese Bullock and Mike Stephens. Located in Jackson, Mississippi, the company is nationally respected for its dedication to authenticity. While their homes look like older homes, all floor plans are designed to accommodate modern lifestyles.

Breland & Farmer Designers

Designer Edsel Breland is the owner and president of Breland & Farmer Designers, Inc., which he founded in 1973. The homes designed by Breland have a definite Southern signature, but fit perfectly in any region.

Chatham Home Planning, Inc.

Chatham Home Planning, Inc., founded over 15 years ago, is a professional member of the AIBD and the National Association of Home Builders. The company specializes in designs that have a strong historical look; early American, Southern cottages, Georgian classics, French Colonials, Southern Louisiana designs and traditional homes.

Design Basics, Inc.

For nearly a decade, Design Basics, a nationally recognized home design service in Omaha, has been developing plans for custom homebuilders. Since 1987, the firm has consistently appeared in Builder magazine, the official magazine of the National Association of Home Builders, as one of the top-selling designers.

Donald A. Gardner Architects, Inc.

The South Carolina firm of Donald A. Gardner was established in response to a growing demand for residential designs that reflect constantly changing lifestyles. The company's specialty is providing homes with refined custom-style details and unique features such as passive-solar designs and open floor plans.

Frank Betz Associates, Inc.

Frank Betz Associates, Inc., located in Smyrna, Georgia, is one of the nation's leaders in the design of stock plans. FBA, Inc. has provided builders and developers with home plans since 1977.

Greg Marquis & Associates

The designs of Greg Marquis have been proven to be popular not only across the United States, but internationally as well. He is a native of New Orleans, and many of his designs incorporate various features of the architectural style of South Louisiana.

Home Design Alternatives, Inc.

Lawrence Rigg, designer, has 40 years of experience in residential design. Growing up in the home building trade, Larry's experience includes 25 years with a prominent St. Louis architect/homebuilder.

Home Design Services

Home Design Services is a full-service design firm that has specialized in residential and multi-family design for thirty years. The firm offers a full complement of services, taking a project from concept through completed construction documents.

Home Planners

Headquartered in Tucson, Arizona, with additional offices in Detroit, Home Planners is one of the longest running and most successful home design firms in the United States. With over 2,500 designs in its portfolio, the company provides a wide range of styles, sizes and types of homes for the residential builder.

Jannis Vann & Associates

Jannis Vann is the president and principle designer of Jannis Vann & Associates, Inc. in Woodstock, Georgia. She has been in business since 1982 and has been publishing since 1987. Her collection showcases traditional, country and European exteriors with contemporary, open flowing interiors.

Larry E. Belk Designs

Through the years, Larry E. Belk has worked with individuals and builders alike to provide a quality product. Flowing, open spaces and interesting angles define his interiors. Great emphasis is placed on providing views that showcase the natural environment.

Larry James & Associates

Larry James has been designing classic homes since 1972. His goal is to create a collection of timeless designs. He likes to design new homes that trigger pleasant memories of times-gone-by. "21st Century living wrapped in a turn-of-the-Century package." He strives to design beautiful homes that will never fade.

Looney Ricks Kiss Architects

Established in 1983, Looney Ricks Kiss is a full-service architectural, interior design, planning and research firm with offices in Memphis, Nashville and Princeton. Their design focus encompasses the full integration of market awareness, land planning and architecture. More than 190 regional and national awards attest to their design excellence.

Nelson Design Group

Michael E. Nelson is a certified member of the American Institute of Building Designers, providing both custom and stock residential home plans. He designs homes that families enjoy now and which also bring maximum appraisal value at resale.

The Sater Design Collection

The Sater Design Collection has a long established tradition of providing South Florida's most diverse and extraordinary custom designed homes. This is exemplified by over 50 national design awards, numerous magazine features and, most important, satisfied clients.

Select Home Designs

Select Home Designs has 50 years of experience delivering top-quality and affordable residential designs to the North American housing market. Since the company's inception in 1948, more than 350,000 new homes throughout North America and overseas have been built from Select's plans.

Stephen Fuller, Inc.

Stephen S. Fuller established Stephen Fuller, Inc. with the tenets of innovation, quality, originality and uncompromising architectural techniques in traditional and European homes. Especially popular throughout the Southeast, Stephen Fuller's plans are known for their extensive detail and thoughtful design.

Studer Residential Designs, Inc.

Studer Residential Designs, Inc. was founded in 1971. Brothers Mike and Paul Studer base their design strategy on the idea that families desire serviceable floor plans with skillfully detailed interiors and exteriors that reflect the homeowner's excellent taste, as well as providing lasting value to their homes.

This home, as shown in the photograph, may differ from the actual blueprints.
For more detailed information, please check the floor plans carefully.

Photo by Ron Kerr, Kerr Studios—Atlanta

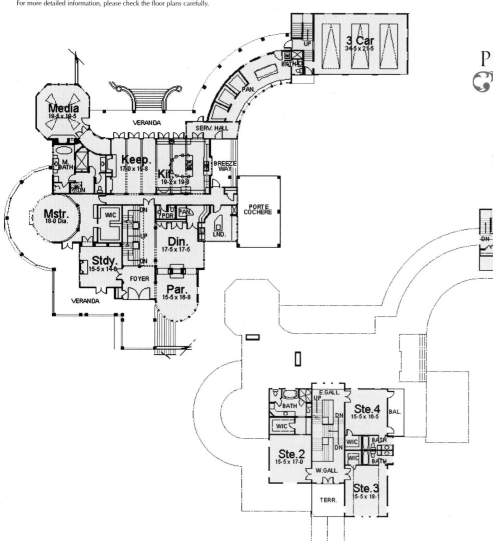

PLAN HPT750001

First Floor: 4,383 square feet
Second Floor: 1,557 square feet
Total: 5,940 square feet
Apartment: 788 square feet
Width: 148'-8" Depth: 120'-5"

Victorian-inspired, this estate home is rife with details and grand appointments. The central foyer opens from double doors on the wrapping veranda and leads to a parlor on the right and a study on the left. The parlor shares a through-fireplace with the formal dining room. A keeping room at the back is open to the island kitchen. A service hall leads to the three-car garage, which has a full apartment above. A media room and the master suite round out the first level. The second level holds three bedrooms with three private baths. A terrace opens from double doors on the west gallery.

5

PLAN HPT750002

First Floor: 2,081 square feet
Second Floor: 1,105 square feet
Total: 3,186 square feet
Bonus Room: 300 square feet
Width: 69'-9" *Depth:* 65'-0"

QUOTE ONE®
Cost to build? See page 310
to order complete cost estimate
to build this house in your area!

From its pediment to the columned porch, this Georgian facade is impressive. Inside, classical symmetry balances the living and dining rooms on either side of the foyer. The two-story great room features built-in cabinetry, a fireplace and a large bay window. The island kitchen opens to the breakfast area. The master suite boasts a tray ceiling, a wall of glass and access to the rear deck, as well as a private bath. This home is designed with a walkout basement foundation.

This home, as shown in the photograph, may differ from the actual blueprints. For more detailed information, please check the floor plans carefully.

Photo courtesy of Stephen Fuller, Inc.

PLAN HPT750003

First Floor: 2,628 square feet

Second Floor: 1,775 square feet

Total: 4,403 square feet

Width: 79'-6" Depth: 72'-4"

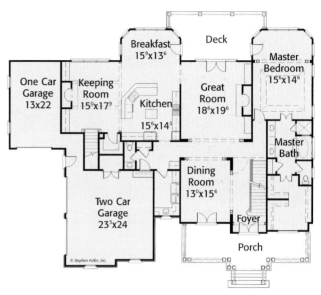

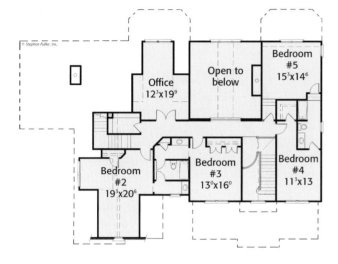

This home, as shown in the photograph, may differ from the actual blueprints.
For more detailed information, please check the floor plans carefully.

With five bedrooms and a wonderful stone-and-siding exterior, this country home will satisfy every need. Two sets of French doors provide access to the dining room and foyer. The great room enjoys a warming fireplace and deck access. The kitchen, breakfast bay and keeping room feature an open floor plan. A charming sitting area in a bay window sets off the master bedroom. The master bath features a large walk-in closet, two-sink vanity, separate tub and shower and compartmented toilet. Four bedrooms, an office and two full baths complete the upper level. This home is designed with a walkout basement foundation.

Photo by Scott W. Moore and Duvaune E. White

This home, as shown in the photograph, may differ from the actual blueprints. For more detailed information, please check the floor plans carefully.

Photo courtesy of Donald A. Gardner Architects, Inc., ©1997 Donald A. Gardner Architects, Inc.

PLAN HPT750004

First Floor: 1,113 square feet
Second Floor: 960 square feet
Total: 2,073 square feet
Bonus Space: 338 square feet
Width: 49'-4" Depth: 58'-10"

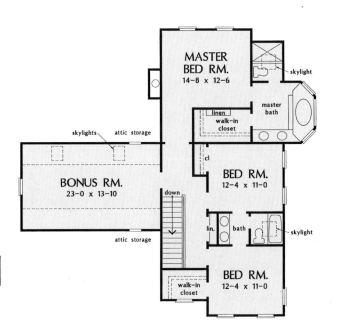

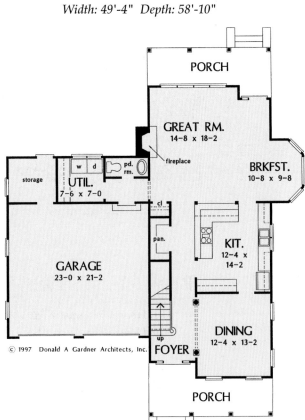

With a perfect blend of country and traditional, this family home fits nicely on a narrow lot. Columns define the entry to the dining room, while the kitchen, breakfast bay and great room remain open for a casual atmosphere. A half-bath and utility room are conveniently located nearby. Upstairs, the master suite has a luxurious bath with a sunny bay window. Two additional bedrooms share a skylit bath. A skylit bonus room over the garage allows the option of future expansion.

This home, as shown in the photograph, may differ from the actual blueprints.
For more detailed information, please check the floor plans carefully.

Photo courtesy of Stephen Fuller, Inc.

QUOTE ONE®
Cost to build? See page 310
to order complete cost estimate
to build this house in your area!

The covered front stoop of this two-story traditionally styled home gives way to the foyer and formal areas inside. A cozy living room with a fireplace sits on the right, and an elongated dining room is on the left. For fine family living, a great room and a kitchen/breakfast area account for the rear of the first-floor plan. A guest room with a nearby full bath finishes off the accommodations. Upstairs, four bedrooms include a master suite fit for royalty. A bonus room rests near Bedroom 2 and would make a great office or additional bedroom. This home is designed with a walkout basement foundation.

PLAN HPT750005

First Floor: 1,700 square feet
Second Floor: 1,585 square feet
Total: 3,285 square feet
Bonus Room: 176 square feet
Width: 60'-0" Depth: 47'-6"

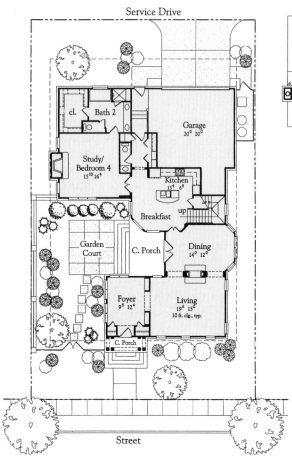

Service Drive

Garage
20⁰ 20⁰

cl. Bath 2

Study/
Bedroom 4
15¹⁰ 16⁴

Kitchen
13⁴ 6⁸

Breakfast

up

Garden
Court

C. Porch

Dining
14⁰ 12⁰

Foyer
9⁸ 12⁴

Living
19⁶ 15⁵
10 ft. clg., typ.

C. Porch

Street

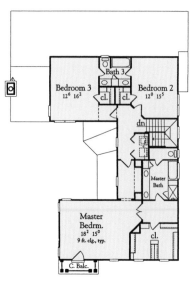

Bath 3

Bedroom 3
12⁶ 16²

cl. cl.

Bedroom 2
12⁰ 15⁵

dn

Master
Bath

Master
Bedrm.
18² 15⁰
9 ft. clg., typ.

cl.

C. Balc.

PLAN HPT750006

First Floor: 1,681 square feet
Second Floor: 1,342 square feet
Total: 3,023 square feet
Width: 46'-9" Depth: 68'-0"

A finely crafted porch and covered balcony complement classical elements, such as a portico and triple symmetrical dormers, on this stately yet charming home. The entry leads to a foyer thatís brightened by three sets of windows. A through-fireplace connects a crowd-size living room and a formal dining room that leads to a side porch and courtyard. The first-floor bedroom has a fireplace and easily converts to a study. A rear-loading garage keeps the car out of public view but handy for errands.

This home, as shown in the photograph, may differ from the actual blueprints.
For more detailed information, please check the floor plans carefully.

Photo by ©Jeffrey Jacobs/Mims Studio

Extra Storage
21'2"x 6'4"

Two-Car Garage
21'2"x 24'

Patio

Porch

Utility

Kitchen
13'8"x 15'8"

WIC

Master Bath

WIC

Family
22'9"x 17'

Master Bedroom
13'8"x 21'

Breakfast
13'8"x 12'

Unfinished Gameroom
14'4"x 15'4"

Living
11'10"x 14'

Dining
11'10"x 14'

Porch

Bath

WIC

Bedroom
13'6"x 12'2"

WIC

Bath

WIC

Balcony

Bedroom
11'10"x 17'6"

Open to Below

Bedroom
11'10"x 17'6"

Shelf

This home combines French styling with Colonial influences to produce a magnificent picture of elegance. A grand two-story foyer introduces the living room to the left and the dining room to the right. The family room reveals a fireplace flanked by two sets of French doors leading to the rear porch. The island kitchen provides plenty of work space and functions well with a breakfast room, a convenient utility room and a powder room. The first-floor master suite is a secluded place to relax. Upstairs, three family bedrooms—all with walk-in closets—and two full baths complete the sleeping quarters. An unfinished bonus room above the two-car garage is great for future space.

PLAN HPT750007

First Floor: 2,183 square feet
Second Floor: 993 square feet
Total: 3,176 square feet
Bonus Room: 221 square feet
Width: 66'-0" Depth: 84'-0"

This home, as shown in the photograph, may differ from the actual blueprints. For more detailed information, please check the floor plans carefully.

Photo by Chris A. Little, Atlanta, courtesy of Chatham Home Planning, Inc.

Photo by Dave Dawson Photography

PORCH

LAUNDRY
6'-0" X 11'-0"

TWO CAR GARAGE
21'-0" X 20'-0"

MASTER BEDROOM
15'-0" X 19'-0"

GREAT ROOM
21'-10" X 15'-2"

BREAKFAST
16'-4" X 10'-0"

PORCH

MASTER BATH
10'-2" X 10'-0"

HERS

STAIR HALL
15'-1" X 12'-0"

POWDER

HIS

KITCHEN
16'-4" X 12'-0"

UP

PANTRY

LIVING ROOM
14'-7" X 17'-0"

FOYER
7'-0" X 13'-0"

DINING ROOM
14'-7" X 15'-0"

PORCH

PLAN HPT750008

First Floor: 2,380 square feet
Second Floor: 1,295 square feet
Total: 3,675 square feet
Width: 77'-4" Depth: 58'-4"

QUOTE ONE®

Cost to build? See page 310
to order complete cost estimate
to build this house in your area!

Finely crafted porches—front, side and rear—
make this home a classic in traditional Southern
living. Past the large French doors, the impressive foyer is
flanked by the formal living and dining rooms. Beyond
the stair is a vaulted great room with an expanse of windows, a fireplace and built-in bookcases. From here, the
breakfast room and kitchen are easily accessible and
open to a private side porch. The master suite provides a
large bath, two spacious closets, a fireplace and a private
entry that opens to the covered rear porch. The second
floor contains three bedrooms with private bath access
and a playroom. This home is designed with a walkout
basement foundation.

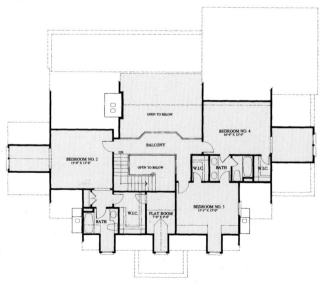

OPEN TO BELOW

BEDROOM NO. 4
16'-0" X 12'-0"

BEDROOM NO. 2
15'-0" X 13'-0"

BALCONY

DN

OPEN TO BELOW

W.I.C.

BATH

W.I.C.

BATH

W.I.C.

PLAY ROOM
7'-0" X 9'-0"

BEDROOM NO. 3
15'-1" X 13'-0"

The double wings, twin chimneys and center portico of this home work in concert to create a classic architectural statement. The two-story foyer is flanked by the spacious dining room and formal living room, each containing its own fireplace. A large family room with a full wall of glass beckons the outside in, while it opens conveniently to the sunlit kitchen and breakfast room. The master suite features a tray ceiling and French doors that open to a covered porch. A grand private bath with all the amenities, including a garden tub and huge closet, completes this suite. Two other bedrooms share a bath while another has its own private bath. The fourth bedroom also features a sunny nook for sitting or reading. This home is designed with a walkout basement foundation.

PLAN HPT750009

First Floor: 1,455 square feet
Second Floor: 1,649 square feet
Total: 3,104 square feet
Width: 53'-0" Depth: 46'-0"

QUOTE ONE®
Cost to build? See page 310
to order complete cost estimate
to build this house in your area!

This home, as shown in the photograph, may differ from the actual blueprints.
For more detailed information, please check the floor plans carefully.

Photo courtesy of Stephen Fuller, Inc.

This home, as shown in the photograph, may differ from the actual blueprints.
For more detailed information, please check the floor plans carefully.

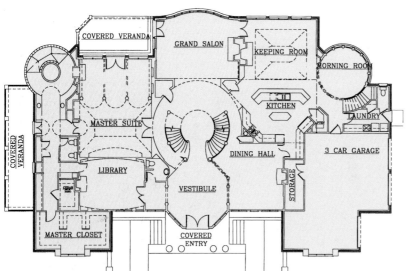

COVERED VERANDA

GRAND SALON

KEEPING ROOM

MORNING ROOM

COVERED VERANDA

MASTER SUITE

KITCHEN

LAUNDRY

LIBRARY

DINING HALL

3 CAR GARAGE

VESTIBULE

STORAGE

MASTER CLOSET

COVERED ENTRY

PLAN HPT750010

First Floor: 3,911 square feet
Second Floor: 2,184 square feet
Total: 6,095 square feet
Width: 102'-1" Depth: 62'-5"

Opulent, but not overstated, this estate plan offers symmetry, elegance and a grand entry. The first floor caters to gatherings both large and small with a grand salon, a keeping room, a formal dining hall, a circular morning room and a very private library. The first-floor master suite opens to both a rear and side veranda. The gourmet kitchen easily serves both casual and formal dining areas. The second floor contains three family bedrooms with private baths. There is also a full guest suite with a sitting room on this level.

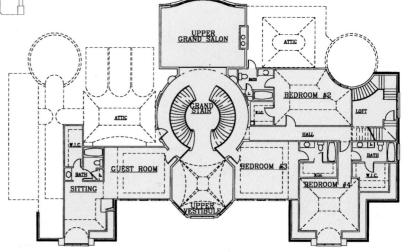

UPPER GRAND SALON

ATTIC

BEDROOM #2

GRAND STAIR

ATTIC

LOFT

W.I.C.

HALL

BATH

GUEST ROOM

BEDROOM #3

SITTING

BEDROOM #4

UPPER VESTIBULE

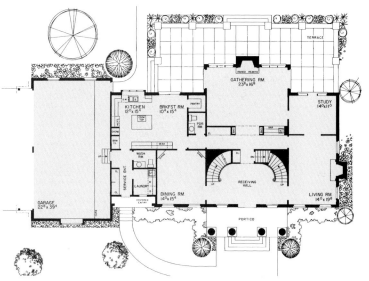

This classic Georgian design contains a variety of features that make it outstanding: a pediment gable with cornice work and dentils, beautifully proportioned columns, and a distinct window treatment. Inside, the foyer's stunning curved staircase introduces you to this Southern-style home. The first floor contains some special appointments: a fireplace in the living room and another fireplace and a wet bar in the gathering room. A study is offered towards the rear of the plan for convenient home office use. A gourmet island kitchen is open to a breakfast room with a pantry. Upstairs, an extension over the garage allows for a huge walk-in closet in the master suite and a full bath in one of the family bedrooms.

PLAN HPT750011

First Floor: 2,348 square feet
Second Floor: 1,872 square feet
Total: 4,220 square feet
Width: 90'-4" Depth: 44'-8"

L|D

QUOTE ONE®
Cost to build? See page 310
to order complete cost estimate
to build this house in your area!

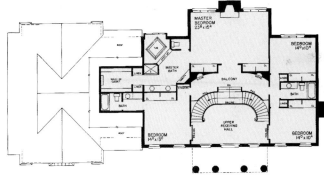

This home, as shown in the photograph, may differ from the actual blueprints.
For more detailed information, please check the floor plans carefully.

Photo by Andy Lautman, Lautman Photography

This home, as shown in the photograph, may differ from the actual blueprints.
For more detailed information, please check the floor plans carefully.

Archival Designs Joanne E. Loftus

PLAN HPT750012

First Floor: 1,920 square feet
Second Floor: 912 square feet
Total: 2,832 square feet
Width: 70'-0" Depth: 40'-0"

The impressive facade of this classic design previews an elegant floor plan. To the left of the large foyer, French doors open to a study filled with natural light. The open dining room, to the right of the foyer, is defined by a single column. To the rear of the plan, the living room/den and kitchen—with a bowed breakfast area—provide space for the family to gather. Also at the rear of the plan, a guest room features its own bath and private access to the outside through a garage entrance. On the left side of the plan, the master suite offers a walk-in closet, a luxurious bath and private access to the study. Upstairs, two bedrooms—each with a private vanity—share a bath. Bookshelves line the library loft, which is lighted by three skylights.

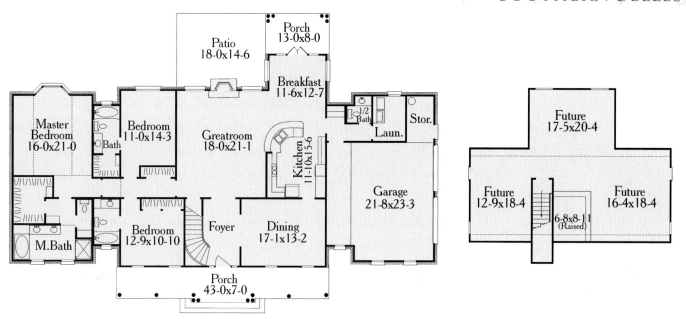

This elegant symmetrical home features a gabled porch complemented by columns. The breakfast room, adjacent to the kitchen, opens to a rear porch. The spacious great room provides a fireplace and a view of the patio. A lovely bayed window brightens the master suite, which includes a walk-in closet and a bath with a garden tub and a separate shower. Two secondary bedrooms each offer a private bath. A winding staircase leads to second-level future space. Please specify basement, crawlspace or slab foundation when ordering.

PLAN HPT750013

Square Footage: 2,497
Bonus Space: 966 square feet
Width: 87'-0" Depth: 57'-3"

This home, as shown in the photograph, may differ from the actual blueprints.
For more detailed information, please check the floor plans carefully.

Photo by Ken Purcell

Photo courtesy of Chatham Home Planning, Inc., photo by Chris A. Little of Atlanta

This home, as shown in the photograph, may differ from the actual blueprints. For more detailed information, please check the floor plans carefully.

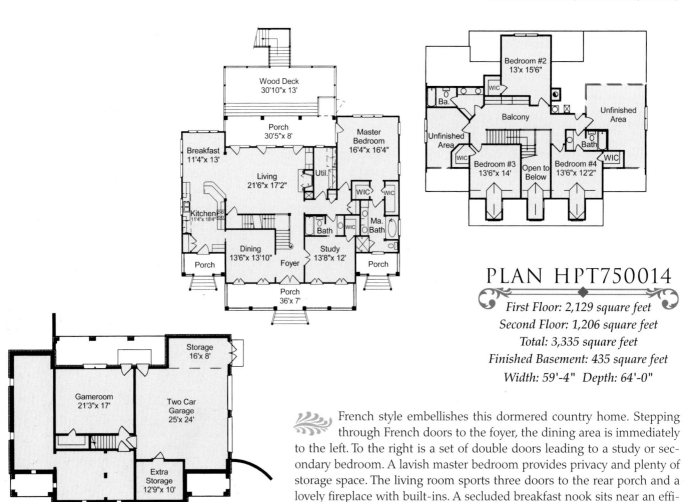

Wood Deck
30'10"x 13'

Porch
30'5"x 8'

Master
Bedroom
16'4"x 16'4"

Breakfast
11'4"x 13'

Living
21'6"x 17'2"

Util.

Kitchen
11'4"x 18'4"

WIC   WIC

Porch

Dining
13'6"x 13'10"

Foyer

Bath

WIC

Study
13'8"x 12'

Ma.
Bath

Porch

Porch
36'x 7'

Bedroom #2
13'x 15'6"

WIC

Ba.

Unfinished
Area

Balcony

Unfinished
Area

Bath

WIC

WIC

Bedroom #3
13'6"x 14'

Open to
Below

Bedroom #4
13'6"x 12'2"

Storage
16'x 8'

Gameroom
21'3"x 17'

Two Car
Garage
25'x 24'

Extra
Storage
12'9"x 10'

PLAN HPT750014

First Floor: 2,129 square feet
Second Floor: 1,206 square feet
Total: 3,335 square feet
Finished Basement: 435 square feet
Width: 59'-4" Depth: 64'-0"

French style embellishes this dormered country home. Stepping through French doors to the foyer, the dining area is immediately to the left. To the right is a set of double doors leading to a study or secondary bedroom. A lavish master bedroom provides privacy and plenty of storage space. The living room sports three doors to the rear porch and a lovely fireplace with built-ins. A secluded breakfast nook sits near an efficient kitchen. Upstairs, two of the three family bedrooms boast dormer windows. Plans include a basement-level garage that adjoins a game room and two handy storage areas.

PLAN HPT750015

First Floor: 2,092 square feet
Second Floor: 1,027 square feet
Total: 3,119 square feet
Width: 66'-0" Depth: 80'-0"

This Southern Plantation home, featuring traditional accents such as front-facing dormers, a covered front porch and a stucco-and-brick facade, will be the delight of any countryside neighborhood. Inside, a study and formal dining room flank the foyer. The family room shares a two-sided fireplace with the refreshing sun room, which overlooks the rear deck. The kitchen opens to an eating area overlooking the front yard. The first-floor master suite features a large closet space and a private bath. A three-car garage completes the first floor. Three additional bedrooms and two baths are located upstairs.

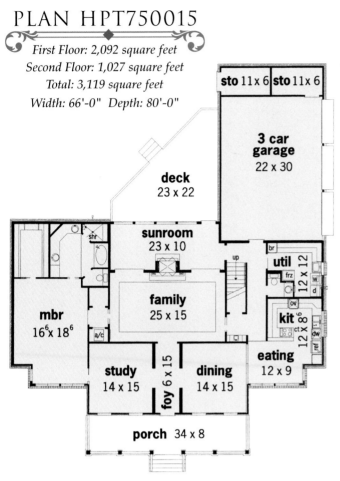

sto 11 x 6   sto 11 x 6

3 car garage 22 x 30

deck 23 x 22

sunroom 23 x 10

up

br

util 12 x 12

frz

w
d

family 25 x 15

mbr 16⁶ x 18⁶

a/c

ov

kit 12 x 8⁶

ct
dw
ref

foy 6 x 15

study 14 x 15

dining 14 x 15

eating 12 x 9

shr

porch 34 x 8

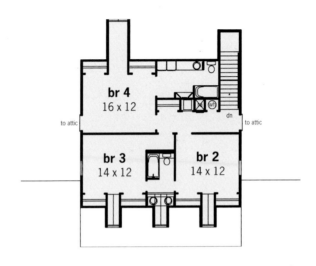

br 4 16 x 12

br 3 14 x 12

br 2 14 x 12

to attic

dn

to attic

This home, as shown in the photograph, may differ from the actual blueprints. For more detailed information, please check the floor plans carefully.

Photo courtesy of Breland & Farmer Designers, Inc.

This home, as shown in the photograph, may differ from the actual blueprints.
For more detailed information, please check the floor plans carefully.

PLAN HPT750016

First Floor: 2,199 square feet
Second Floor: 1,235 square feet
Total: 3,434 square feet
Bonus Room: 150 square feet
Width: 62'-6" Depth: 54'-3"

QUOTE ONE®

Cost to build? See page 310
to order complete cost estimate
to build this house in your area!

The covered front porch of this home warmly welcomes family and visitors. To the right of the foyer is a versatile option room. On the other side is the formal dining room. A comfortable great room boasts French doors to a rear deck and easy access to a large breakfast area and sun room. The adjacent kitchen includes a cooking island/breakfast bar. Secluded on the main level for privacy, the master suite features a private deck and a lavish bath loaded with amenities. Three additional bedrooms and two baths occupy the second level. This home is designed with a walkout basement foundation.

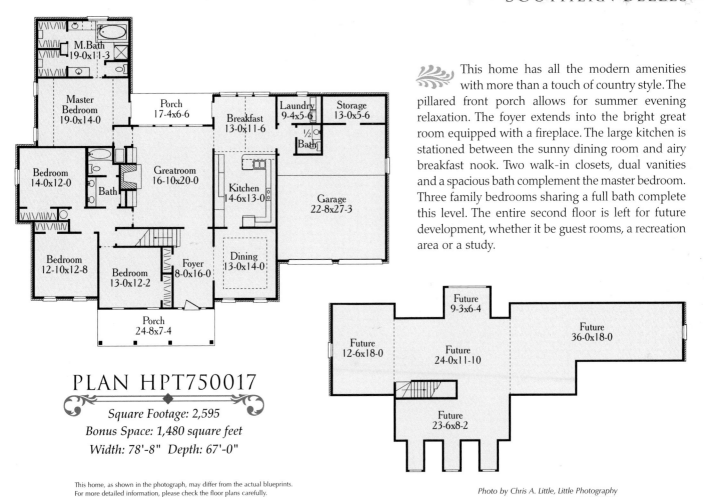

This home has all the modern amenities with more than a touch of country style. The pillared front porch allows for summer evening relaxation. The foyer extends into the bright great room equipped with a fireplace. The large kitchen is stationed between the sunny dining room and airy breakfast nook. Two walk-in closets, dual vanities and a spacious bath complement the master bedroom. Three family bedrooms sharing a full bath complete this level. The entire second floor is left for future development, whether it be guest rooms, a recreation area or a study.

PLAN HPT750017

Square Footage: 2,595

Bonus Space: 1,480 square feet

Width: 78'-8"   Depth: 67'-0"

This home, as shown in the photograph, may differ from the actual blueprints. For more detailed information, please check the floor plans carefully.

Photo by Chris A. Little, Little Photography

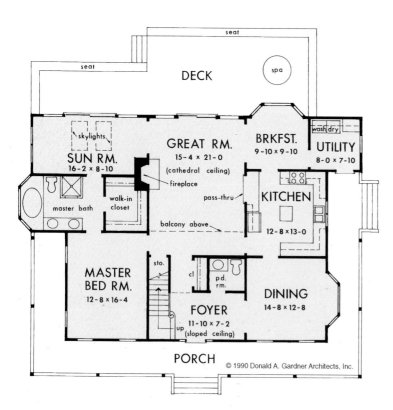

DECK

spa

seat

seat

seat

SUN RM.
16-2 x 8-10

skylights

GREAT RM.
15-4 x 21-0
(cathedral ceiling)
fireplace

pass-thru

BRKFST.
9-10 x 9-10

UTILITY
8-0 x 7-10

wash dry

walk-in closet

master bath

KITCHEN
12-8 x 13-0

balcony above

MASTER BED RM.
12-8 x 16-4

sto.

cl

p.d. rm.

DINING
14-8 x 12-8

FOYER
11-10 x 7-2
(sloped ceiling)

up

PORCH

© 1990 Donald A. Gardner Architects, Inc.

PLAN HPT750018

First Floor: 1,651 square feet
Second Floor: 567 square feet
Total: 2,218 square feet
Width: 55'-0" Depth: 53'-10"

QUOTE ONE®

Cost to build? See page 310
to order complete cost estimate
to build this house in your area!

A wonderful wraparound covered porch at the front and sides of this house and the open deck with a spa at the back provide plenty of outside living area. Inside, the spacious great room is appointed with a fireplace, cathedral ceiling and clerestory with an arched window. The kitchen is centrally located for maximum flexibility in layout and features a food-preparation island for convenience. Besides the master bedroom with access to the sun room, there are two second-level bedrooms that share a full bath.

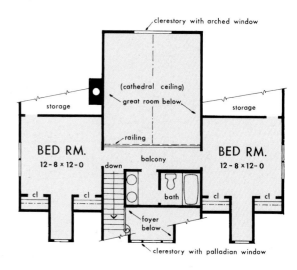

clerestory with arched window

(cathedral ceiling)

great room below

railing

storage

storage

BED RM.
12-8 x 12-0

BED RM.
12-8 x 12-0

balcony

down

cl

cl

bath

cl

cl

foyer below

clerestory with palladian window

PLAN HPT750019

First Floor: 1,977 square feet
Second Floor: 650 square feet
Total: 2,627 square feet
Bonus Room: 280 square feet
Width: 72'-4" Depth: 48'-4"

This fine brick three-bedroom home is great for the growing family. This elegant facade is accented with triple dormers and highlighted with a porch that was created for rocking chairs. Enter through a columned front porch to the foyer, which is flanked by a formal dining room and either a study or a private guest suite. A huge master suite is located on the first floor for privacy and is complete with two walk-in closets and a sumptuous bath. Please specify basement, crawlspace or slab foundation when ordering.

This home, as shown in the photograph, may differ from the actual blueprints.
For more detailed information, please check the floor plans carefully.

Photo courtesy of Nelson Design Group, LLC

This home, as shown in the photograph, may differ from the actual blueprints. For more detailed information, please check the floor plans carefully.

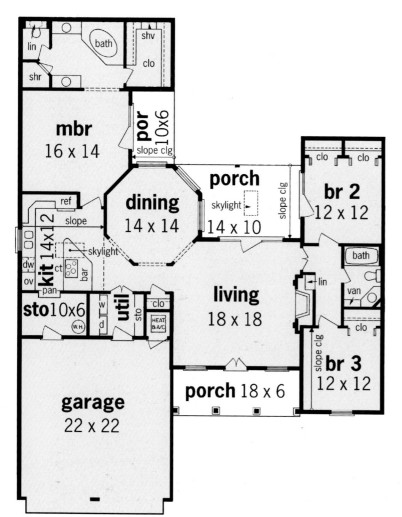

PLAN HPT750020

Square Footage: 1,655
Width: 52'-0" Depth: 66'-0"

 Elegantly arched doors and windows decorate the exterior of this fine home, which offers an intriguing floor plan. The living room features a soaring fifteen-foot ceiling and adjoins the octagonal dining room. Both rooms offer views of the skylit rear porch; a skylight also brightens the kitchen. The lavish master suite includes a walk-in closet, access to a small side porch, and a full bath with a corner marble tub. Two additional bedrooms, thoughtfully placed apart from the master suite, share a full bath. Please specify crawlspace or slab foundation when ordering.

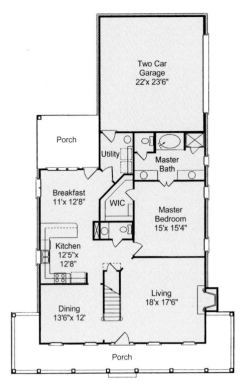

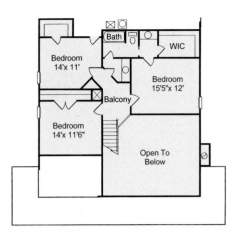

PLAN HPT750021

First Floor: 1,516 square feet
Second Floor: 840 square feet
Total: 2,356 square feet
Width: 46'-10" Depth: 73'-5"

Looking for a home with a country attitude and modern amenities? Welcome home! A wide columned porch graced by tall shuttered windows will greet guests with a feeling of comfort. The formal living room is enhanced by a central fireplace, while the dining room is situated just off the U-shaped kitchen. Sunshine pours in from the breakfast area, flooding the kitchen with light. The master bedroom features a walk-in closet and double doors to the dual-vanity bathroom. Upstairs, three family bedrooms—two enjoy walk-in closets—share a compartmented bath. The rear-loading two-car garage doesn't detract from the symmetry of the home.

This home, as shown in the photograph, may differ from the actual blueprints. For more detailed information, please check the floor plans carefully.

Photo courtesy of Chatham Home Planning, Inc., photo by Chris A. Little of Atlanta

This home, as shown in the photograph, may differ from the actual blueprints.
For more detailed information, please check the floor plans carefully.

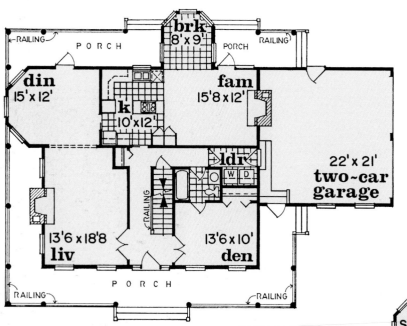

PLAN HPT750022

First Floor: 1,291 square feet
Second Floor: 1,291 square feet
Total: 2,582 square feet
Width: 64'-6" Depth: 47'-0"

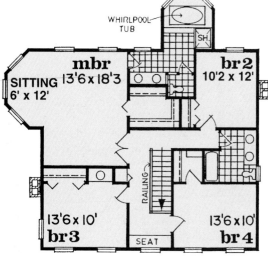

Traditional with an essence of farmhouse flavor, this four-bedroom home begins with a wraparound covered porch. The floor plan revolves around a central hall with a formal living room and dining room on the left and private den on the right. The bayed breakfast room is located near the L-shaped kitchen with an island work center. Both the family room and the living room are warmed by hearths. Two rear porches are reached through doors in the family room and the bayed dining room. The master suite on the second level has a bayed sitting room. Note the window seat on the second-floor landing.

PLAN HPT750023

Square Footage: 1,787
Bonus Room: 326 square feet
Width: 66'-2" Depth: 66'-8"

A neighborly porch as friendly as a handshake wraps around this charming country home. Inside, cathedral ceilings promote a feeling of spaciousness. The great room is enhanced with a fireplace and built-in bookshelves. A uniquely shaped formal dining room separates the kitchen and breakfast area. Outdoor pursuits—rain or shine—will be enjoyed from the screened porch. The master suite is located at the rear of the plan for privacy and features a walk-in closet and a luxurious bath. Two additional bedrooms—one with a walk-in closet—share a skylit bath.

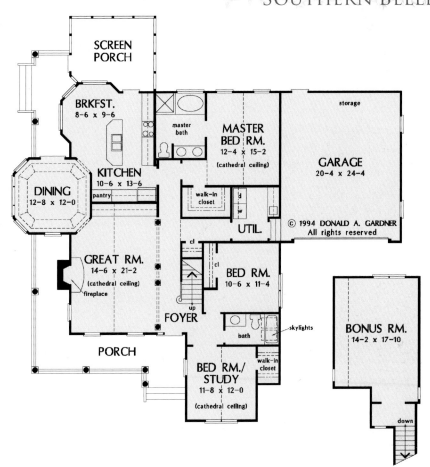

This home, as shown in the photograph, may differ from the actual blueprints.
For more detailed information, please check the floor plans carefully.

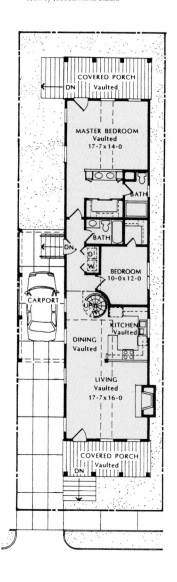

PLAN HPT750024

Square Footage: 1,278
Bonus Room: 256 square feet
Width: 18'-3" Depth: 70'-0"

The gently rustic facade of this design bears a mild resemblance to a seaside cottage. But a carefree interior provides amenities for both traditional entertaining and casual gatherings. A vaulted open living and dining space includes a fireplace and a stunning interior vista of the winding wrought-iron staircase. The center of the plan provides a flex room, which can serve as a family bedroom, guest room or home office. A privacy door leads to the master bedroom, bath and dressing area. The homeowner's bedroom leads out to the covered rear porch.

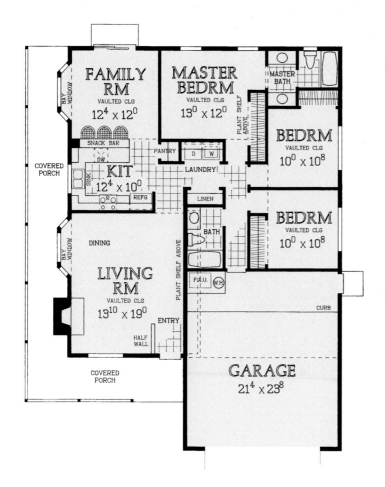

Floor plan labels:

FAMILY RM
VAULTED CLG
12⁴ x 12⁰

MASTER BEDRM
VAULTED CLG
13⁰ x 12⁰

MASTER BATH

BEDRM
VAULTED CLG
10⁰ x 10⁸

COVERED PORCH

SNACK BAR

DW

KIT
12⁴ x 10⁰

SINK

R

REFG

PANTRY

D   W

LAUNDRY

PLANT SHELF ABOVE

LINEN

BAY WINDOW

DINING

BATH

BEDRM
VAULTED CLG
10⁰ x 10⁸

LIVING RM
VAULTED CLG
13¹⁰ x 19⁰

PLANT SHELF ABOVE

F.A.U.   W.H.

CURB

BAY WINDOW

ENTRY

HALF WALL

COVERED PORCH

GARAGE
21⁴ x 23⁸

PLAN HPT750025

Square Footage: 1,389
Width: 44'-8" Depth: 54'-6"

L

Simple rooflines and an inviting porch enhance the floor plan. A formal living room has a warming fireplace and a delightful bay window. The U-shaped kitchen shares a snack bar with the bayed family room. Note the sliding glass doors to the rear yard here. The sleeping quarters are found to the right of the plan. Three bedrooms include two family bedrooms served by a full bath and a lovely master suite with its own private bath.

Quote One®

Cost to build? See page 310
to order complete cost estimate
to build this house in your area!

Photo by Bob Greenspan, Greenspan Photography

This home, as shown in the photograph, may differ from the actual blueprints. For more detailed information, please check the floor plans carefully.

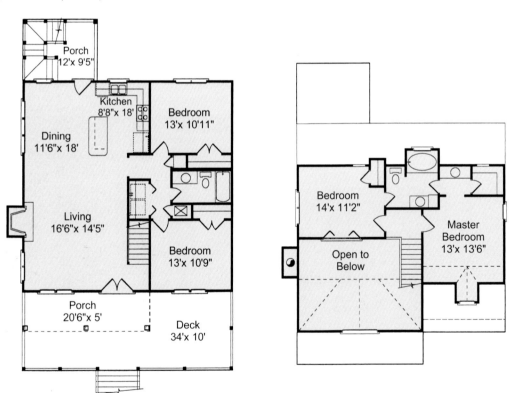

Porch
12'x 9'5"

Kitchen
8'8"x 18'

Dining
11'6"x 18'

Bedroom
13'x 10'11"

Living
16'6"x 14'5"

Bedroom
13'x 10'9"

Porch
20'6"x 5'

Deck
34'x 10'

Bedroom
14'x 11'2"

Master
Bedroom
13'x 13'6"

Open to
Below

PLAN HPT750026

First Floor: 1,122 square feet
Second Floor: 528 square feet
Total: 1,650 square feet
Width: 34'-0" Depth: 52'-5"

This lovely seaside vacation home is perfect for seasonal family getaways or for the family that lives coastal year-round. The spacious front deck is great for private sunbathing or outdoor barbecues and provides breathtaking ocean views. The two-story living room is warmed by a fireplace on breezy beach nights, while the island kitchen overlooks the open dining area nearby. Two first-floor family bedrooms share a hall bath. Upstairs, the master bedroom features a walk-in closet, a dressing area with a vanity, and access to a whirlpool tub shared with an additional family bedroom—perfect for a nursery or home office.

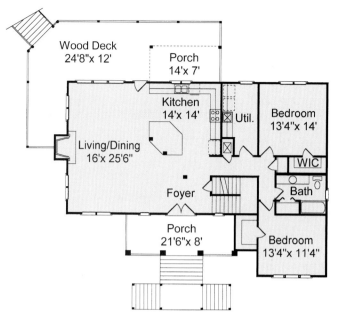

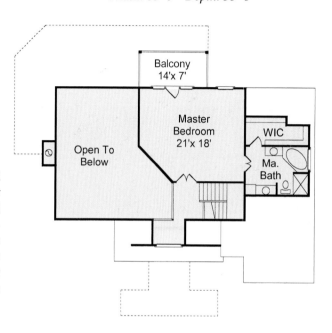

PLAN HPT750027

First Floor: 1,552 square feet
Second Floor: 653 square feet
Total: 2,205 square feet
Width: 60'-0" Depth: 50'-0"

A split staircase adds flair to this European-style coastal home where a fireplace brings warmth on chilly evenings. The foyer opens to the expansive living/dining area and island kitchen. A multitude of windows fills the interior with sunlight and ocean breezes. The wraparound rear deck finds access near the kitchen. The utility room is conveniently tucked between the kitchen and the two first-floor bedrooms. The second-floor master suite offers a private balcony and a luxurious bath with a garden tub, shower and walk-in closet.

This home, as shown in the photograph, may differ from the actual blueprints.
For more detailed information, please check the floor plans carefully.

Photo courtesy of Chatham Home Planning, Inc., Chris A. Little of Atlanta

This home, as shown in the photograph, may differ from the actual blueprints. For more detailed information, please check the floor plans carefully.

Photo courtesy of The Sater Design Collection, ©Oscar Thompsom

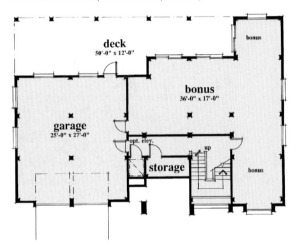

deck
50'-0" x 12'-0"

bonus

bonus
36'-0" x 17'-0"

garage
25'-0" x 27'-0"

opt. elev.

storage

up

bonus

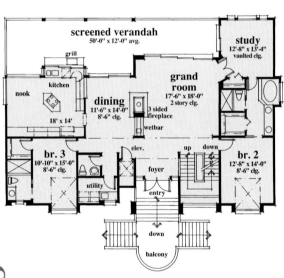

screened verandah
50'-0" x 12'-0" avg.

study
12'-8" x 13'-4"
vaulted clg.

grill

kitchen

nook

grand room
17'-6" x 18'-0"
2 story clg.

dining
11'-6" x 14'-0"
8'-6" clg.

3 sided fireplace

18' x 14'

wetbar

br. 3
10'-10" x 15'-0"
8'-6" clg.

elev.

up   down

br. 2
12'-8" x 14'-0"
8'-6" clg.

foyer

utility

entry

down

balcony

PLAN HPT750028

First Floor: 2,066 square feet

Second Floor: 810 square feet

Total: 2,876 square feet

Bonus Space: 1,260 square feet

Width: 64'-0" Depth: 45'-0"

L

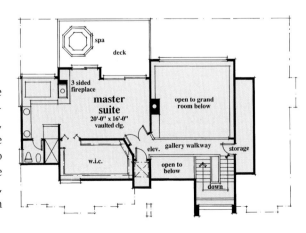

spa

deck

3 sided fireplace

master suite
20'-0" x 16'-0"
vaulted clg.

open to grand room below

w.i.c.

elev.   gallery walkway

storage

open to below

down

This striking Floridian plan is designed for entertaining. A large open floor plan offers soaring, sparkling space for planned gatherings. The foyer leads to the grand room, highlighted by a glass fireplace, a wet bar and wide views of the outdoors. Both the grand room and the formal dining room open to a screened veranda. The first floor includes two spacious family bedrooms and a secluded study which opens from the grand room. The second-floor master suite offers sumptuous amenities, including a private deck and spa, a three-sided fireplace, a sizable walk-in closet and a gallery hall with an overlook to the grand room.

PLAN HPT750029

First Floor: 1,252 square feet

Second Floor: 1,209 square feet

Total: 2,461 square feet

Width: 60'-6" Depth: 38'-9"

This Colonial home offers a historically correct exterior design with an updated interior for modern living. The foyer is flanked by the living and dining rooms while the more intimate family room is found in the rear where a fireplace brings warmth and atmosphere. The U-shaped kitchen adjoins the sunny breakfast bay in the rear. The two-car garage is accessed from the kitchen via the utility room for added convenience. The grand staircase in the foyer rises to three family bedrooms, a full bath and a luxurious master suite.

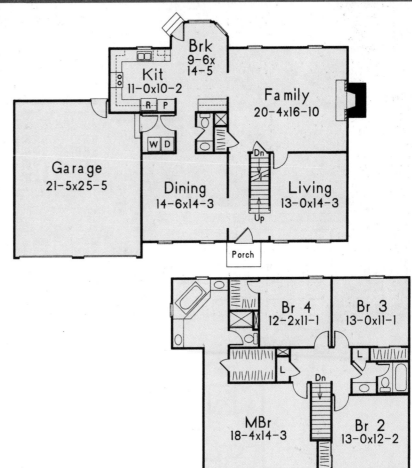

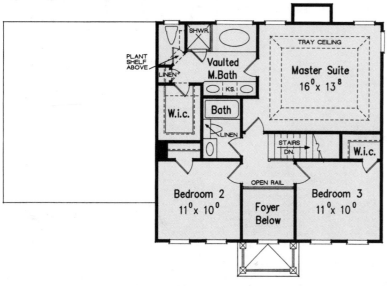

PLAN HPT750030

First Floor: 840 square feet
Second Floor: 766 square feet
Total: 1,606 square feet
Width: 50'-0" Depth: 34'-4"

Gabled dormers, keystone lintels and a covered entry display a pleasant exterior. Inside, the kitchen and breakfast area opens to the grand room, which features a warming fireplace. A powder room is located just across from the dining room. On the second floor, three bedrooms provide plenty of room for the family, including the master suite with a vaulted private bath and a large walk-in closet. Don't miss the two-car garage that enters through the breakfast area. Please specify basement or crawlspace foundation when ordering.

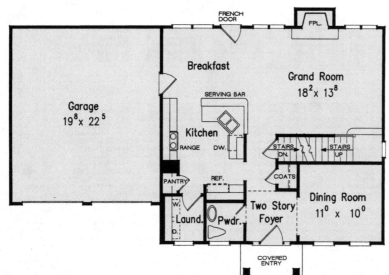

PLAN HPT750031

First Floor: 2,615 square feet
Second Floor: 1,726 square feet
Total: 4,341 square feet
Apartment: 437 square feet
Width: 124'-0" Depth: 31'-0"

L

Designed to resemble the St. George Tucker house in Williamsburg, this stately home offers a floor plan for today's family. First-floor rooms include a family room with informal dining space at one end of the plan and a formal living room at the other end. In between are the media room, guest powder room, dining room and kitchen. Three second-floor bedrooms include a luxurious master suite with a sitting room. There is also a guest room or apartment with a private bath over the garage.

QUOTE ONE®

Cost to build? See page 310 to order complete cost estimate to build this house in your area!

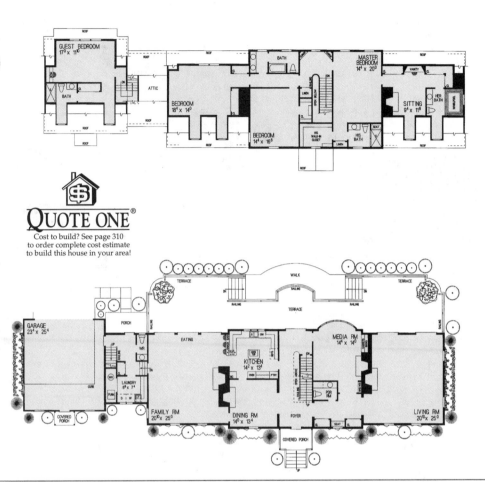

PLAN HPT750032

First Floor: 1,341 square feet
Second Floor: 1,299 square feet
Total: 2,640 square feet
Width: 50'-0" Depth: 42'-6"

Stately Colonial accents and classical symmetry enhance the facade of this two-story design. Inside, the two-story foyer is flanked by formal living and dining rooms. The two-story family room is warmed by a cozy fireplace. The kitchen with a pantry and serving bar easily serves the bayed breakfast room, which features a French door to the backyard. The home office easily converts to a guest suite, located near a hall bath. A two-car garage completes the first floor. Upstairs, the master suite features a bayed sitting area, vaulted master bath and walk-in closet. Three additional family bedrooms share a hall bath. The second-floor laundry room is a convenient bonus. Please specify basement or crawlspace foundation when ordering.

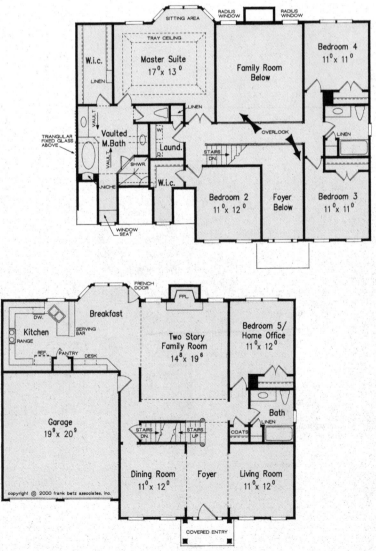

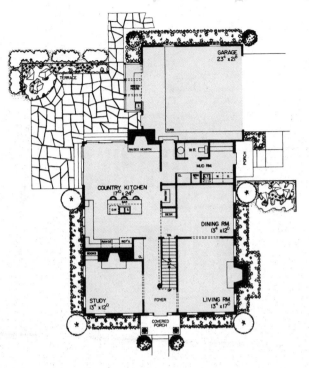

Perfect for a narrow site, this historic adaptation is in "temple form"—the gable end of the house faces the street, as in a Greek temple. Three chimneys support four fireplaces—in the living room, study, kitchen and master bedroom. Family members and guests will love the huge country kitchen, with room for relaxing, a snack bar for quick meals, and access to the terrace. The master suite has a deluxe bath and a private balcony. Three bedrooms and two full baths complete the plan.

PLAN HPT750033

First Floor: 1,440 square feet

Second Floor: 1,394 square feet

Total: 2,834 square feet

Width: 38'-0" Depth: 62'-0"

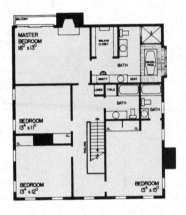

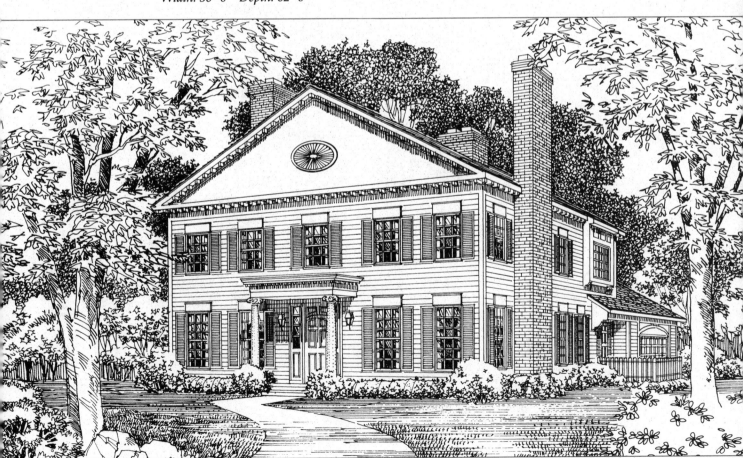

Nothing on a home says "Americana" like open pediment and covered porch detailing. Step into the two-story foyer and be formally introduced to the dining room on the left and the living room on the right. The two-story family room is a place of comfort and open space featuring a central fireplace and rear access. The kitchen and breakfast bay work well together. Five bedrooms, including a luxurious master suite, complete this plan. Please specify basement or crawlspace foundation when ordering.

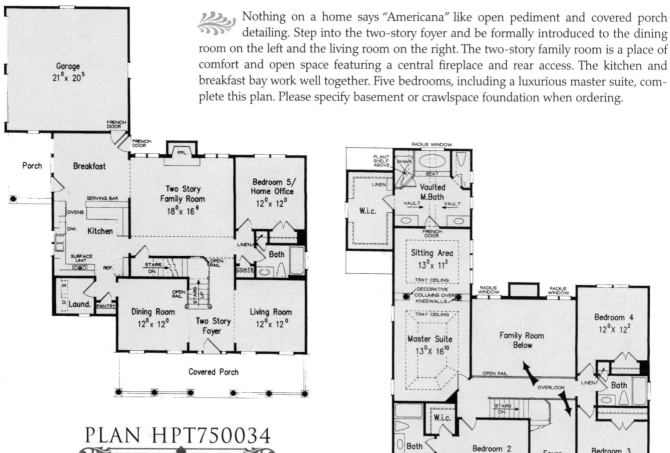

PLAN HPT750034

First Floor: 1,438 square feet
Second Floor: 1,464 square feet
Total: 2,902 square feet
Width: 52'-0" Depth: 64'-6"

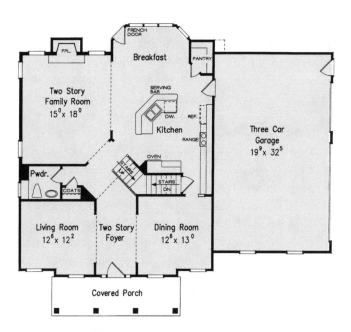

PLAN HPT750035

First Floor: 1,265 square feet

Second Floor: 1,492 square feet

Total: 2,757 square feet

Width: 53'-0" *Depth:* 53'-6"

This Greek Revival-style home brings back the charm of the past. Inside, the first floor features a two-story family room, with multiple windows and a fireplace, that is open to the kitchen and spacious breakfast nook. The living and dining rooms flank the two-story foyer. The second floor enjoys three family bedrooms and a master suite that includes a private bath, an enormous walk-in closet and a bedroom with a tray ceiling. Please specify basement or crawlspace foundation when ordering.

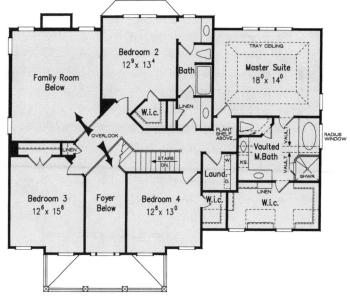

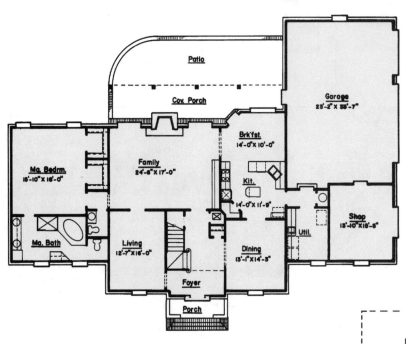

PLAN HPT750036

First Floor: 2,190 square feet
Second Floor: 1,418 square feet
Total: 3,608 square feet
Width: 84'-10"   Depth: 61'-10"

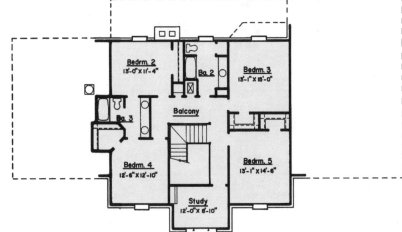

Luxury is highly evident in this fine brick mansion. The master bedroom is one example, with its two walk-in closets, huge bedroom area and lavish bath. Another example of luxury is the four secondary bedrooms upstairs, with access to a private study. Take note of the spacious family room, complete with a fireplace and access to the rear covered patio. The island kitchen is sure to please, serving the formal dining room or the sunny breakfast room with ease. The three-car garage will shelter the family fleet.

PLAN HPT750037

First Floor: 1,904 square feet
Second Floor: 922 square feet
Total: 2,826 square feet
Width: 60'-6" Depth: 74'-0"

Massive stone quoins outline the vertical dimensions of this imposing two-story Georgian design. A recessed entryway looks through the large family room with a fireplace to the covered rear porch. Formal living and dining rooms flank the two-story foyer, and stairs lead up to three bedrooms and two full baths. The first-floor master suite features a large walk-in closet and a full bath. The kitchen opens to a corner breakfast room. The utility room sits just off the kitchen and opens to a hall that leads from the house to the two-car garage. Please specify crawlspace or slab foundation when ordering.

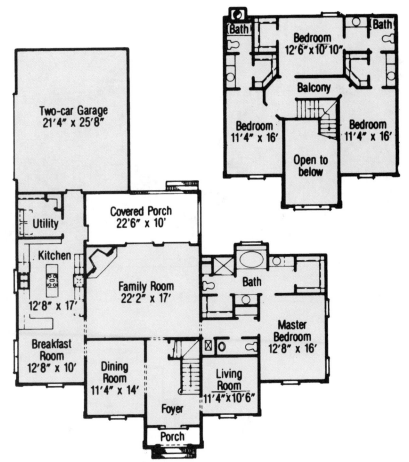

PLAN HPT750038

First Floor: 1,355 square feet
Second Floor: 1,046 square feet
Total: 2,401 square feet
Width: 56'-0" Depth: 36'-0"

Classic in design, this handsome Colonial home brightens the neighborhood with its hipped roof and prominent pedimented entry. An open floor plan allows for circular movement throughout the living spaces using the grand staircase as the central hub. The adjoining dining room and breakfast nook are conveniently situated near the elaborate island kitchen that leads to the garage via the utility area. The cozy family room and more formal living room reside on the left. Two family bedrooms share a full bath on the second floor while the master suite enjoys privacy with a vaulted bath.

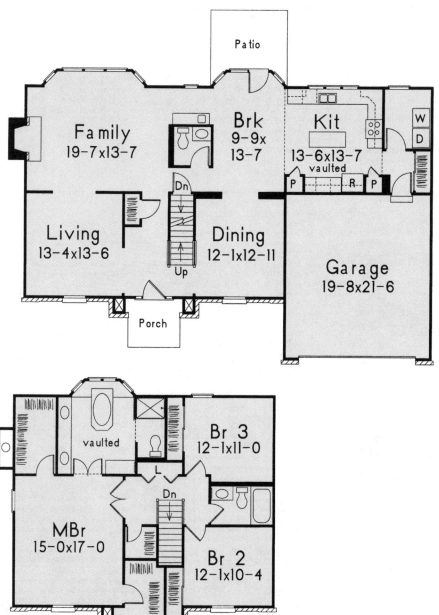

PLAN HPT750039

First Floor: 1,208 square feet

Second Floor: 1,218 square feet

Total: 2,426 square feet

Width: 62'-0" Depth: 36'-0"

Twin bay windows, an elegant Palladian window and corner quoins help create symmetry on this spectacular Southern home. The formal dining and living rooms are filled with natural light from the bay windows. The more casual family room also enjoys wonderful views with its generous window wall. The island kitchen serves both the dining room and the breakfast nook with ease and efficiency. Three bedrooms and a full bath join the lavish master suite on the second floor where the master bedroom delights with a tray ceiling. A second staircase leads from the kitchen to the second-floor utility room. A bonus room over the two-car garage offers more space to grow.

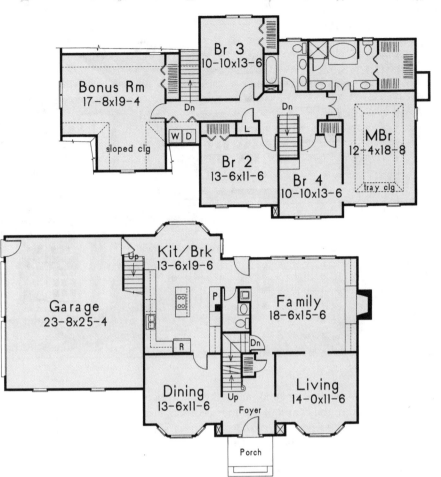

A shed dormer and a pedimented porch enhance the charm of this four-bedroom farmhouse. Inside, the first floor provides plenty of shared living space away from the second-floor sleeping zone. The foyer introduces the formal dining room with its view of the front yard. The nearby kitchen features a pantry, work island, pass-through to the family room, and a sunny breakfast nook. A coffered ceiling adds elegance to the hearth-warmed family room. Four bedrooms and a laundry room reside on the second level. A tray ceiling adorns the master suite, which includes a vaulted bath and a walk-in closet. Please specify basement or crawlspace foundation when ordering.

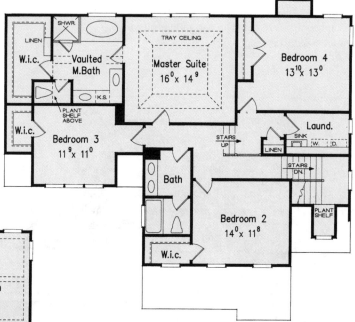

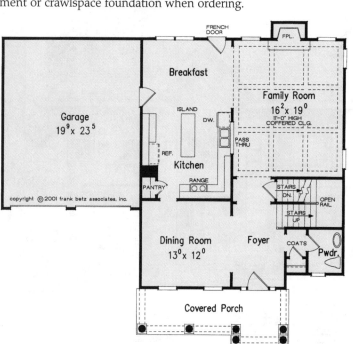

PLAN HPT750040

First Floor: 1,033 square feet
Second Floor: 1,359 square feet
Total: 2,392 square feet
Width: 50'-0" Depth: 42'-6"

From the columned front porch to the curved patio in back, this house is filled with elegance and style. The foyer, featuring a graceful curving staircase, opens to the formal living and dining rooms. The focal point of the large family room is its fireplace, but windows will beckon you to the covered porch and patio outside. Multiple windows also highlight the kitchen, with its large work island, and the round breakfast room. The master suite is in a private wing and contains a large walk-in closet, an amenity-laden bath and its own exit to the back porch. A nearby guest room could serve as a study or a library. Four bedrooms, two full baths and a sitting room reside upstairs. Please specify slab or crawlspace foundation when ordering.

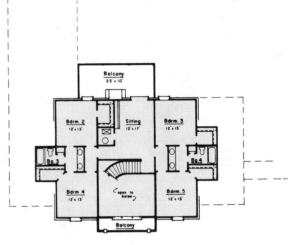

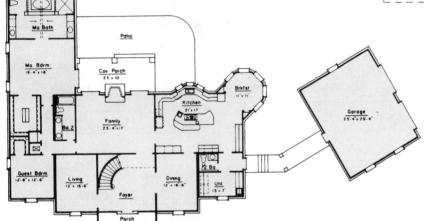

PLAN HPT750041

First Floor: 3,117 square feet
Second Floor: 1,411 square feet
Total: 4,528 square feet
Width: 76'-10" Depth: 68'-10"

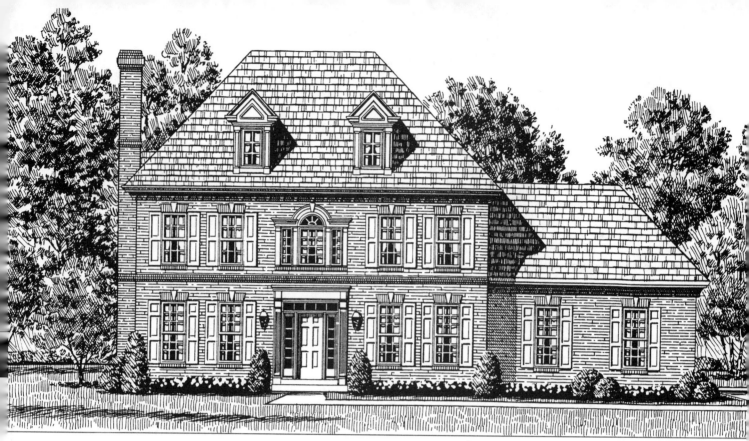

PLAN HPT750042

First Floor: 1,365 square feet
Second Floor: 1,288 square feet
Total: 2,653 square feet
Width: 61'-0" Depth: 38'-0"

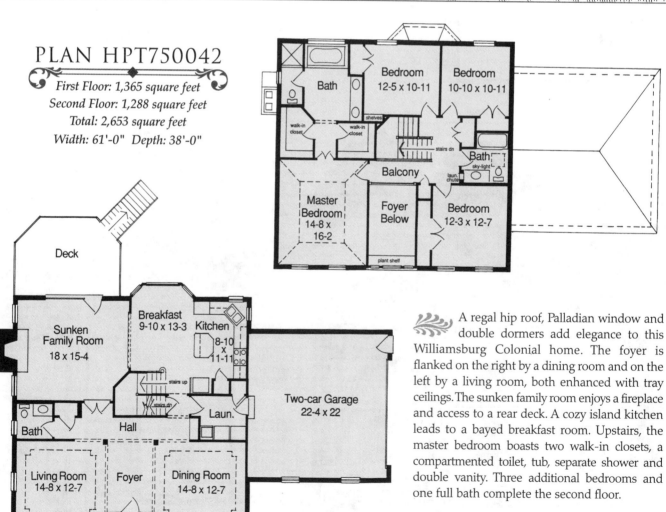

Second floor plan labels:
Bath
Bedroom 12-5 x 10-11
Bedroom 10-10 x 10-11
walk-in closet
shelves
walk-in closet
stairs dn
Bath
sky-light
laun. chute
Master Bedroom 14-8 x 16-2
Balcony
Foyer Below
Bedroom 12-3 x 12-7
plant shelf

First floor plan labels:
Deck
Sunken Family Room 18 x 15-4
Breakfast 9-10 x 13-3
Kitchen 8-10 x 11-11
stairs up
stairs dn
Laun.
Two-car Garage 22-4 x 22
Bath
Hall
Living Room 14-8 x 12-7
Foyer
Dining Room 14-8 x 12-7
Porch

A regal hip roof, Palladian window and double dormers add elegance to this Williamsburg Colonial home. The foyer is flanked on the right by a dining room and on the left by a living room, both enhanced with tray ceilings. The sunken family room enjoys a fireplace and access to a rear deck. A cozy island kitchen leads to a bayed breakfast room. Upstairs, the master bedroom boasts two walk-in closets, a compartmented toilet, tub, separate shower and double vanity. Three additional bedrooms and one full bath complete the second floor.

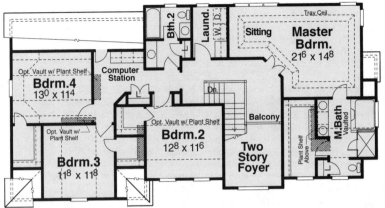

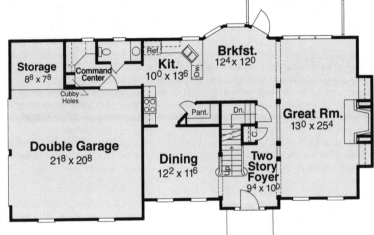

PLAN HPT750043

First Floor: 1,105 square feet
Second Floor: 1,432 square feet
Total: 2,537 square feet
Width: 58'-4" Depth: 31'-0"

The elegant facade of this traditional home is enhanced by an attractive combination of siding and stone. Plentiful windows and two country dormers illuminate interior spaces on both floors. Inside, the spacious two-story foyer is flanked by the great room featuring a fireplace and the formal dining room, which connects to the kitchen. A bayed breakfast area accesses a rear patio/deck. A two-car garage with storage completes the first floor. Upstairs, the master bedroom features a sitting area and a master bath with an enormous walk-in closet. Three additional family bedrooms—each with a walk-in closet—share a hall bath and a family computer station.

PLAN HPT750044

First Floor: 1,670 square feet
Second Floor: 1,741 square feet
Total: 3,411 square feet
Width: 64'-0" Depth: 78'-2"

Symmetry is everything in the Georgian style, and this home is a classic Georgian in both plan and elevation. The facade as a whole balances a one-story extended porch under a two-story hipped roof box. Inside, a traditional foyer with a central staircase is flanked by the living/dining rooms on one side and the great room on the other. Rear stairs allow private access to a secluded guest suite over the garage. This home is designed with a basement foundation.

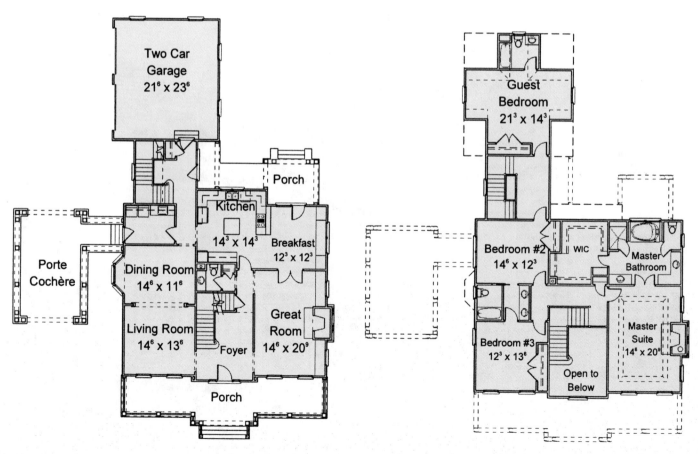

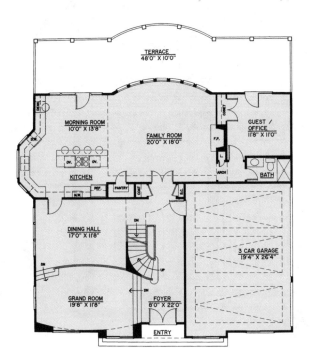

TERRACE
48'0" X 10'0"

MORNING ROOM
10'0" X 13'8"

FAMILY ROOM
20'0" X 18'0"

GUEST /
OFFICE
11'8" X 11'0"

F.P.

KITCHEN

PANTRY

BATH

ARCH

DINING HALL
17'0" X 11'8"

DN

UP

DN

3 CAR GARAGE
19'4" X 26'4"

GRAND ROOM
19'8" X 11'8"

FOYER
8'0" X 22'0"

ENTRY

PLAN HPT750045

First Floor: 1,593 square feet
Second Floor: 1,559 square feet
Total: 3,152 square feet
Width: 51'-0" Depth: 46'-6"

Symmetry is exhibited though the use of brick details, shutters and graceful columns on this design. Inside, to the left of the two-story foyer and down a few steps, is the grand room, which is slightly oval. A spacious dining hall is just up three steps and offers direct access from the huge island kitchen. The family room, located to the rear of the home, features a bowed wall of windows and a warming fireplace. A guest room or office accesses the rear deck as well as a full bath. Upstairs, the master bedroom is full of amenities, including two walk-in closets, a private porch and a lavish bath. Three family bedrooms, each with direct access to a bath, finish out this floor.

BEDROOM #2
13'4" X 11'4"

OPEN TO
FAMILY ROOM
BELOW

PORCH
13'4" X 8'2"

CLOSET

BATH

GALLERY

MASTER
BEDROOM
15'4" X 22'0"

BEDROOM #3
11'4" X 11'8"

DN

W.
D.
LAUN.

TREY CEILING

W.I.C.

BEDROOM #4
11'8" X 12'8"

OPEN
TO FOYER
BELOW

W.I.C.

VAULT

M. BATH

PLANT
SHELF

BATH

CLOSET

C. Rosen

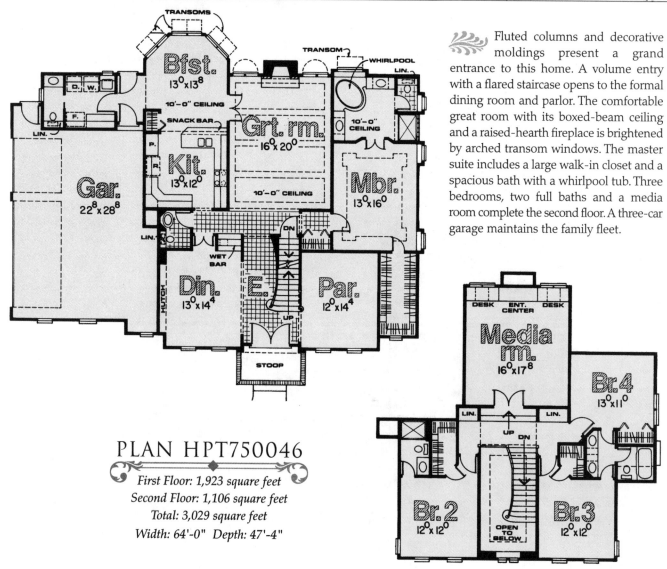

Fluted columns and decorative moldings present a grand entrance to this home. A volume entry with a flared staircase opens to the formal dining room and parlor. The comfortable great room with its boxed-beam ceiling and a raised-hearth fireplace is brightened by arched transom windows. The master suite includes a large walk-in closet and a spacious bath with a whirlpool tub. Three bedrooms, two full baths and a media room complete the second floor. A three-car garage maintains the family fleet.

PLAN HPT750046

First Floor: 1,923 square feet
Second Floor: 1,106 square feet
Total: 3,029 square feet
Width: 64'-0" Depth: 47'-4"

QUOTE ONE®
Cost to build? See page 310
to order complete cost estimate
to build this house in your area!

PLAN HPT750047

First Floor: 2,063 square feet
Second Floor: 894 square feet
Total: 2,957 square feet
Width: 72'-8" Depth: 51'-4"

An elegant brick elevation and rows of shuttered windows lend timeless beauty to this two-story Colonial design. The volume entry opens to the formal dining and living rooms and the magnificent great room. Sparkling floor-to-ceiling windows flank the fireplace in the great room, which offers a cathedral ceiling. French doors, bay windows and a decorative ceiling, plus a wet bar, highlight the private den. Special lifestyle amenities in the kitchen and bayed breakfast area include a built-in desk, wrapping counters and an island. A boxed ceiling adds elegance to the master suite. In the master bath/dressing area, note the large walk-in closet, built-in dresser, His and Hers vanities, oval whirlpool tub and plant shelves. Upstairs, each secondary bedroom contains a roomy closet and private bath.

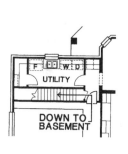

**Optional Basement
Stair Location**

PLAN HPT750048

First Floor: 2,595 square feet

Second Floor: 1,652 square feet

Total: 4,247 square feet

Bonus Room: 766 square feet

Width: 74'-11" Depth: 60'-3"

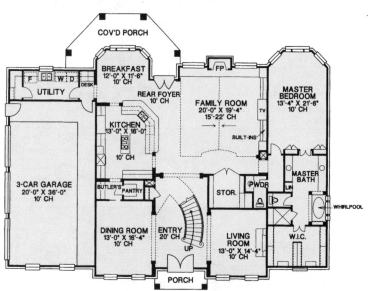

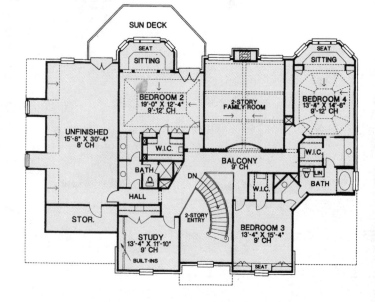

Dressed in white-as-lace snowfall, red-orange fall leaves, or the greens and pastels of spring and summer, this home is handsome in all seasons. Its pediment and porch detailing enrich a facade ripe with traditional elements. Indulgent feautres are prominent on both floors: grand bedrooms with sitting areas, abundant storage space and closets with built-ins, and formal and informal living areas. A study on the second floor is a handy student's reading room. Unfinished bonus space can be completed later for a hobby room, game room or additional bedroom. Please specify basement or slab foundation when ordering.

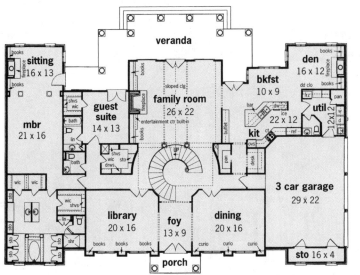

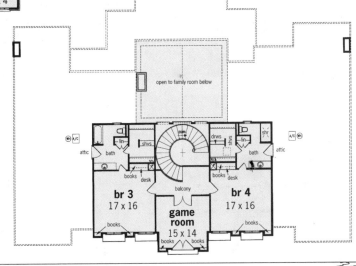

open to family room below

Two-story pilasters create a sense of the Old South on the facade of this modern home, updating the classic Adam's style. The foyer opens through an archway, announcing the breathtaking circular staircase. The formal dining room is situated on the right while the private library is found to the left. The grand family room is crowned with a sloped ceiling. The angled galley kitchen adjoins the breakfast nook while the butler's pantry facilitates service to the dining room. The master suite finds privacy on the left with an elegant sitting area defined by pillars. Two bedroom suites, each with a walk-in closet, share the second floor with the game room. Please specify crawlspace or slab foundation when ordering.

PLAN HPT750049

First Floor: 4,208 square feet
Second Floor: 1,352 square feet
Total: 5,560 square feet
Width: 94'-0" Depth: 68'-0"

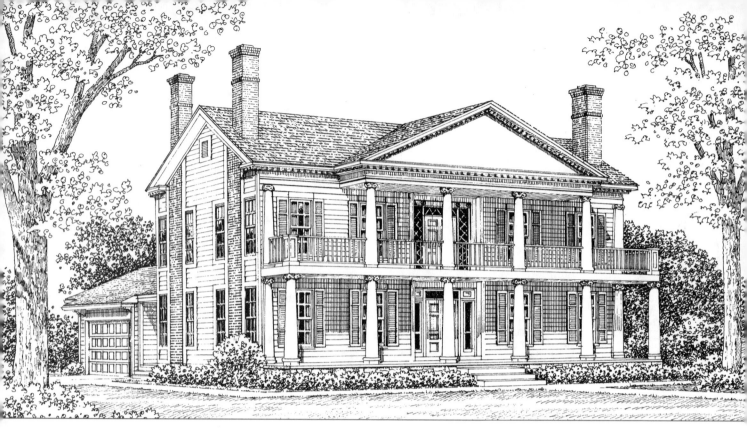

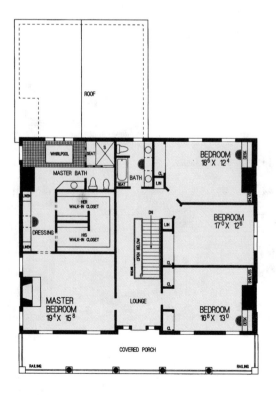

Covered porches upstairs and down are a charming addition to this well-appointed two-story Colonial home. Four chimneys herald four hearths inside: living room, dining room, family room and study. The family room is enhanced by a kitchen snack bar for informal meals or interaction between guests and the cook. A rear patio can be viewed and accessed from here. The second floor holds four bedrooms. The master suite includes a warm fireplace, oversized walk-in closet and relaxing master bath. Three family bedrooms share a full hall bath and a lounge that includes covered porch access.

PLAN HPT750050

First Floor: 2,191 square feet
Second Floor: 1,928 square feet
Total: 4,119 square feet
Width: 50'-0" Depth: 80'-0"

L|D

Quote One®
Cost to build? See page 310
to order complete cost estimate
to build this house in your area!

PLAN HPT750051

First Floor: 1,944 square feet
Second Floor: 1,427 square feet
Total: 3,371 square feet
Width: 52'-0" Depth: 84'-0"

The dazzling exterior of this Southern estate is true to form with six magnificent columns creating an awe-inspiring facade. The foyer leads to the living room with its fifteen-foot ceiling and paired window walls. Access to both the rear covered porch and the side courtyard is gained from the living room. The angled kitchen is flanked by the sunny eating bay and the convenient utility room. The side-loading, two-car garage at the rear contains an expansive storage area. The second floor holds the game room, an ancillary kitchen and three bedrooms while the master suite finds seclusion on the first floor. Note that Bedroom 4 includes a dressing area, a private bath and access to the balcony. Please specify basement, crawlspace or slab foundation when ordering.

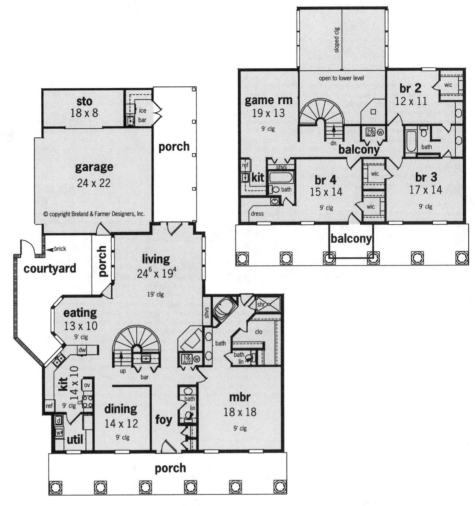

© copyright Breland & Farmer Designers, Inc.

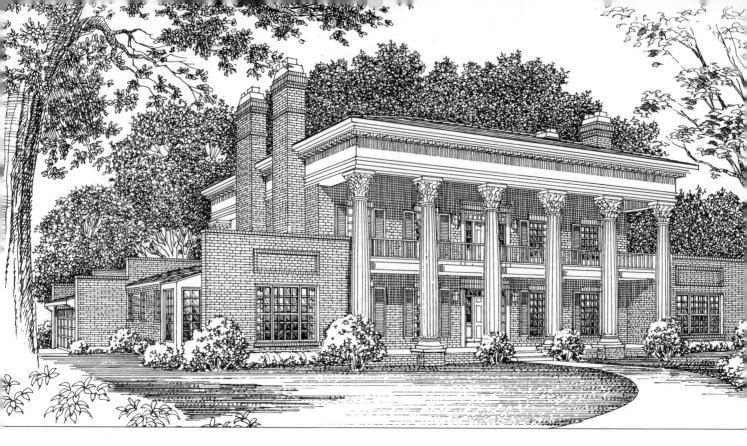

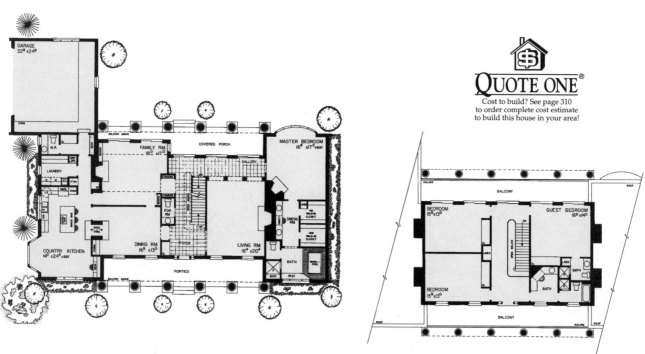

Andrew Jackson's dream of white-pillared splendor resulted in the building of The Hermitage from 1819 to 1834 near Nashville, Tennessee. Like its forebear, this adaptation has six soaring Corinthian columns on both the front and the rear, sheltering balconies accessible from the second floor. Two sets of twin chimneys and two projecting wings balance the central portion of the house. Living and dining rooms are at the front of the plan, as is the country kitchen, highlighted by a bay window, a through-fireplace to the dining room and a cooktop island/snack bar. The rear covered porch is reached through sliding glass doors in the family room and along the gallery. The amenity-laden master suite fills the right wing, while three other bedrooms are upstairs.

PLAN HPT750052

First Floor: 2,822 square feet
Second Floor: 1,335 square feet
Total: 4,157 square feet
Width: 88'-8" Depth: 68'-0"

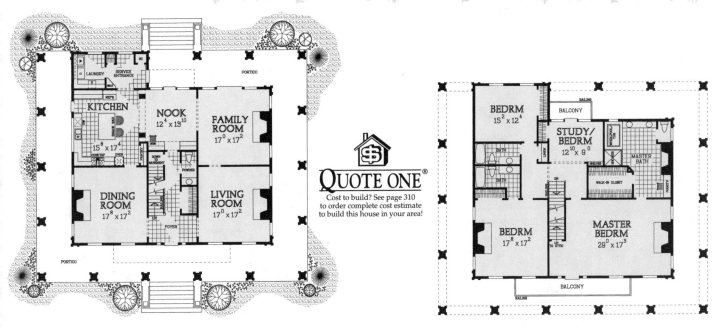

QUOTE ONE®
Cost to build? See page 310
to order complete cost estimate
to build this house in your area!

PLAN HPT750053

First Floor: 1,877 square feet

Second Floor: 1,877 square feet

Total: 3,754 square feet

Width: 65'-0" Depth: 53'-0"

L D

The gracious hospitality and the genteel, easy lifestyle of the South are brought to life in this elegant Southern Colonial home. Contributing to the exterior's stucco warmth are shutters, a cupola and square columns surrounding the home. Inside, the warmth continues with six fireplaces throughout the home: in the formal dining room, living room, family room—and on the second floor—family bedroom, master bedroom and master bath. The second floor contains two family bedrooms—each with its own bath—and a lavish master bedroom with a balcony and a pampering bath. A study/bedroom with a balcony completes the upstairs. Plans for a detached garage with an enclosed lap pool are included with the blueprints.

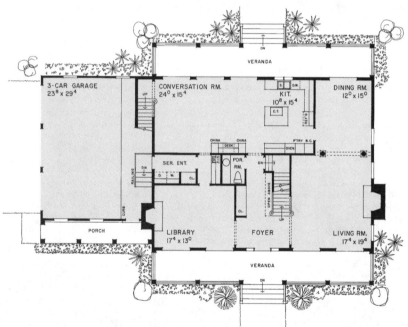

Spring breezes and summer nights will be a joy to take in on the verandas and balcony of this gorgeous Southern Colonial home. Or, if you prefer, sit back and enjoy a good book in the library, or invite a friend over for a chat in the conversation room. The first floor also includes formal dining and living rooms, a service entry with a laundry and a three-car garage. You'll find a bonus room over the garage; you may decide to turn it into a media room or an exercise room. The master bedroom sports a fireplace, two walk-in closets, a double-bowl vanity, a shower and a whirlpool tub. Three other bedrooms occupy the second floor—one has its own full bath. Of course, the balcony is just a step away.

PLAN HPT750054

First Floor: 1,778 square feet
Second Floor: 1,663 square feet
Total: 3,441 square feet
Bonus Room: 442 square feet
Width: 72'-0" Depth: 50'-0"

LD

QUOTE ONE®
Cost to build? See page 310
to order complete cost estimate
to build this house in your area!

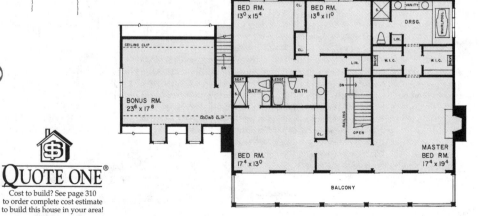

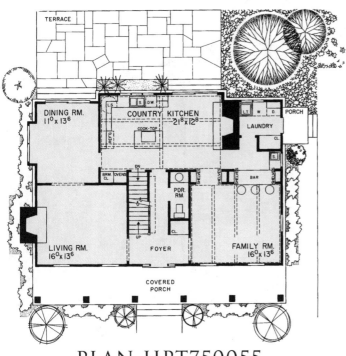

PLAN HPT750055

First Floor: 1,308 square feet

Second Floor: 1,262 square feet

Total: 2,570 square feet

Width: 44'-8" Depth: 36'-0"

A covered porch and a balcony highlight the exterior of this family farmhouse. Gathering areas dominate the front of the first floor: a living room with a fireplace to the left and a family room with a wet bar to the right. Directly to the back is the country kitchen with another fireplace and an island cooktop. The dining room flanks the kitchen on one side and a laundry room on the other. Four bedrooms are found on the second floor. The large master suite showcases a curved counter and a large walk-in closet in its private bath. Three other bedrooms share a full bath that includes double vanities.

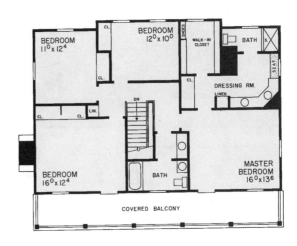

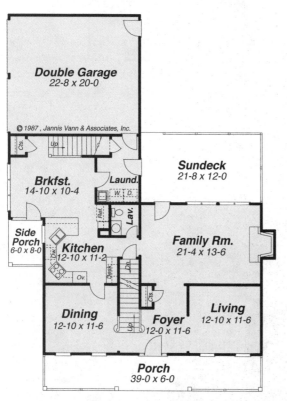

Double Garage
22-8 x 20-0

© 1987, Jannis Vann & Associates, Inc.

Up.

Brkfst.
14-10 x 10-4

Laund.

Sundeck
21-8 x 12-0

W. D.

Side Porch
6-0 x 8-0

Kitchen
12-10 x 11-2

Ref.

Lav.

Family Rm.
21-4 x 13-6

Desk

Dn.

Dining
12-10 x 11-6

Foyer
12-0 x 11-6

Living
12-10 x 11-6

Porch
39-0 x 6-0

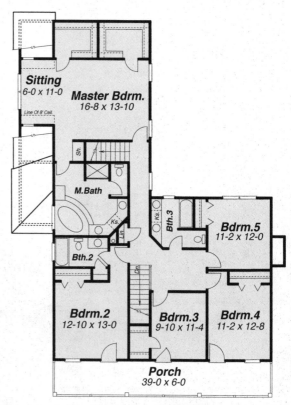

Sitting
6-0 x 11-0

Master Bdrm.
16-8 x 13-10

Line Of 8' Ceil.

Sh.

M.Bath

Bth.2

Bth.3

Bdrm.5
11-2 x 12-0

Bdrm.2
12-10 x 13-0

Bdrm.3
9-10 x 11-4

Bdrm.4
11-2 x 12-8

Dn.

Porch
39-0 x 6-0

PLAN HPT750056

First Floor: 1,286 square feet
Second Floor: 1,675 square feet
Total: 2,961 square feet
Width: 35'-0" Depth: 64'-0"

The Southern plantation comes to mind when looking at this two-story home complete with a porch and terrace. Formal elegance is the order of the day as you enter the foyer flanked by the living and dining rooms. The family room features a full window wall overlooking the deck, which is also accessible from the rear entry of the garage. Corner cabinets house the sink and surface unit, keeping everything within a few steps of each other. Rear stairs lead to the master suite, located over the garage, providing privacy from the rest of the second floor. Four additional bedrooms—one with its own private bath—are also on the second floor. Please specify basement or slab foundation when ordering.

PLAN HPT750057

First Floor: 2,473 square feet

Second Floor: 1,233 square feet

Total: 3,706 square feet

Bonus Room: 155 square feet

Width: 60'-0" Depth: 64'-2"

This twin-gabled farmhouse is sure to please, with its covered front porch, large screened back porch and many amenities. Inside, the foyer is flanked by a formal dining room and a cozy study. Double doors separate the foyer from the spacious great room, which is complete with a fireplace and twin French doors to the screened porch. The homeowner will definitely feel pampered in the master suite. Here, two walk-in closets, a separate exercise room and a lavish bath wait to help with relaxation. Upstairs, an absolutely luxurious bath will make family or guests feel like royalty. Note the optional media room. Please specify basement, crawlspace or slab foundation when ordering.

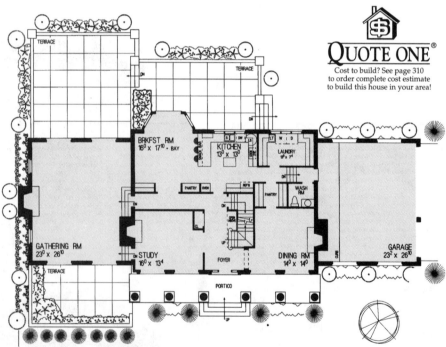

PLAN HPT750058

First Floor: 2,167 square feet
Second Floor: 1,992 square feet
Total: 4,159 square feet
Width: 94'-4" Depth: 42'-9"

L

The elegant facade of this design, with its columned portico, fanlights and dormers, houses an amenity-filled interior. The gathering room, study and dining room, each with a fireplace, provide plenty of room for relaxing and entertaining. A large work area contains a kitchen with a breakfast room, a snack bar, a laundry room and a pantry. The four-bedroom second floor includes a master suite with a sumptuous private bath and an exercise room. Attic storage is available above the gathering room.

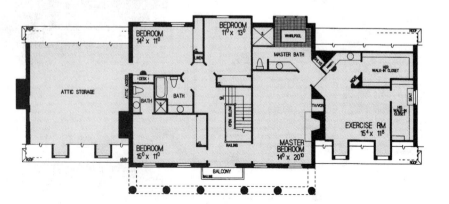

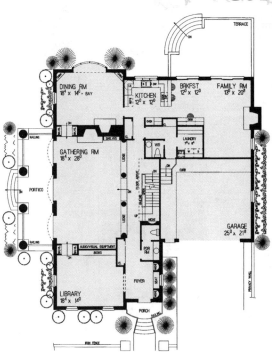

18th-Century Charleston, South Carolina, w…
"single house," one room deep, with the narr…
street. This adaptation recalls the 1750 home of Robe…
with tall pillars and a handsome brick exterior crowned…
The original has a fragment of a Civil War cannon on its roof, lodged
there in 1865 when the cannon was blown up to keep it from Sherman's
troops. (It was deemed safer to leave it there than to try to remove it.)
This version adds a family room and a garage to the floor plan. The
sunken gathering room opens to the long hall through a colonnade and
is flanked by the dining room and a library. Upstairs is a sumptuous
master suite with a through-fireplace and three other bedrooms.

PLAN HPT750059

First Floor: 2,440 square feet

Second Floor: 2,250 square feet

Total: 4,690 square feet

Width: 65'-6" Depth: 64'-0"

QUOTE ONE®

Cost to build? See page 310
to order complete cost estimate
to build this house in your area!

PLAN HPT750060

First Floor: 1,598 square feet

Second Floor: 1,675 square feet

Total: 3,273 square feet

Bonus Room: 534 square feet

Width: 54'-8" Depth: 68'-0"

Main- and second-level covered porches, accompanied by intricate detailing, and many multi-pane windows create a splendid Southern mansion. The prominent entry opens to formal dining and living rooms. The grand family room is warmed by a fireplace and views a screened porch with a cozy window seat. The roomy breakfast area provides access to the porch and the three-car garage. French doors open to the second-floor master suite, which features decorative ceiling details, His and Hers walk-in closets, a large dressing area, dual lavs, a whirlpool bath and a separate shower area.

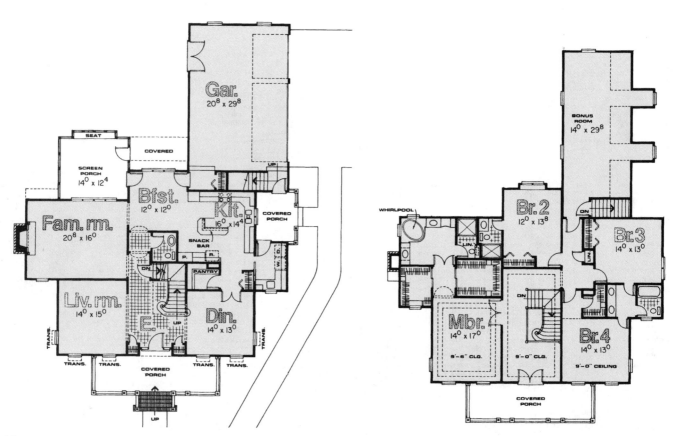

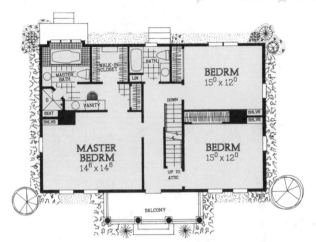

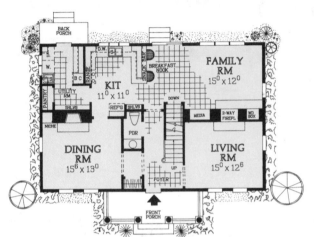

PLAN HPT750061

First Floor: 1,232 square feet
Second Floor: 1,232 square feet
Third Floor: 421 square feet
Total: 2,885 square feet
Width: 44'-0" Depth: 34'-0"

The drama of a porch, a balcony and a widow's walk will make this Colonial home a showpiece in any neighborhood. The formal living and dining rooms both feature fireplaces—the perfect backdrop for elegant entertaining. The large country kitchen offers a convenient U-shaped counter with a snack bar, and is open to the family room. Upstairs, the luxurious master bedroom is partnered with two family bedrooms and a full hall bath. The third floor holds a large studio with a full bath.

Quote One®
Cost to build? See page 310
to order complete cost estimate
to build this house in your area!

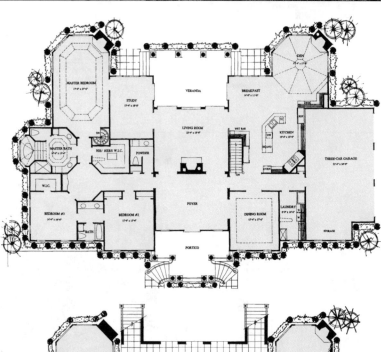

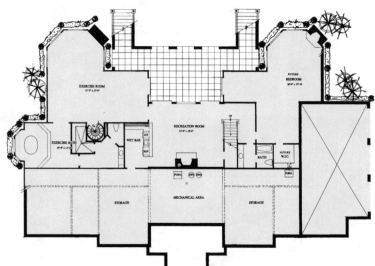

PLAN HPT750062

Square Footage: 4,646
Finished Basement: 1,974 square feet
Width: 111'-10" Depth: 76'-0"

Timeless in every detail, this home displays a stately manner through the use of brick, symmetrical design and classic elements. The tremendous foyer offers an ideal location for greeting guests and provides a double entrance to the living room. The kitchen easily serves the formal dining room, the breakfast room and the octagonal den. With a vaulted master bath, access to the study and a private stair to the health spa below, the master suite is complete in every detail. The lower terrace level contains an exercise room with a large bath and a recreation room with a fireplace and wet bar. This home is designed with a walkout basement foundation.

PLAN HPT750063

First Floor: 1,895 square feet
Second Floor: 1,661 square feet
Total: 3,556 square feet
Width: 86'-10" Depth: 39'-1"

A two-story pillared entrance portico and tall multi-paned windows, flanking the double front doors, together accentuate the facade of this Southern Colonial design. This brick home is stately and classic in its exterior appeal. The three-car garage opens to the side so it does not disturb the street view. Formal living and dining rooms are at each end of the foyer. The living room is complemented by a music room or an optional bedroom with a full bath nearby. The formal dining room and the informal breakfast room are easily served by the kitchen. The spacious family room features a built-in wet bar. The second floor contains two family bedrooms and the luxurious master suite with a private bath.

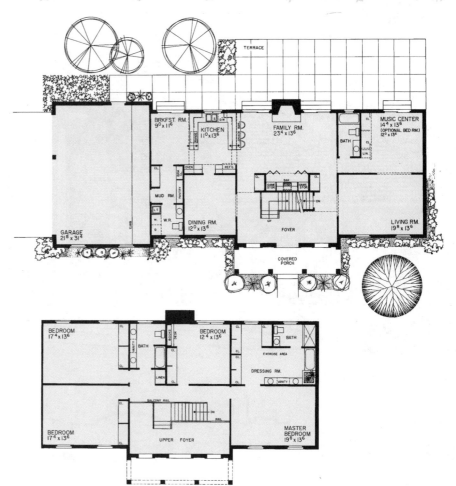

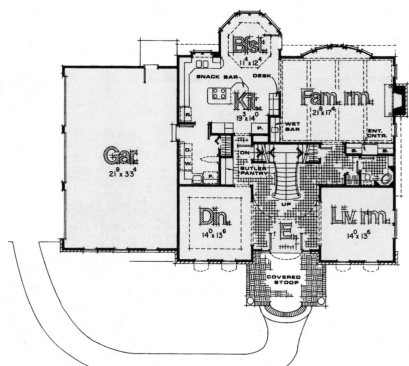

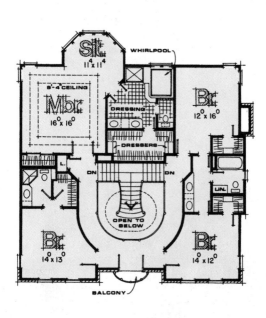

PLAN HPT750064

First Floor: 1,675 square feet
Second Floor: 1,605 square feet
Total: 3,280 square feet
Width: 65'-0" Depth: 46'-0"

A grand and glorious split staircase makes a lasting first impression in this stately two-story home. The impressive family room is lit by a beveled wall of windows—while a wet bar, built-in bookcases and an entertainment center provide the finishing touches. The spacious kitchen is sure to please, featuring an island cooktop with a snack bar, a planning desk and a sunny bayed breakfast area. Upstairs, each secondary bedroom enjoys a walk-in closet and two bedrooms share a hollywood bath while a third features a private bath. The master suite offers uncommon elegance with French doors, a tray ceiling, gazebo sitting area and a separate off-season closet. Enter the master bath through yet more French doors and enjoy its relaxing whirlpool tub, open shower and built-in dressers in the large walk-in closet.

PLAN HPT750065

First Floor: 3,509 square feet

Second Floor: 1,564 square feet

Total: 5,073 square feet

Attic: 740 square feet

Width: 86'-6" Depth: 67'-3"

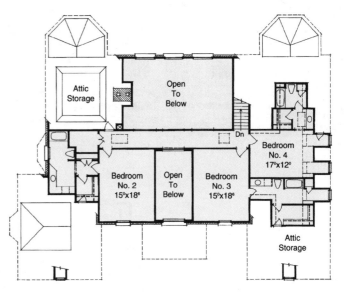

Symmetry combined with classical detailing proclaims this estate as the very finest in elegant architecture. Designed on the traditional center-hall principle, the home sustains both grand formal spaces and intimate casual areas. The study connects to the master suite, but also is accessed directly from the foyer, making it a fine home office. The master suite spotlights a tray ceiling, a huge walk-in closet and a resplendent bath. This home is designed with a walkout basement foundation.

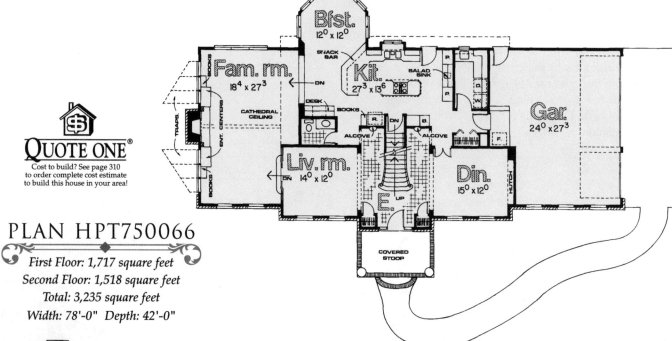

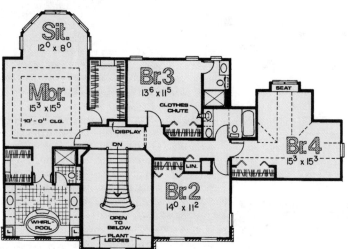

QUOTE ONE®

Cost to build? See page 310
to order complete cost estimate
to build this house in your area!

PLAN HPT750066

First Floor: 1,717 square feet

Second Floor: 1,518 square feet

Total: 3,235 square feet

Width: 78'-0" Depth: 42'-0"

Stately columns highlight the facade of this beautiful Southern Colonial home. The open entry allows for views into formal areas and up the tapering staircase. The dining room joins the kitchen through double doors. The living room can be divided from the sunken family room by pocket doors. Step down into the huge family room to find large windows, a fireplace, a built-in entertainment center and bookcases. The kitchen features a gazebo breakfast area, serving bar and cooktop island. Upstairs, three family bedrooms share two full baths. The private master suite features a tiered ceiling, two walk-in closets and a roomy bayed sitting area.

PLAN HPT750067

First Floor: 3,504 square feet
Second Floor: 1,725 square feet
Total: 5,229 square feet
Width: 56'-9" Depth: 122'-0"

Classic elements—such as double columns capped by a pediment—contribute to this lovely home's curb appeal. A carefully planned interior begins with spacious, open formal rooms and, to the opposite side of the foyer, a flex room that easily converts to a guest suite. A butler's pantry leads to the gourmet kitchen, which has a breakfast area. The master bedroom provides twin walk-in closets and a luxurious bath. The family room provides leisure space and features a centerpiece fireplace. Four family bedrooms and two full baths occupy the second floor.

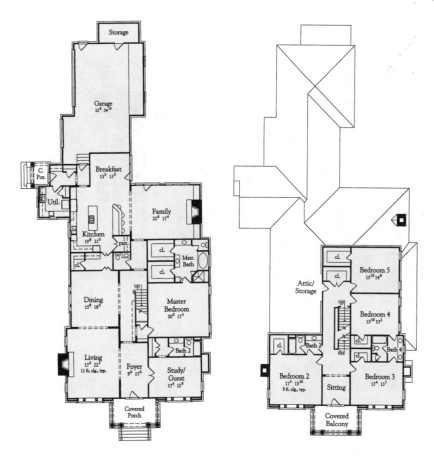

This home, as shown in the photograph, may differ from the actual blueprints. For more detailed information, please check the floor plans carefully.

©Jeffrey Jacobs/Architectural Photography

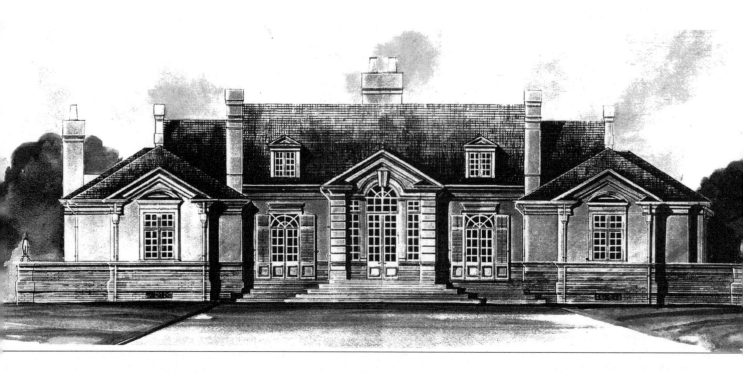

This Neoclassical home has plenty to offer! The elegant entrance is flanked by a formal dining room on the left and a beam-ceilinged study—complete with a fireplace—on the right. An angled kitchen is sure to please with a work island, plenty of counter and cabinet space, and a snack counter that it shares with the sunny breakfast room. A family room with a second fireplace is nearby. The lavish master suite features many amenities, including a huge walk-in closet, a three-sided fireplace and a lavish bath. Two secondary bedrooms have private baths. Finish the second-floor bonus space to create an office, a play room and a full bath. A three-car garage easily shelters the family fleet.

PLAN HPT750068

Square Footage: 3,828
Bonus Space: 1,018 square feet
Width: 80'-6" Depth: 70'-8"

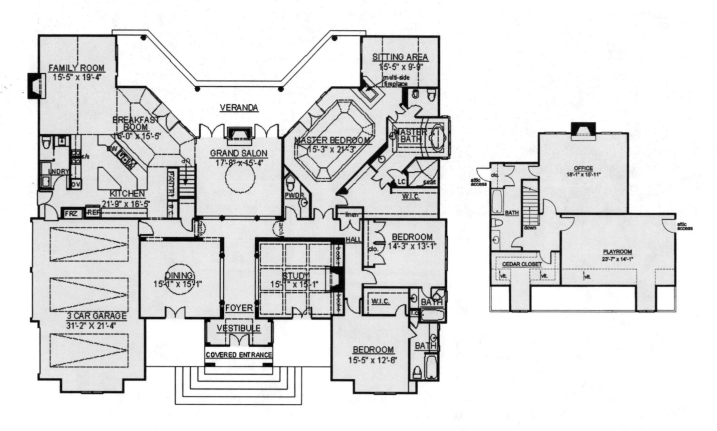

PLAN HPT750069

First Floor: 2,714 square feet
Second Floor: 2,529 square feet
Total: 5,243 square feet
Width: 94'-0" Depth: 48'-0"

You've probably seen homes like this—on BBC or PBS specials. They're usually inhabited by landed gentry who've inherited the structure from generations of ancestors. But this rendition is thoroughly modern and completely yours to decorate and enjoy. And you won't find any cramped, drafty areas inside—the floor plan is spacious and flexible enough for formal dinners and raucous Superbowl parties. Note the guest suite on the first floor near the library (a loggia access enhances the beamed-ceiling library). The family room is huge, and close enough to the breakfast room and kitchen to make it practical. A screened porch is a bonus. The grand staircase separates the master suite on the second floor from secondary bedrooms. A large cedar closet, sitting area and private porch reinforce the luxury here.

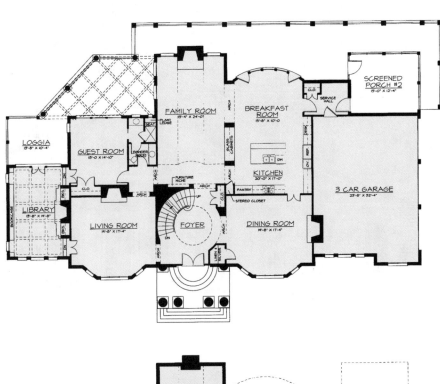

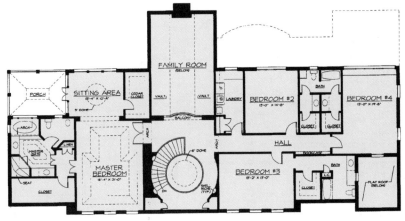

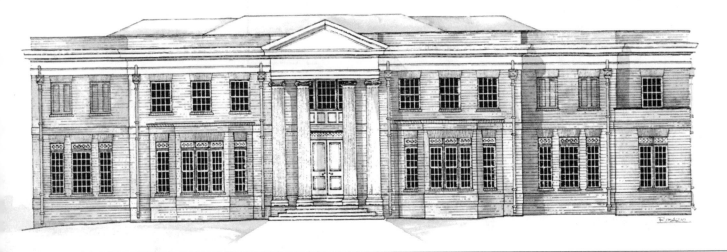

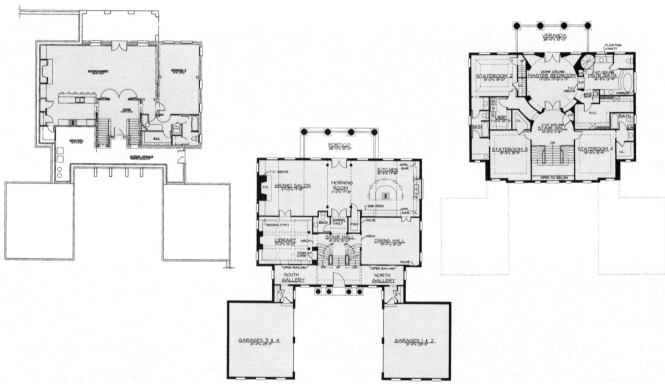

Simply elegant, with dignified details, this beautiful home is reminiscent of English estate homes. Two double garages flank a columned front door and are attached to the main floor by galleries leading to the entry foyer. Here a double staircase leads upstairs and encourages a view beyond the morning room, grand salon and rear portico. The gourmet kitchen has a uniquely styled island counter with a cooktop. For formal meals, the dining hall is nearby. The elaborate master bedroom and three staterooms reside on the second level. The master bedroom features a circular shape and enjoys a private lanai, a through-fireplace to the master bath, and numerous alcoves and built-in amenities.

PLAN HPT750070

First Floor: 2,175 square feet
Second Floor: 1,927 square feet
Total: 4,102 square feet
Finished Basement: 1,927 square feet
Width: 74'-0" Depth: 82'-0"

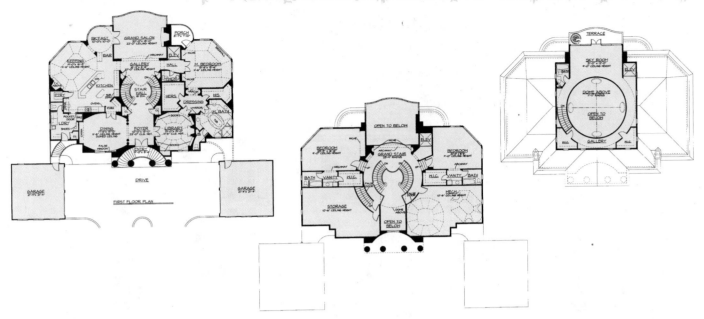

PLAN HPT750071

First Floor: 3,340 square feet
Second Floor: 1,540 square feet
Third Floor: 850 square feet
Total: 5,730 square feet
Width: 106'-0" Depth: 82'-0"

This is a grand design—there is no denying it. Symmetrical, ornate, historical and complex, it speaks to those with the discretion to investigate a very particular kind of estate home. Interior spaces are adorned with distinctive details. The entry and gallery focus on circular stairs with double access to the second-floor landing. Each of the living areas has a unique and decorative ceiling treatment. Even the master bath is enhanced beyond the ordinary. Aspects to appreciate: a formal library, two walk-in pantries, a master bedroom vestibule, double garages, a private master bedroom porch, an elevator, and a gigantic storage area on the second floor.

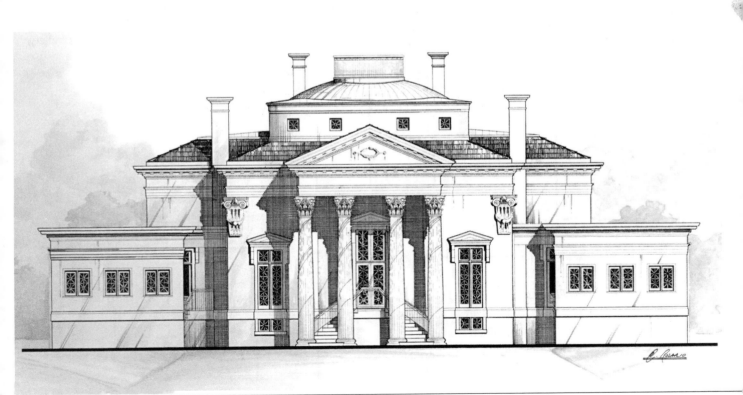

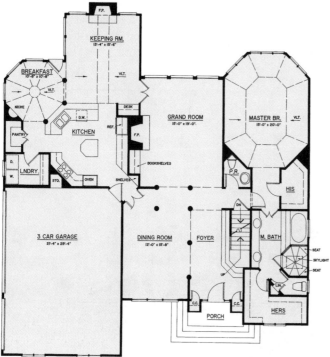

This narrow-lot design would be ideal for a golf course or lakeside lot. Inside the arched entry, the formal dining room is separated from the foyer and the massive grand room by decorative pillars. At the end of the day, the family will enjoy gathering in the cozy keeping room with its fireplace and easy access to the large island kitchen and the sunny gazebo-style breakfast room. The master suite, located on the first floor for privacy, features a uniquely designed bedroom and a luxurious bath with His and Hers walk-in closets. Your family portraits and favorite art treasures can be displayed along the upstairs gallery, which shares space with three family bedrooms and two full baths.

PLAN HPT750072

First Floor: 2,035 square feet
Second Floor: 1,030 square feet
Total: 3,065 square feet
Width: 55'-8" Depth: 62'-0"

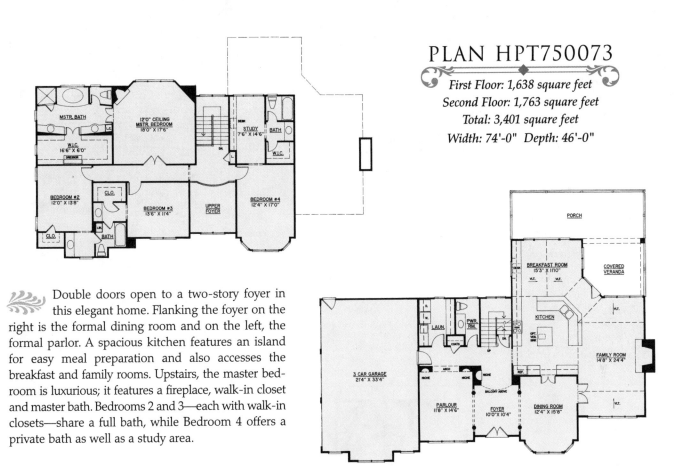

PLAN HPT750073

First Floor: 1,638 square feet
Second Floor: 1,763 square feet
Total: 3,401 square feet
Width: 74'-0" Depth: 46'-0"

Double doors open to a two-story foyer in this elegant home. Flanking the foyer on the right is the formal dining room and on the left, the formal parlor. A spacious kitchen features an island for easy meal preparation and also accesses the breakfast and family rooms. Upstairs, the master bedroom is luxurious; it features a fireplace, walk-in closet and master bath. Bedrooms 2 and 3—each with walk-in closets—share a full bath, while Bedroom 4 offers a private bath as well as a study area.

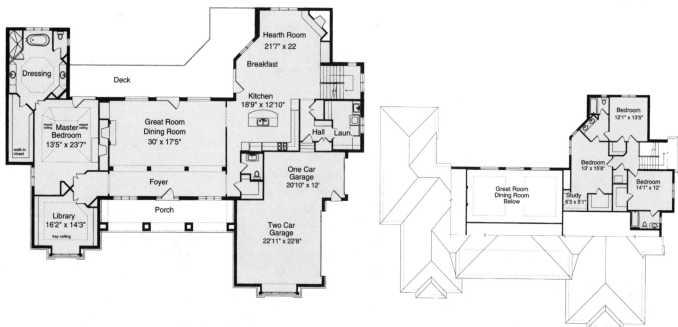

An elegant front porch, columns inside and out, various ceiling treatments and decorative windows create a spectacular home. An open floor plan provides large formal and informal spaces. The island kitchen with extensive counter space offers easy access to the formal dining and breakfast areas. Located for privacy, the impressive master bedroom suite showcases a deluxe dressing room with a whirlpool tub, dual vanities, an oversized shower and a walk-in closet. A library is located near the master bedroom. Split stairs are positioned for family convenience and lead to three bedrooms, each with a large walk-in closet and private access to a bath. A three-car garage and full basement complete this exciting showplace.

PLAN HPT750074

First Floor: 3,087 square feet
Second Floor: 1,037 square feet
Total: 4,124 square feet
Width: 92'-2" Depth: 70'-10"

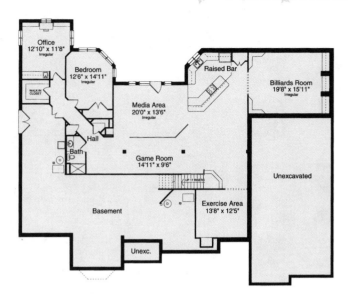

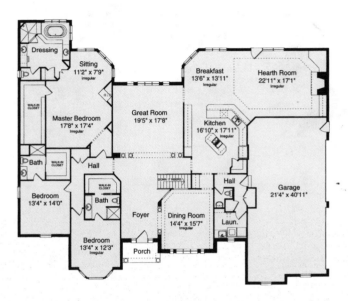

PLAN HPT750075

Square Footage: 3,570
Finished Basement: 2,367 square feet
Width: 84'-6" Depth: 69'-4"

The stone and brick exterior with multiple gables and a side-entry garage creates a design that boasts great curb appeal. The gourmet kitchen with an island and snack bar combines with the spacious breakfast room and hearth room to create a warm and friendly atmosphere for family living. The luxurious master bedroom with a sitting area and a fireplace is complemented by a deluxe dressing room and walk-in closet. The basement level contains an office, media room, billiards room, exercise area and plenty of storage.

PLAN HPT750076

Square Footage: 4,038
Width: 98'-0" Depth: 90'-0"

Reminiscent of the old Newport mansions, this luxury house has volume ceilings, a glamorous master suite with a hearth-warmed sitting area, a glassed-in sun room, a home office, three porches with a deck, and a gourmet kitchen with a pantry. Graceful French doors are used for all the entrances and in the formal living and dining rooms. The kitchen is magnificent and boasts a large pantry. A centrally positioned family room is graced with a large fireplace and is accessed by the rear porch, living room and dining room. Please specify basement, crawlspace or slab foundation when ordering.

PLAN HPT750077

Square Footage: 2,311
Bonus Space: 720 square feet
Width: 74'-0" Depth: 50'-0"

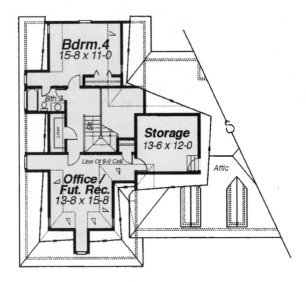

This timeless Colonial design boasts both contemporary and classical elements. Double doors enter to formal living and dining rooms flanking the foyer. The spacious family room boasts a cozy fireplace, built-ins and access to the rear sun deck. The first-floor master bedroom, brightened by a bay window, features a private bath and a roomy walk-in closet. Two family bedrooms are placed just behind the two-car garage. Bedroom 4, a home office and storage space are all located on the second floor.

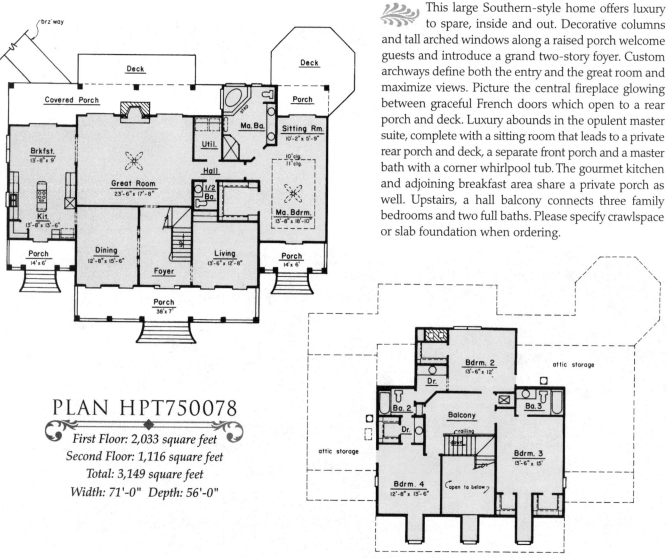

This large Southern-style home offers luxury to spare, inside and out. Decorative columns and tall arched windows along a raised porch welcome guests and introduce a grand two-story foyer. Custom archways define both the entry and the great room and maximize views. Picture the central fireplace glowing between graceful French doors which open to a rear porch and deck. Luxury abounds in the opulent master suite, complete with a sitting room that leads to a private rear porch and deck, a separate front porch and a master bath with a corner whirlpool tub. The gourmet kitchen and adjoining breakfast area share a private porch as well. Upstairs, a hall balcony connects three family bedrooms and two full baths. Please specify crawlspace or slab foundation when ordering.

PLAN HPT750078

First Floor: 2,033 square feet
Second Floor: 1,116 square feet
Total: 3,149 square feet
Width: 71'-0" Depth: 56'-0"

PLAN HPT750079

First Floor: 3,732 square feet

Second Floor: 1,080 square feet

Total: 4,812 square feet

Bonus Room: 903 square feet

Width: 108'-4" Depth: 73'-6"

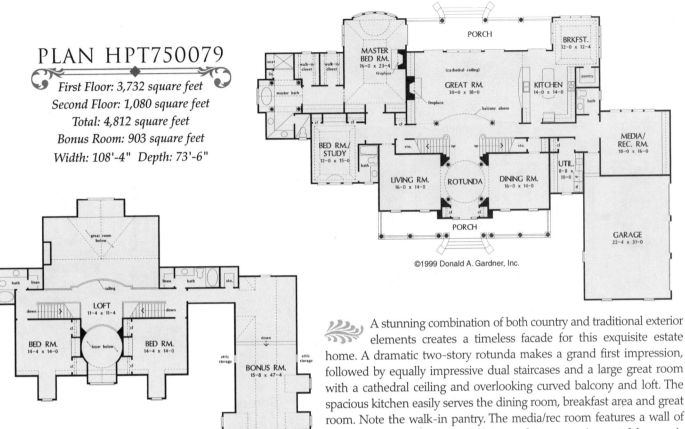

©1999 Donald A. Gardner, Inc.

A stunning combination of both country and traditional exterior elements creates a timeless facade for this exquisite estate home. A dramatic two-story rotunda makes a grand first impression, followed by equally impressive dual staircases and a large great room with a cathedral ceiling and overlooking curved balcony and loft. The spacious kitchen easily serves the dining room, breakfast area and great room. Note the walk-in pantry. The media/rec room features a wall of built-in cabinets to house television and stereo equipment. More oasis than bedroom, the master suite is enhanced by a deep tray ceiling and enjoys a fireplace, built-in dressing cabinetry, His and Hers walk-in closets and a luxurious bath with every amenity. Two bedrooms, two baths and an oversized bonus room are on the second floor.

© 1998 Donald A. Gardner, Inc.

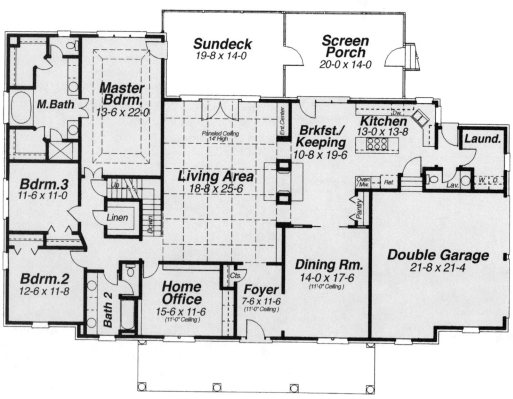

Sundeck
19-8 x 14-0

Screen Porch
20-0 x 14-0

Master Bdrm.
13-6 x 22-0

M. Bath

Paneled Ceiling 14' High

Ent. Center

Brkfst./ Keeping
10-8 x 19-6

Kitchen
13-0 x 13-8

Laund.

Living Area
18-8 x 25-6

Oven/Mw.   Ref.   Lav.   W. D.

Pantry

Bdrm. 3
11-6 x 11-0

Up

Linen

Down

Dining Rm.
14-0 x 17-6
(11'-0" Ceiling)

Double Garage
21-8 x 21-4

Bdrm. 2
12-6 x 11-8

Bath 2

Home Office
15-6 x 11-6
(11'-0" Ceiling)

Cts.

Foyer
7-6 x 11-6
(11'-0" Ceiling)

PLAN HPT750080

Square Footage: 2,788
Width: 83'-2"   Depth: 60'-5"

Southern plantation elegance on a generous scale for everyday living. The side-loading two-car garage, home office, screened porch and sun deck are all bonuses in this refined design. The foyer opens to the living area that shares a double-sided fireplace with the breakfast/keeping room. The adjoining kitchen accesses the garage and the utility room. The master suite enjoys a tray-ceilinged bedroom and a lavish private bath. Two family bedrooms share a full bath nearby. The living room and master bedroom open to the sun deck while the breakfast area leads to the screened porch.

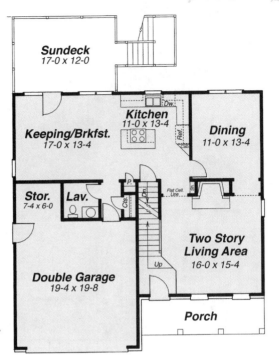

Sundeck
17-0 x 12-0

Keeping/Brkfst.
17-0 x 13-4

Kitchen
11-0 x 13-4

Dining
11-0 x 13-4

Stor.
7-4 x 6-0

Lav.

Two Story Living Area
16-0 x 15-4

Up

Double Garage
19-4 x 19-8

Porch

PLAN HPT750081

First Floor: 998 square feet
Second Floor: 1,156 square feet
Total: 2,154 square feet
Width: 40'-0" Depth: 42'-0"

The two-story columned front porch gives flair and style to this Colonial-inspired home. The two-story living area and foyer generates a spacious feeling as you enter the home. The keeping/breakfast area provides expanded views to the sun deck and rear property. An open flow between the oversized keeping/breakfast area and kitchen allows for interaction with family and friends. The second floor holds the master suite, which includes a large walk-in closet, private bath and tray ceiling. Three additional bedrooms share a full bath. Bedroom 4 may be converted to a nursery or a private sitting room for the master suite.

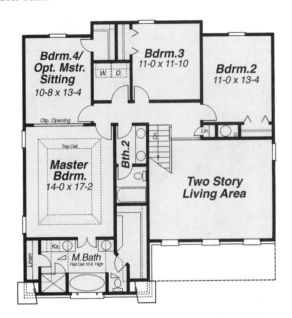

Bdrm.4/ Opt. Mstr. Sitting
10-8 x 13-4

Bdrm.3
11-0 x 11-10

Bdrm.2
11-0 x 13-4

Master Bdrm.
14-0 x 17-2

Bth.2

Two Story Living Area

M.Bath

PLAN HPT750082

First Floor: 2,247 square feet
Second Floor: 637 square feet
Total: 2,884 square feet
Bonus Room: 235 square feet
Width: 64'-0" Depth: 55'-2"

This astonishing traditional home looks great with its gables, muntin windows with keystone lintels, and turret-style bay. The heart of the home is the vaulted family room with a fireplace. The master bath leads into a walk-in closet. The home office near the hall bath is illuminated by a bayed wall of windows and is flexible as an additional family bedroom. The kitchen conveniently connects to the dining room, breakfast room and garage. Family bedrooms upstairs share a loft that overlooks the family room. Please specify basement or crawlspace foundation when ordering.

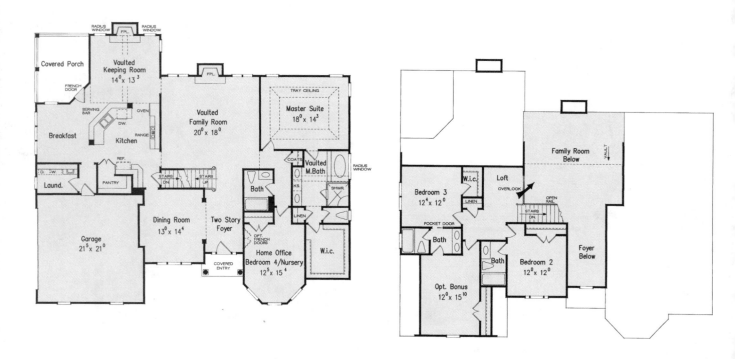

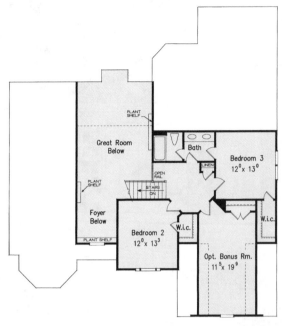

The two-story traditional home takes its inspiration from the Georgian era with its window placement, hipped roof and gable arrangement. The bay window, a more modern element, adds a multitude of sunlight to the sitting area in the master suite. The two-story foyer leads past the grand staircase to the vaulted great room where a warming fireplace creates an inviting atmosphere. The island kitchen, breakfast nook and sun room/keeping room enjoy the visual benefits of the multitude of windows in these areas. The master suite finds privacy on the first floor while the two family bedrooms rest on the second floor with a shared bath. Please specify basement or crawlspace foundation when ordering.

PLAN HPT750083

First Floor: 2,003 square feet
Second Floor: 579 square feet
Total: 2,582 square feet
Bonus Room: 262 square feet
Width: 54'-0" *Depth:* 60'-0"

This two-story traditional design offers a narrow-lot layout—perfect for any family. The foyer opens to the formal dining room and the two-story grand room warmed by a fireplace. The kitchen features a pantry and easily serves the breakfast and dining rooms. A first-floor bedroom easily converts to a home office and is placed near a hall bath, just behind the two-car garage. Upstairs, the master suite enjoys a vaulted master bath with a walk-in closet. Two additional family bedrooms on the second floor share a hall bath. Please specify basement or crawlspace foundation when ordering.

PLAN HPT750084

First Floor: 1,099 square feet
Second Floor: 966 square feet
Total: 2,065 square feet
Width: 47'-0" Depth: 38'-4"

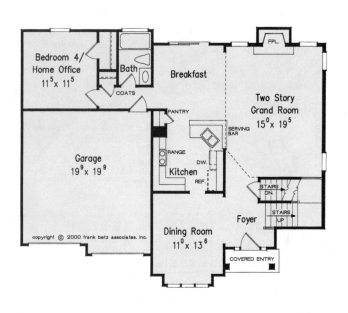

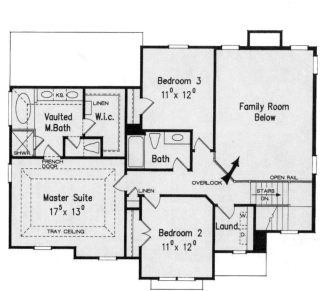

Beautiful brickwork and traditional styling create this home's classic exterior. Inside, the grand foyer introduces the formal dining room to the left. Down the hall, a powder room is convenient to the dining room and the spacious great room. The galley-style kitchen passes through to the breakfast area, which borders the great room with its fireplace and built-in shelving. The first-floor master suite features private porch access. The second floor houses three family bedrooms—one with a private bath—a loft and a future study or office space. This home is designed with a basement foundation.

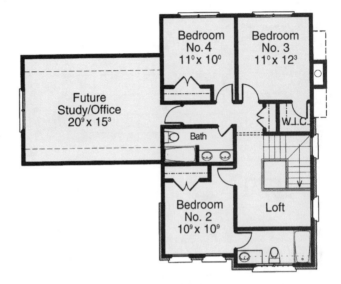

PLAN HPT750085

First Floor: 1,353 square feet

Second Floor: 623 square feet

Total: 1,976 square feet

Bonus Room: 300 square feet

Width: 46'-0" Depth: 53'-2"

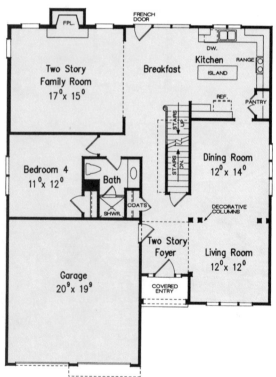

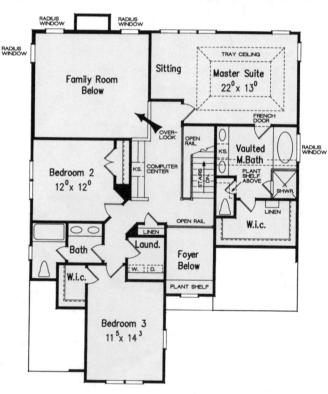

PLAN HPT750086

First Floor: 1,330 square feet
Second Floor: 1,195 square feet
Total: 2,525 square feet
Width: 40'-0" Depth: 51'-4"

This traditional home enjoys shingles, gables and muntin windows. Entertain extended family and guests with ease in either the informal or formal living areas of this plan. Some amenities include the two-story family room and a kitchen with an island counter. The master suite enjoys a tray ceiling with a French door leading to a vaulted bath. The master bath features a radius window by the soaking tub, a separate shower, compartmented toilet, two-sink vanity and plant shelf. Note the convenient second-floor laundry set between Bedrooms 2 and 3. Please specify basement or crawlspace foundation when ordering. Entertain extended family and guests with ease in either the informal or formal living areas of this plan.

Muntin windows and a transom door fill the interior of this home with natural light. A covered front porch welcomes you inside to a two-story foyer. The first floor features a two-story family room with a fireplace and a kitchen with an island counter. The vaulted formal living room combines with the dining area. The breakfast room accesses the rear through a French door. A bedroom—perfect for a guest suite—is placed just behind the three-car garage. Upstairs, the master suite offers a vaulted sitting area, a bath with an angled oval tub, and His and Hers walk-in closets. Three additional family bedrooms reside on the second floor. Please specify basement or crawlspace foundation when ordering.

PLAN HPT750087

First Floor: 1,658 square feet
Second Floor: 1,600 square feet
Total: 3,258 square feet
Width: 52'-4" Depth: 55'-6"

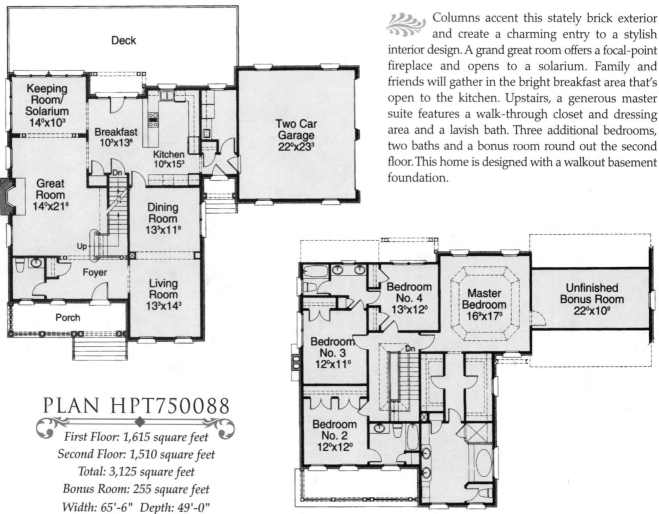

Columns accent this stately brick exterior and create a charming entry to a stylish interior design. A grand great room offers a focal-point fireplace and opens to a solarium. Family and friends will gather in the bright breakfast area that's open to the kitchen. Upstairs, a generous master suite features a walk-through closet and dressing area and a lavish bath. Three additional bedrooms, two baths and a bonus room round out the second floor. This home is designed with a walkout basement foundation.

PLAN HPT750088

First Floor: 1,615 square feet

Second Floor: 1,510 square feet

Total: 3,125 square feet

Bonus Room: 255 square feet

Width: 65'-6" Depth: 49'-0"

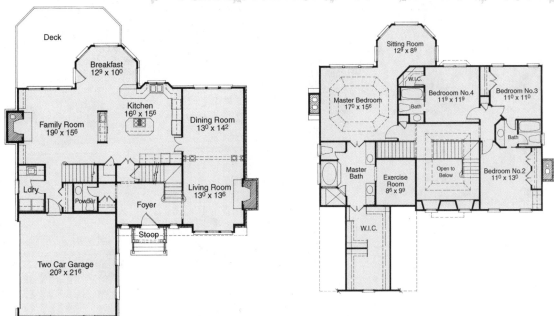

First floor plan labels:

Deck

Breakfast
12⁹ x 10⁰

Kitchen
16⁰ x 15⁶

Dining Room
13⁰ x 14²

Family Room
19⁰ x 15⁶

Living Room
13⁰ x 13⁶

Ldry

Powder

Foyer

Stoop

Two Car Garage
20⁹ x 21⁶

Second floor plan labels:

Sitting Room
12⁹ x 8⁹

W.I.C.

Master Bedroom
17⁰ x 15⁶

Bath

Bedrooom No.4
11⁹ x 11⁹

Bedroom No.3
11⁰ x 11⁰

Bath

Master Bath

Exercise Room
8⁶ x 9⁹

Open to Below

Bedroom No.2
11⁰ x 13⁰

W.I.C.

Complete with widow's walk detailing and a pedimented front entry, this wood-and-stone cottage is a true delight. Formal living and dining rooms dominate the right side of the plan, while more casual gathering and eating areas are found to the rear. The open family room, bayed breakfast area and island kitchen provide a fantastic layout for gatherings of all kinds. The counter-filled kitchen is truly a gourmet's delight. A double stairway leads to the second floor, which revels in an incredible master suite with a sitting room and an exercise room, in addition to three family bedrooms. Bedroom 4 includes its own private bath and a walk-in closet. This home is designed with a walkout basement foundation.

PLAN HPT750089

First Floor: 1,495 square feet
Second Floor: 1,600 square feet
Total: 3,095 square feet
Width: 49'-0" Depth: 57'-0"

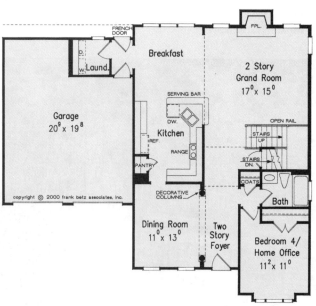

This two-story traditional design features elegant early American elements and a modern array of amenities within. The brick facade makes a stately first impression. Inside, the narrow two-story foyer is flanked by a home office on the right and a formal dining room on the left. With a hall bath located just next door, the home office can convert to a first-floor bedroom. The rear breakfast room is easily served from the kitchen and is open to the two-story grand room warmed by a fireplace. A laundry room is located behind the two-car garage. The second floor offers a sumptuous master suite that includes a vaulted master bath and His and Hers walk-in closets. Two additional family bedrooms share a hall bath. Please specify basement or crawlspace foundation when ordering.

PLAN HPT750090

First Floor: 1,220 square feet
Second Floor: 963 square feet
Total: 2,183 square feet
Width: 50'-0" Depth: 45'-0"

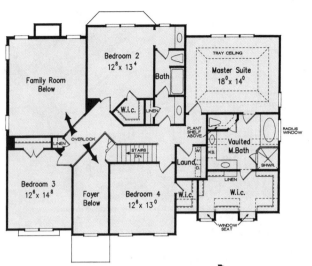

Variety abounds across the facade of this classic Colonial design. The pedimented entry gives way to the two-story foyer that opens to the living room, dining room and the engaging two-story family room. The kitchen overlooks the bayed breakfast room. A walk-in pantry is placed next to the entry to the three-car garage. The second floor holds the master suite along with three bedrooms and a shared full bath. The vaulted master bath is a luxurious retreat for the homeowners and extends into an enormous walk-in closet. Please specify basement or crawlspace foundation when ordering.

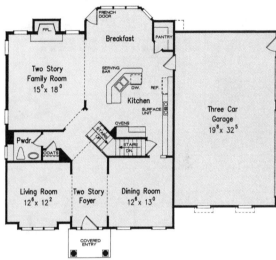

PLAN HPT750091

First Floor: 1,279 square feet

Second Floor: 1,499 square feet

Total: 2,778 square feet

Guest Room: 240 square feet

Width: 53'-0" Depth: 46'-6"

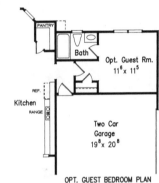

OPT. GUEST BEDROOM PLAN

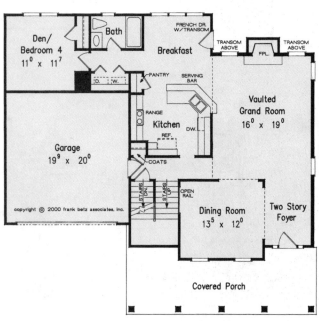

Den/
Bedroom 4
11^0 x 11^7

Bath

Breakfast

FRENCH DR.
W/ TRANSOM

TRANSOM
ABOVE

FPL.

TRANSOM
ABOVE

PANTRY

SERVING
BAR

D. W.

RANGE

Kitchen

Garage
19^9 x 20^0

REF.

DW.

COATS

Vaulted
Grand Room
16^0 x 19^0

STAIRS
DN

STAIRS

OPEN
RAIL

copyright © 2000 frank betz associates, inc.

Dining Room
13^5 x 12^0

Two Story
Foyer

Covered Porch

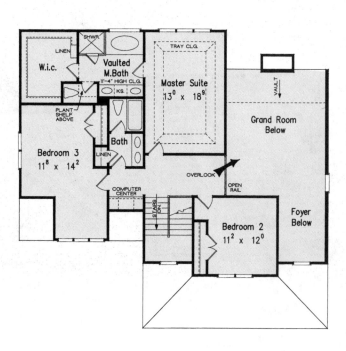

LINEN

SHWR

Vaulted
M.Bath
$11'-4"$ HIGH CLG.

W.i.c.

TRAY CLG.

Master Suite
13^0 x 18^9

VAULT

PLANT
SHELF
ABOVE

KS.

Bath

LINEN

Grand Room
Below

Bedroom 3
11^8 x 14^2

COMPUTER
CENTER

OVERLOOK

OPEN
RAIL

STAIRS
DN

Bedroom 2
11^2 x 12^0

Foyer
Below

This traditional two-story cottage is perfect for a narrow lot. Colonial elements enhance the exterior, while modern amenities are abundant inside. The two-story foyer opens to the formal dining room and the vaulted grand room warmed by a fireplace. The kitchen easily serves the casual breakfast room, which accesses the rear through a French door. The first-floor bedroom, secluded behind the garage, is placed near a hall bath and laundry facilities. Upstairs, the master bedroom features a vaulted bath with a walk-in closet. Bedrooms 2 and 3 share a hall bath. Please specify basement or crawlspace foundation when ordering.

PLAN HPT750092

First Floor: 1,252 square feet
Second Floor: 1,112 square feet
Total: 2,364 square feet
Width: 50'-0" Depth: 46'-0"

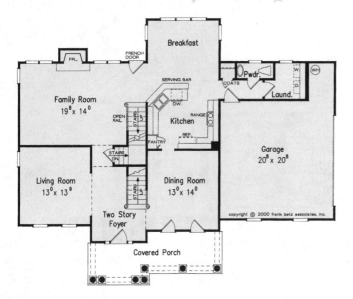

Family Room
19⁸ x 14⁰

Breakfast

Kitchen

Living Room
13⁰ x 13⁹

Dining Room
13⁰ x 14⁰

Garage
20⁸ x 20⁸

Two Story Foyer

Covered Porch

copyright © 2000 frank betz associates, inc.

PLAN HPT750093

First Floor: 1,332 square feet
Second Floor: 1,457 square feet
Total: 2,789 square feet
Width: 58'-0" *Depth:* 46'-6"

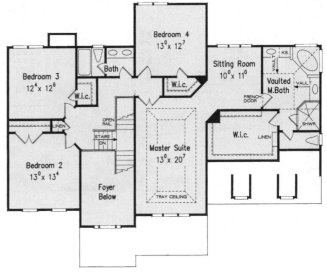

Bedroom 3
12⁴ x 12⁶

Bath

Bedroom 4
13⁰ x 12⁷

Sitting Room
10⁰ x 11⁰

Vaulted M.Bath

Bedroom 2
13⁰ x 13⁴

Foyer Below

Master Suite
13⁰ x 20⁷

TRAY CEILING

This dream home features dormers, multi-pane windows and a pediment supported by columns at the entry to accent its brick-and-siding facade. To the right of the entry the dining room accesses both the covered front porch and the angled kitchen. The adjoining breakfast nook offers expansive views to the rear while the spacious family room to the left creates a friendly atmosphere with a warming fireplace. For more formal entertaining, the living room resides to the left of the foyer. Upstairs three bedrooms share a full bath. The extravagant master suite enjoys a sunny sitting area and an enormous walk-in closet. Please specify basement or crawlspace foundation when ordering.

This luxury farmhouse design is reserved for the large family. A front covered porch that wraps around the side adds a country accent to the exterior. Inside, a study and formal dining room flank the two-story foyer. A guest suite is placed to the right of the two-story family room warmed by a fireplace. The kitchen is open to the nook and casual keeping room. A three-car garage is located nearby. Upstairs, the master suite is sumptuous with a hearth-warmed sitting room, private bath and two large walk-in closets. Three additional bedrooms, two additional baths and a laundry room complete the second floor. Please specify basement or crawlspace foundation when ordering.

First Floor Plan

- FPL.
- Keeping Room 13⁵ x 14⁶
- Breakfast
- FRENCH DOOR
- FPL.
- SERVING BAR
- DW.
- REF.
- PANTRY
- WINE RACK
- Kitchen
- BUTLERS PANTRY
- OVENS
- SURFACE UNIT
- Two Story Family Room 16⁰ x 21⁰
- Guest Bedroom 12⁰ x 13³
- Bath
- COATS
- Pwdr.
- STAIRS DN.
- STAIRS UP
- FRENCH DOORS
- Two Story Foyer
- Study 12⁰ x 12⁶
- Garage 21⁵ x 32⁶
- Dining Room 13⁵ x 15⁶
- Covered Porch
- copyright © 2001 frank betz associates, inc.

PLAN HPT750094

First Floor: 1,999 square feet
Second Floor: 2,046 square feet
Total: 4,045 square feet
Width: 66'-4" Depth: 64'-0"

Second Floor Plan

- FPL.
- Sitting Area
- TRAY CEILING
- RADIUS WINDOW
- RADIUS WINDOW
- Master Suite 21² x 15²
- Family Room Below
- Bedroom 4 12⁰ x 12⁰
- His
- FRENCH DOOR
- Laund.
- SINK
- NICHE
- LINEN
- W.D.
- OVERLOOK
- W.i.c.
- LINEN
- Bath
- TRAY CEILING
- Master Bath
- LINEN
- OPEN RAIL
- STAIRS DN.
- Bath
- Bedroom 2 13⁵ x 14⁰
- Foyer Below
- PLANT SHELF
- Bedroom 3 12⁰ x 13⁶
- SHWR
- W.i.c.
- LINEN
- Hers

98

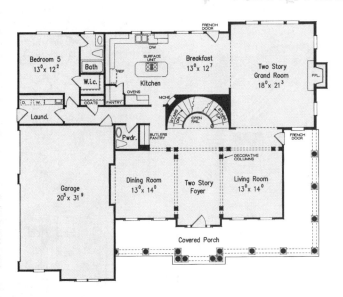

PLAN HPT750095

First Floor: 1,992 square feet
Second Floor: 1,851 square feet
Total: 3,843 square feet
Width: 66'-4" Depth: 53'-0"

This Southern home's strong classic nature is enhanced by the asymmetrical patterns created by the hipped roofline and window placement. A spacious open floor plan greets you upon entering with an array of columns defining the formal dining and living rooms. The focal point of the two-story entry is the sweeping circular staircase that rises to a balcony overlooking both the foyer and the great room. The breakfast nook is situated between the island kitchen and the great room where a wall of windows looks out to the rear property. Bedroom 5 is tucked away on the left, creating privacy for overnight guests. The immensely lavish master suite resides on the second floor where a sitting room offers a quiet retreat. Please specify basement or crawlspace foundation when ordering.

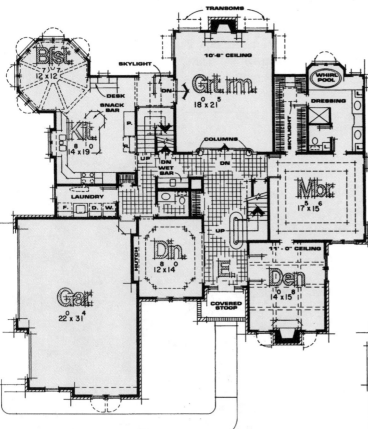

Brick, stone quoins, a hipped roof, and unusual window treatments lend a European air to this striking home. A two-story entry, flanked by a formal dining room with a tray ceiling and a den with fireplace, leads to the enormous great room which features a columned doorway. The master suite features a huge walk-in closet, access to the den, and a large bath with a dressing area and a whirlpool tub. Upstairs are three spacious bedrooms and two baths.

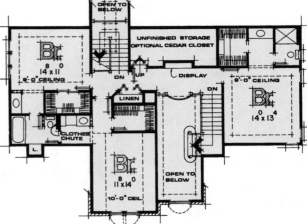

PLAN HPT750096

First Floor: 2,355 square feet
Second Floor: 1,135 square feet
Total: 3,490 square feet
Width: 64'-8" Depth: 65'-4"

A two-story foyer introduces the formal living zones of this plan—a den with a ten-foot ceiling, a dining room with an adjoining butler's pantry, and a living room with a fireplace and a twelve-foot ceiling. For more casual living, the gathering room shares space with the octagonal breakfast area and the amenity-filled kitchen. Sleeping arrangements include a first-floor master suite, which offers a sitting area with a fireplace, a bath with a corner whirlpool tub and compartmented toilet, and an extensive closet. The second floor holds three bedrooms, each with a walk-in closet and private bath.

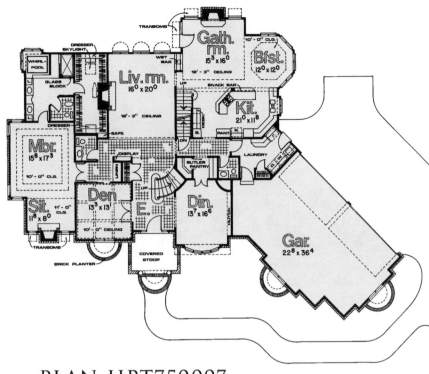

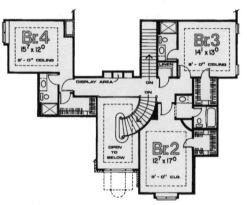

PLAN HPT750097

First Floor: 2,839 square feet
Second Floor: 1,111 square feet
Total: 3,950 square feet
Width: 95'-9" Depth: 70'-2"

PLAN HPT750098

First Floor: 3,520 square feet
Second Floor: 1,638 square feet
Total: 5,158 square feet
Bonus Room: 411 square feet
Width: 96'-6" *Depth:* 58'-8"

This custom-designed estate home elegantly combines stone and stucco, arched windows and stunning exterior details under its formidable hipped roof. The two-story foyer is impressive with its grand staircase, tray ceiling and overlooking balcony. Equally remarkable is the generous living room with a fireplace and a coffered two-story ceiling. The kitchen, breakfast bay and family room with a fireplace are all open to one another for a comfortable, casual atmosphere. The first-floor master suite indulges with numerous closets, a dressing room and a fabulous bath. Upstairs, four more bedrooms are topped by tray ceilings—three have walk-in closets and two have private baths. The three-car garage boasts additional storage and a bonus room above.

PLAN HPT750099

First Floor: 1,741 square feet
Second Floor: 1,375 square feet
Total: 3,116 square feet
Bonus Room: 345 square feet
Width: 78'-0" Depth: 36'-0"

L

Symmetrical but for the nested gables, this delightful home gives a twist to the classical Georgian style. The second-story Palladian window floods the entry with sunlight as it opens to the living areas within. On the right, the living room leads to the vaulted family room that in turn opens to the rear deck. To the left of the entry is the formal dining room, conveniently situated near the island kitchen/breakfast nook. The second floor is devoted to the family bedrooms while the master suite finds privacy on the first floor.

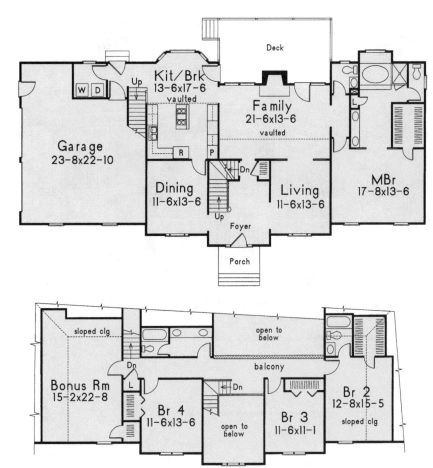

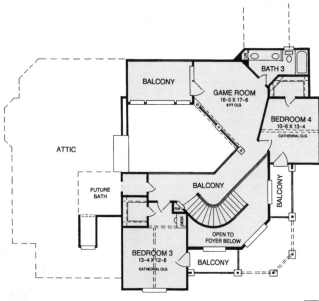

BALCONY

GAME ROOM
16-0 X 17-6
8 FT CLG

BATH 3

BEDROOM 4
10-6 X 13-4
CATHEDRAL CLG

ATTIC

FUTURE
BATH

BALCONY

BALCONY

OPEN TO
FOYER BELOW

BEDROOM 3
13-4 X 12-6
CATHEDRAL CLG

BALCONY

PLAN HPT750100

First Floor: 2,515 square feet
Second Floor: 978 square feet
Total: 3,493 square feet
Width: 69'-5" Depth: 81'-1"

L

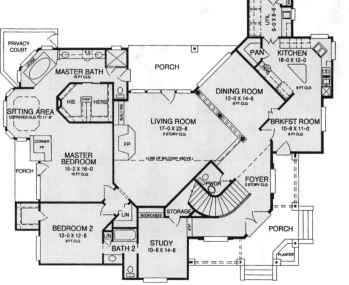

This gorgeous home is tailor-made for a corner or pie-shaped lot. Featuring mirror-image gables on both sides, this elevation is stunning from any direction. A two-story entry and a great room command attention upon entering the home. The master suite includes a masonry fireplace situated between the sitting area and the bedroom. A study conveniently located off the foyer can be used as a bedroom. A gourmet kitchen with a triangular work island, corner sink and large pantry is located on the opposite side of the home. Upstairs, one bedroom with a private outside balcony is ideal for an office. A game room, a bath and another bedroom with a private outside balcony provide the finishing touches to this elegant home.

PLAN HPT750101

First Floor: 2,154 square feet

Second Floor: 845 square feet

Total: 2,999 square feet

Width: 65'-4" Depth: 66'-4"

L

The stacked bay window adds drama to this charming home. The dining room is distinguished by arches with round column supports between the foyer and the dining area. The kitchen combines a cooktop island and a bay-windowed breakfast area. A beautiful bayed bedroom is located downstairs with the master bedroom, which features a curved wall. Upstairs are two family bedrooms—one with a bay window—that share a full bath and a game room. Please specify crawlspace or slab foundation when ordering.

PLAN HPT750102

First Floor: 869 square feet
Second Floor: 963 square feet
Total: 1,832 square feet
Width: 44'-0" Depth: 36'-0"

This beautiful home is highlighted by keystones and lintels decorating the windows and garage doors. The pedimented entryway leads to a lavish living room where a large fireplace and a ribbon of windows await. The cozy breakfast room and L-shaped kitchen are quite spacious and include access to the rear deck. The stairs wrap around and lead the family up to the sleeping quarters. The master suite is complete with a walk-in closet and bath.

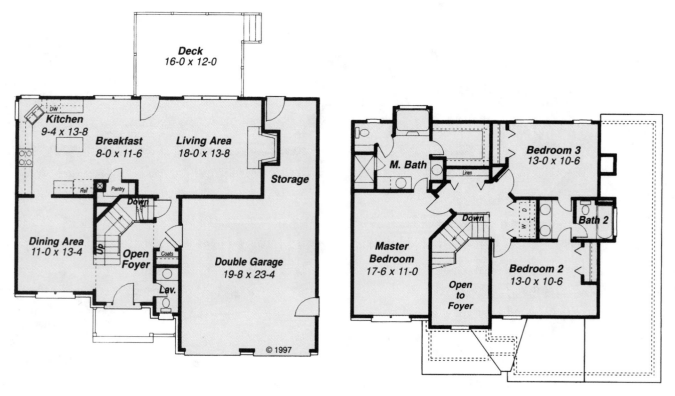

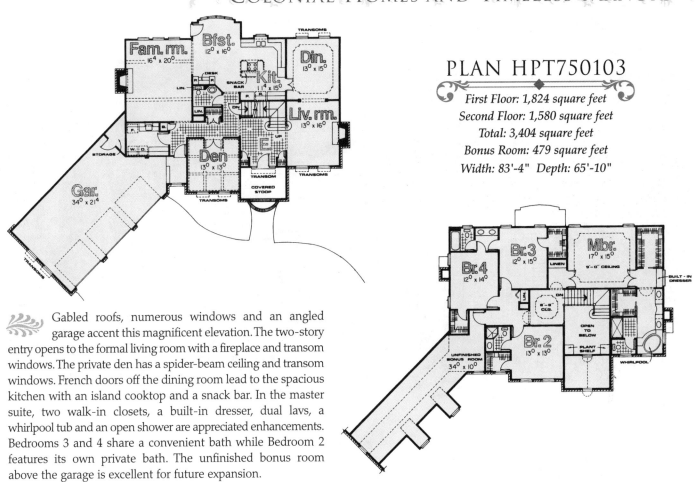

PLAN HPT750103

First Floor: 1,824 square feet
Second Floor: 1,580 square feet
Total: 3,404 square feet
Bonus Room: 479 square feet
Width: 83'-4"   Depth: 65'-10"

Gabled roofs, numerous windows and an angled garage accent this magnificent elevation. The two-story entry opens to the formal living room with a fireplace and transom windows. The private den has a spider-beam ceiling and transom windows. French doors off the dining room lead to the spacious kitchen with an island cooktop and a snack bar. In the master suite, two walk-in closets, a built-in dresser, dual lavs, a whirlpool tub and an open shower are appreciated enhancements. Bedrooms 3 and 4 share a convenient bath while Bedroom 2 features its own private bath. The unfinished bonus room above the garage is excellent for future expansion.

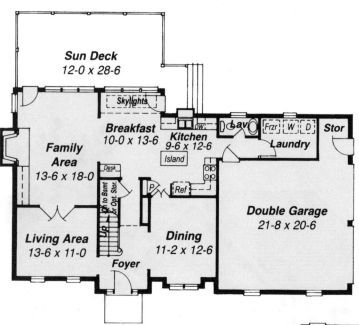

Sun Deck
12-0 x 28-6

Skylights

Breakfast
10-0 x 13-6

Kitchen
9-6 x 12-6

Island

Family Area
13-6 x 18-0

Desk

Ft to Bsmt or Opt. Stor.

Lav

Frzr *W* *D*

Laundry

Stor

Living Area
13-6 x 11-0

P

Ref

Dining
11-2 x 12-6

Double Garage
21-8 x 20-6

Foyer

This grand two-story home has plenty of space and a variety of rooms for flexible entertaining. First impressions include a large arched window that adds interest and plenty of light to the front entrance. Formal living and dining areas are located at the front of the home, while the rear-facing family room with its fireplace provides a more informal atmosphere. The open kitchen and sunny breakfast area are perfect for casual meals and quiet moments. The luxurious master suite, three family bedrooms and a second bath are on the second floor. Please specify basement, crawlspace or slab foundation when ordering.

PLAN HPT750104

First Floor: 1,122 square feet
Second Floor: 1,428 square feet
Total: 2,550 square feet
Width: 56'-0" Depth: 32'-0"

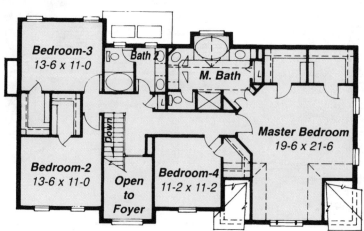

Bedroom-3
13-6 x 11-0

Bath 2

M. Bath

Bedroom-2
13-6 x 11-0

Down

Open to Foyer

Bedroom-4
11-2 x 11-2

Master Bedroom
19-6 x 21-6

108

A variety of textures, arches and angles adds interest to this impressive elevation. Inside, columns define the living areas, separating the living room from the foyer and the dining room, and marking the entrance to the breakfast area. The family room is a delight, with a wall of windows and a cheery fireplace. The family cook will enjoy the efficient island kitchen, with views of the back porch, a convenient butler's pantry and a spacious laundry room nearby. The deluxe master suite offers two immense walk-in closets and a bath that is sure to please.

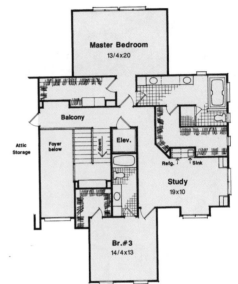

PLAN HPT750105

First Floor: 2,192 square feet
Second Floor: 1,417 square feet
Total: 3,609 square feet
Width: 62'-0" Depth: 64'-0"

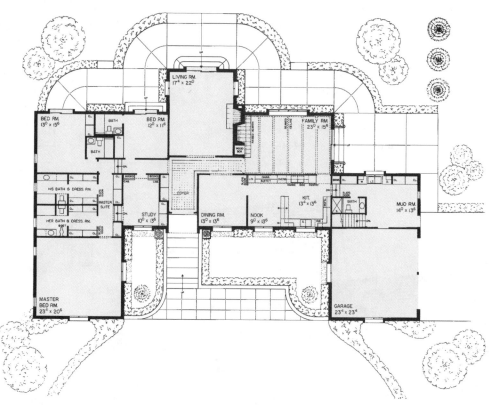

PLAN HPT750106

Square Footage: 3,577

Width: 105'-0" Depth: 65'-8"

[L]

From the graceful curving drive court to the formal living room, this expansive, hospitable French country home is loaded with charm. Formal garden areas at the entry are enclosed by low retaining walls and allow room for shrubs and fanciful flowers. A double-door entry opens to an L-shaped foyer flanked by a study with built-ins and the formal living room and dining room. The casual family room features a beamed ceiling and a raised-hearth fireplace with a convenient wood box. Access the wrapping patio through sliding glass doors at one end of the family room, at the center wall of the living room and from each of two family bedrooms. The master suite is a stunning example of luxury with His and Hers baths and study access. The kitchen with an attached nook leads down two steps to an enormous mudroom with a half-bath, laundry area and closet space.

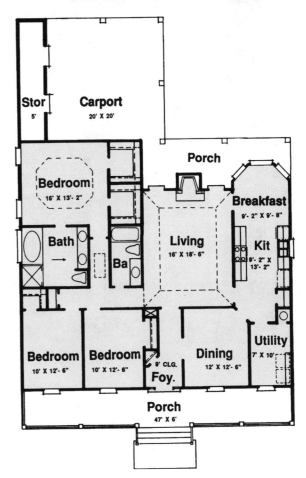

PLAN HPT750107

Square Footage: 1,704
Width: 47'-0" Depth: 66'-0"

This Southern cottage provides spacious front and rear porches, along with many other amenities. The entry leads to the formal dining room on the right and a grand living space with a tray ceiling just beyond. The open kitchen and breakfast areas allow courtyard views and connect directly to the living areas. The large master suite features separate walk-in closets and a bath with two lavatories, a whirlpool tub and a separate shower. Two family bedrooms share a full bath.

Floor plan labels:

Stor 5'
Carport 20' X 20'
Porch
Bedroom 16' X 13'-2"
Breakfast 9'-2" X 9'-8"
Bath
Living 16' X 18'-6"
Kit 9'-2" X 13'-2"
Ba
Bedroom 10' X 12'-6"
Bedroom 10' X 12'-6"
9' CLG.
Foy.
Dining 12' X 12'-6"
Utility 7' X 10'
Porch 47' X 6'

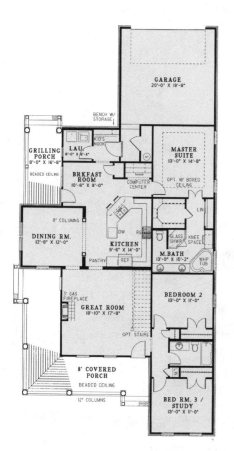

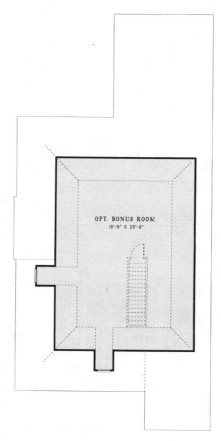

PLAN HPT750108

Square Footage: 1,845
Bonus Room: 1,191 square feet
Width: 41'-4" Depth: 83'-8"

Tradition is embodied in this Southern-style home that features a proposed bonus area. A wraparound entry porch with classic Southern columns allows you to enjoy the view from every direction. A large great room features a gas fireplace and an open stairway leading to the upper level. Two family bedrooms feature a connecting full bath. A breakfast area with access to a spacious kitchen and rear grilling porch conveniently provides entertaining and relaxing family dinners. Just off the computer center, the master suite features an optional boxed ceiling and a large walk-in closet. The upper level could be a huge bonus area for use as a game room. Please specify crawlspace or slab foundation when ordering.

PLAN HPT750109

Square Footage: 1,934
Width: 36'-8" Depth: 85'-0"

 Decorative lintels and stylish shuttered windows complement the columned L-shaped porch and gables for a simple traditional look. The entryway reveals the great room with a boxed ceiling and gas fireplace and leads to an open dining room defined by columns. The master suite includes a whirlpool tub, separate shower, dual vanities, compartmented toilet and two walk-in closets. The two family bedrooms share a full hall bath. Please specify crawlspace or slab foundation when ordering.

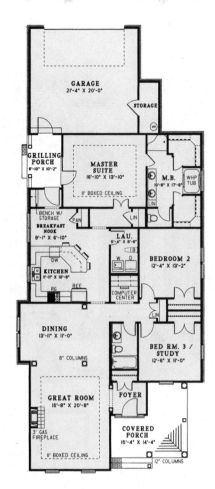

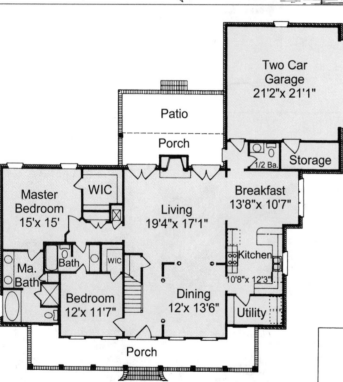

PLAN HPT750110

First Floor: 1,796 square feet
Second Floor: 610 square feet
Total: 2,406 square feet
Width: 65'-9" Depth: 64'-9"

Two Car Garage 21'2"x 21'1"

Patio

Porch

1/2 Ba.

Storage

Breakfast 13'8"x 10'7"

WIC

Master Bedroom 15'x 15'

Living 19'4"x 17'1"

Bath

WIC

Kitchen 10'8"x 12'3"

Ma. Bath

Bedroom 12'x 11'7"

Dining 12'x 13'6"

Utility

Porch

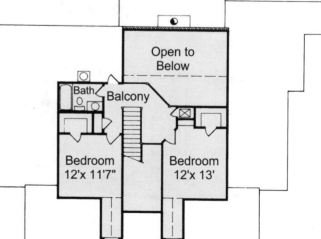

Open to Below

Bath

Balcony

Bedroom 12'x 11'7"

Bedroom 12'x 13'

Eye-catching details create an elegant entry for this Southern cottage. The interior is just as inviting. Walk through the foyer to a two-story living room with a dramatic sloped ceiling. The family room opens to a large kitchen and an informal eating area with access to a guest bath. Upstairs, a balcony hall overlooks the stunning living room and leads to two large family bedrooms that share a bath. Please specify crawlspace or slab foundation when ordering.

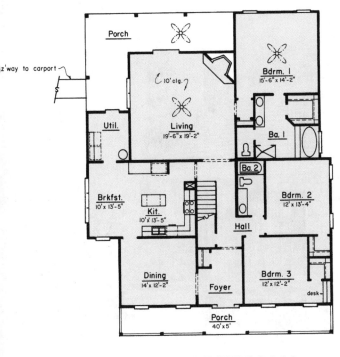

PLAN HPT750111

First Floor: 2,020 square feet
Second Floor: 352 square feet
Total: 2,372 square feet
Width: 46'-0" Depth: 58'-0"

The stylish exterior of this charming Southern cottage will be a pleasing addition to any neighborhood. Lead guests leisurely through the foyer and central hall to a magnificent living area with a corner fireplace and views of the side and rear yards. Step out onto the L-shaped covered porch and enjoy a quiet evening of conversation. The spacious breakfast area/kitchen will appeal to the whole family—views of the side courtyard and lots of room to relax will invite them to stay awhile. A secluded master suite affords comfort to spare with a walk-in closet, linen closet and twin-lavatory bath with a whirlpool tub and separate shower. A quiet study is found upstairs.

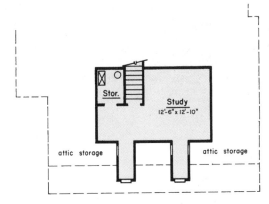

PLAN HPT750112

Square Footage: 2,355
Width: 56'-0" Depth: 81'-0"

 Round columns and arched windows grace the elegant entry of this Savannah cottage. Front and rear porches offer plenty of room to sit and relish a sweet breeze on a warm summer evening—and further embellish an easy-care stucco exterior. Inside, delightful views of the rear covered porch abound. The breakfast area, family room and master suite all enjoy this amenity. Raised ceilings in these last two rooms expand the plan and add drama to the interior. The convenient kitchen/breakfast area, just off the family room, features a snack bar and a view to the rear yard. Please specify crawlspace or slab foundation when ordering.

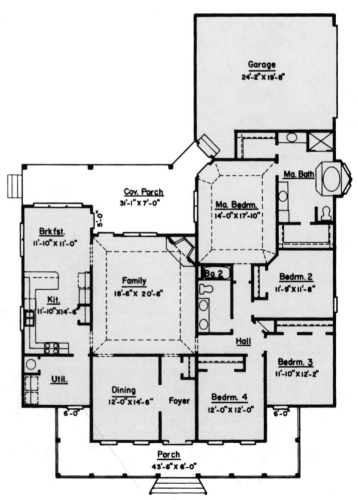

This unique design borrows style from European farmhouses as well as American plantations. Warm country charm is captured by the welcoming details of this Louisiana farmhouse. Enjoy pleasant moments by the fireplace, enhanced by flanking French doors that open to a sprawling rear covered porch. A luxurious master suite offers an oversized corner tub, compartmentalized toilet, walk-in closet and access to a private rear patio. Please specify crawlspace or slab foundation when ordering.

PLAN HPT750113

First Floor: 1,977 square feet
Second Floor: 687 square feet
Total: 2,664 square feet
Bonus Room: 346 square feet
Width: 69'-6" Depth: 69'-9"

Here is a wonderful contemporary home with three porches—perfect for warmer climates or vacation property. A stunning circular staircase is the centerpiece of the foyer. The kitchen is ideal for the chef in the family with its island work area and expansive counter space. The dining room is connected to the kitchen by a butler's pantry. The living room has a warming fireplace and access to a porch. A skylit sun room leads to a guest room through French doors. Two family bedrooms and a full bath are on the second level, while the master suite is secluded for privacy on the first level. Please specify crawlspace or slab foundation when ordering.

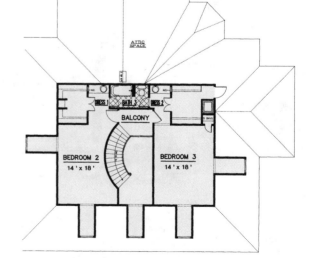

PLAN HPT750114

First Floor: 2,575 square feet
Second Floor: 911 square feet
Total: 3,486 square feet
Width: 64'-0" Depth: 89'-0"

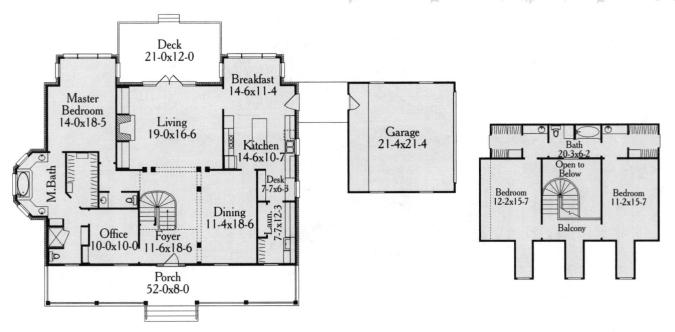

Deck
21-0x12-0

Breakfast
14-6x11-4

Master
Bedroom
14-0x18-5

Living
19-0x16-6

Kitchen
14-6x10-7

Garage
21-4x21-4

M.Bath

Desk
7-7x6-3

Office
10-0x10-0

Dining
11-4x18-6

Laun.
7-7x12-3

Foyer
11-6x18-6

Porch
52-0x8-0

Bath
20-3x6-2

Open to
Below

Bedroom
12-2x15-7

Bedroom
11-2x15-7

Balcony

PLAN HPT750115

First Floor: 2,109 square feet
Second Floor: 896 square feet
Total: 3,005 square feet
Width: 90'-4" Depth: 56'-4"

This American classic home boasts a full-length covered porch and a two-car garage with a connecting breezeway. The U-shaped staircase creates a lasting first impression as the focal point of the foyer. The formal dining room and the living room are defined by decorative columns for an open effect. French doors in the living room lead to the rear deck. The master suite, on the left, offers a sunny bedroom, a private bath with a garden tub, and direct access to the office which is easily converted to a study or sitting room. Two bedrooms and a shared full bath comprise the second floor. Please specify basement, crawlspace or slab foundation when ordering.

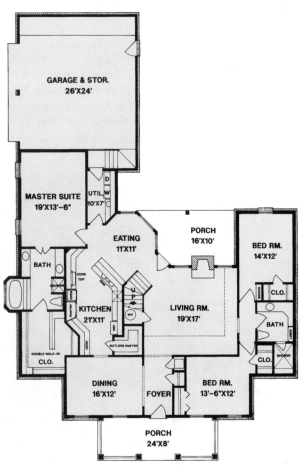

This plan charms instantly with its muntin windows, decorative French-style shutters, stucco exterior and steeply sloping roof complete with dormers. A large living room accesses the rear porch. The kitchen is replete with luxuries: a desk, butler's pantry and plenty of counter space. An adjacent eating area boasts bay windows and looks out to the rear property. On the right side of the plan, two bedrooms share a full bath and feature private walk-in closets. On the left side, a luxurious master suite is complete with double walk-in closets, His and Hers sinks, a garden tub and a separate shower. Future living space can be found on the second level, as well as a library with built-ins; this area is open to the living room below. Please specify basement, crawlspace or slab foundation when ordering.

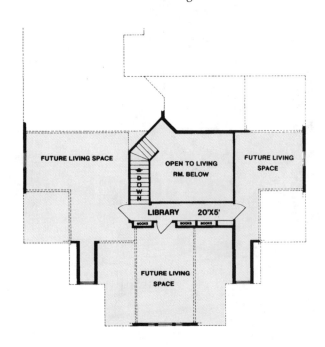

PLAN HPT750116

First Floor: 2,159 square feet
Second Floor: 96 square feet
Total: 2,255 square feet
Bonus Space: 878 square feet
Width: 59'-0" Depth: 86'-0"

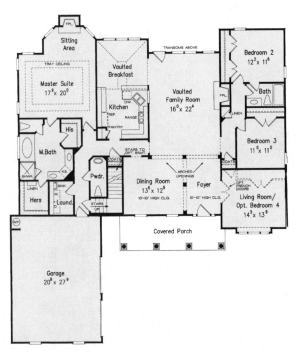

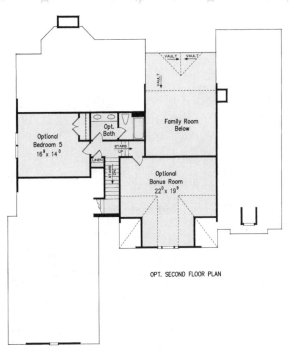

OPT. SECOND FLOOR PLAN

The covered front porch adds an element of Greek Revival to this Southern Country home. The dining room is defined by archways that open to the foyer and vaulted family room, where a fireplace offers warmth and a window wall offers beautiful views. The vaulted breakfast area adjoins the kitchen. The master wing is impressive with a bayed sitting area with a private fireplace. The lavish master bath features His and Hers walk-in closets. Two family bedrooms on the opposite side of the home share a hall bath. The formal living room converts to a fourth bedroom, providing flexible space. Please specify basement or crawlspace foundation when ordering.

PLAN HPT750117

Square Footage: 2,426
Bonus Space: 767 square feet
Width: 63'-0" Depth: 72'-4"

© 1993 Donald A. Gardner Architects, Inc.

B. NATHAN

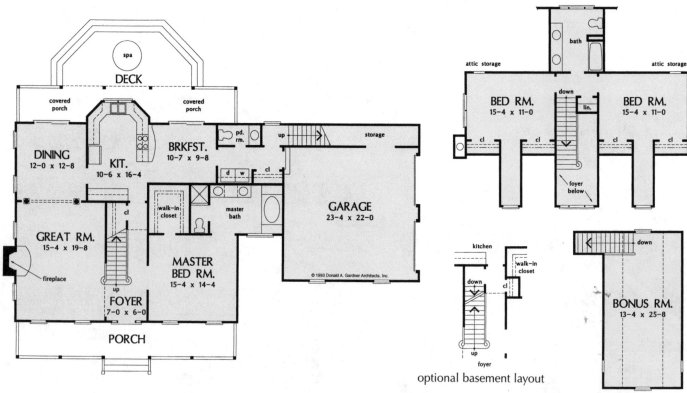

DECK

spa

covered porch

covered porch

DINING
12-0 x 12-8

KIT.
10-6 x 16-4

BRKFST.
10-7 x 9-8

pd. rm.

up

storage

GREAT RM.
15-4 x 19-8

fireplace

cl

walk-in closet

d w cl

master bath

GARAGE
23-4 x 22-0

© 1993 Donald A. Gardner Architects, Inc.

up

FOYER
7-0 x 6-0

MASTER BED RM.
15-4 x 14-4

PORCH

bath

attic storage

attic storage

BED RM.
15-4 x 11-0

down

lin.

BED RM.
15-4 x 11-0

cl

cl

cl

cl

foyer below

kitchen

walk-in closet

down

cl

down

BONUS RM.
13-4 x 25-8

up

foyer

optional basement layout

PLAN HPT750118

First Floor: 1,484 square feet
Second Floor: 660 square feet
Total: 2,144 square feet
Bonus Room: 389 square feet
Width: 72'-8"   Depth: 54'-4"

Overlooking a covered porch and a deck with a spa, this home's kitchen will be a gourmet's delight. A wraparound counter gives plenty of space, while a snack bar opens to the breakfast nook. In the great room—which delights with a fireplace—quiet gatherings and entertaining will be a pleasure. The master bedroom, complete with a spa-style bath, rests to the right side of the first floor. Upstairs, two bedrooms and a full hall bath comfortably house family and guests. Please specify a basement or crawlspace foundation when ordering.

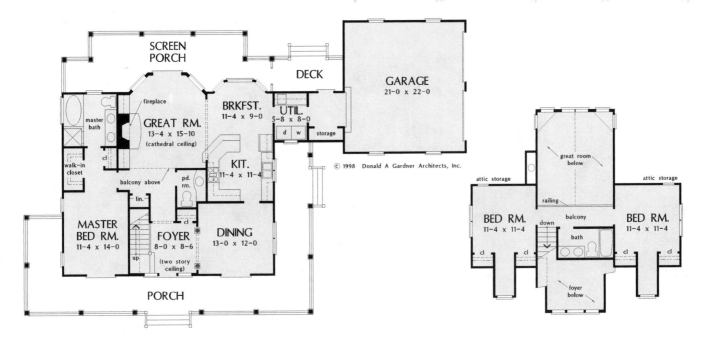

SCREEN PORCH

DECK

GARAGE
21-0 x 22-0

fireplace

master bath

GREAT RM.
13-4 x 15-10
(cathedral ceiling)

BRKFST.
11-4 x 9-0

UTIL.
5-8 x 8-0

d w   storage

© 1998 Donald A Gardner Architects, Inc.

walk-in closet

cl

KIT.
11-4 x 11-4

balcony above

pd. rm.

lin.

cl

MASTER BED RM.
11-4 x 14-0

FOYER
8-0 x 8-6

up

(two story ceiling)

DINING
13-0 x 12-0

PORCH

great room below

attic storage

railing

attic storage

BED RM.
11-4 x 11-4

down

balcony

bath

BED RM.
11-4 x 11-4

cl   cl

foyer below

cl   cl

PLAN HPT750119

First Floor: 1,271 square feet
Second Floor: 490 square feet
Total: 1,761 square feet
Width: 77'-8" Depth: 50'-0"

This farmhouse looks and lives larger than its square footage due to its wrapping front porch and generous screened back porch. The large center dormer directs light through clerestory windows into the dramatic two-story foyer, where interior columns mark the entrance to the formal dining room. The heart of the home is the central great room, where a fireplace is the focal point. The master suite occupies one entire wing of the first floor, while two bedrooms share a full bath upstairs. The compact design possesses all the amenities available in larger homes.

B. NATHAN

© 1998 Donald A. Gardner Architects, Inc.

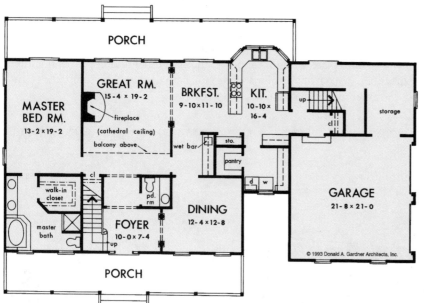

PORCH

GREAT RM.
15-4 x 19-2

BRKFST.
9-10 x 11-10

KIT.
10-10 x
16-4

up

storage

MASTER
BED RM.
13-2 x 19-2

fireplace
(cathedral ceiling)
balcony above

wet bar

cl

walk-in
closet

cl

master
bath

FOYER
10-0 x 7-4

sto.

pantry

pd.
rm

d w

DINING
12-4 x 12-8

up

GARAGE
21-8 x 21-0

PORCH

This open country plan boasts front and rear covered porches and a bonus room for future expansion. The slope-ceilinged foyer has a Palladian window clerestory to let in natural light. The spacious great room presents a fireplace, cathedral ceiling and clerestory with arched windows. The second-floor balcony overlooks the great room. A U-shaped kitchen provides the ideal layout for food preparation. For flexibility, access is provided to the bonus room from both the first and second floors. The first-floor master bedroom features a bath with dual lavatories, a separate tub and shower and a walk-in closet. Two large bedrooms and a full bath are located on the second floor.

PLAN HPT750120

First Floor: 1,632 square feet
Second Floor: 669 square feet
Total: 2,301 square feet
Bonus Room: 528 square feet
Width: 72'-6" Depth: 46'-10"

QUOTE ONE®

Cost to build? See page 310
to order complete cost estimate
to build this house in your area!

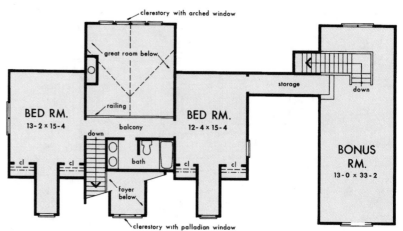

clerestory with arched window

great room below

railing

storage

down

BED RM.
13-2 x 15-4

balcony

BED RM.
12-4 x 15-4

BONUS
RM.
13-0 x 33-2

down

cl

cl

bath

cl

cl

foyer
below

clerestory with palladian window

124

PLAN HPT750121

First Floor: 1,506 square feet
Second Floor: 513 square feet
Total: 2,019 square feet
Bonus Room: 397 square feet
Width: 65'-4" Depth: 67'-10"

With a casually elegant exterior, this three-bedroom farmhouse celebrates sunlight with a Palladian window dormer and a rear arched window. The clerestory window in the two-story foyer shines natural light into the entry, while the arched window lights the great room with its fireplace and cathedral ceiling. The L-shaped kitchen features an island cooktop and a bayed breakfast area with views of the backyard. The master suite is a calm retreat and includes a walk-in closet and luxurious bath. Two family bedrooms and a bonus room are located upstairs.

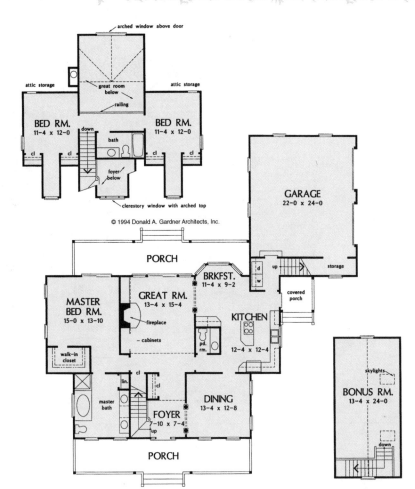

© 1994 Donald A. Gardner Architects, Inc.

© 1994 Donald A. Gardner Architects, Inc.

PLAN HPT750122

Square Footage: 1,561
Width: 60'-10" Depth: 51'-6"

Combining the finest country details with the most modern livability, this one-story home makes modest budgets really stretch. The welcoming front porch encourages you to stop and enjoy the summer breezes. The entry foyer leads to a formal dining room defined by columns. Beyond it is the large great room with a cathedral ceiling and a fireplace. The kitchen and the breakfast room are open to the living area and include porch access. The master suite is tucked away in its own private space. It is conveniently separated from the family bedrooms, which share a full bath. The two-car garage contains extra storage space.

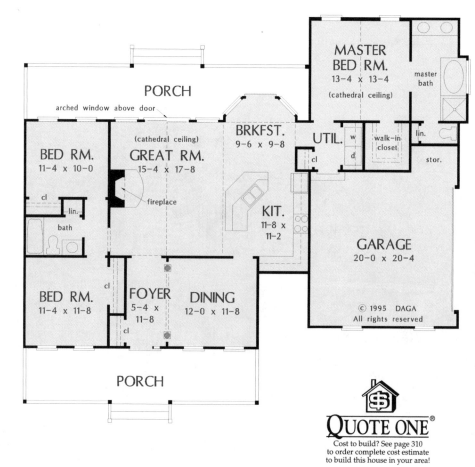

PORCH

arched window above door

BED RM.
11-4 x 10-0

(cathedral ceiling)
GREAT RM.
15-4 x 17-8

cl

lin.

bath

fireplace

BED RM.
11-4 x 11-8

cl

FOYER
5-4 x 11-8

cl

DINING
12-0 x 11-8

PORCH

BRKFST.
9-6 x 9-8

KIT.
11-8 x 11-2

MASTER BED RM.
13-4 x 13-4

(cathedral ceiling)

master bath

UTIL.

w   d

walk-in closet

lin.

stor.

GARAGE
20-0 x 20-4

QUOTE ONE®
Cost to build? See page 310
to order complete cost estimate
to build this house in your area!

PLAN HPT750123

First Floor: 1,766 square feet
Second Floor: 670 square feet
Total: 2,436 square feet
Width: 93'-10" *Depth:* 62'-0"

This farmhouse celebrates sunlight with a Palladian window dormer, a skylit screened porch and a rear arched window. The clerestory window in the foyer throws natural light across the loft to a great room with a fireplace and a cathedral ceiling. The central island kitchen and the breakfast area are open to the great room. The master suite is a calm retreat and opens to the screened porch through a bay area. Upstairs, a loft overlooking the great room connects two family bedrooms, each with a private bath.

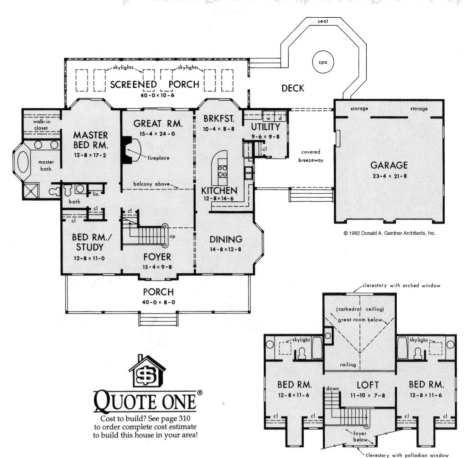

© 1992 Donald A. Gardner Architects, Inc.

QUOTE ONE®

Cost to build? See page 310
to order complete cost estimate
to build this house in your area!

© 1992 Donald A. Gardner Architects, Inc.

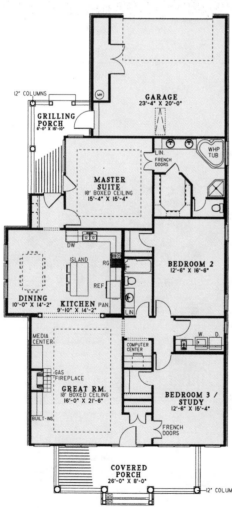

PLAN HPT750124

Square Footage: 1,832
Width: 39'-0" Depth: 81'-0"

This traditional design is the perfect choice for a narrow lot. Great curb appeal is evident, with the exterior's combination brick/wood facade and covered front porch with columns. Once inside, guests are cheered by a glowing fire, flanked by the built-in media center in the great room. The master suite is at the back of the home for privacy and features French doors leading to the luxurious private bath. Please specify block, crawlspace or slab foundation when ordering.

PLAN HPT750125

First Floor: 1,713 square feet
Second Floor: 610 square feet
Total: 2,323 square feet
Bonus Room: 384 square feet
Width: 37'-0" Depth: 73'-0"

This inviting country home includes a covered front porch with columns and railings, double-hung casement windows, wood and brick siding, and dormer windows. The formal dining room at the front of the house begins with an entrance flanked by two columns. The U-shaped kitchen has a pantry and a snack bar. A built-in computer desk lies adjacent to the breakfast room, and a box-ceilinged great room with a fireplace and media center sits at the back of the home. The master suite also has a boxed ceiling and a luxurious master bath with all of the amenities. On the second floor are two bedrooms, each with its own walk-in closet. Please specify basement, crawlspace or slab foundation when ordering.

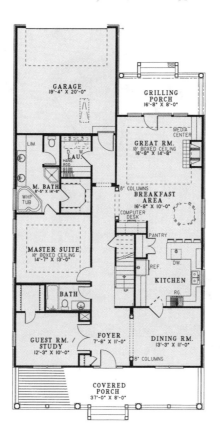

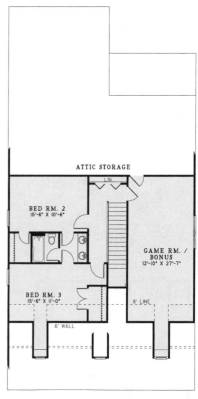

©1995 Donald A. Gardner Architects, Inc.

– B. NATHAN –

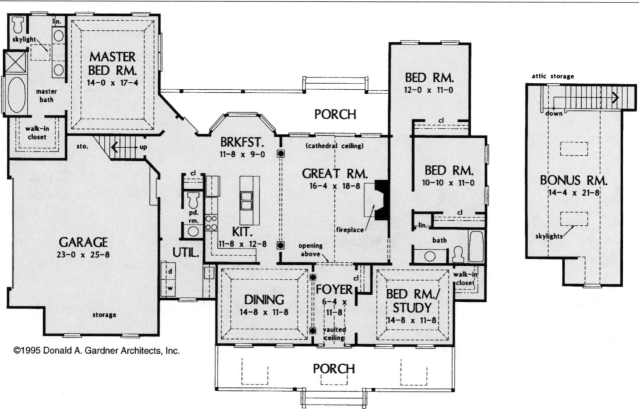

MASTER BED RM. 14-0 x 17-4

skylight

lin.

master bath

walk-in closet

sto.

up

BRKFST. 11-8 x 9-0

cl

pd. rm.

KIT. 11-8 x 12-8

UTIL.

d

w

GARAGE 23-0 x 25-8

storage

PORCH

(cathedral ceiling)

GREAT RM. 16-4 x 18-8

fireplace

opening above

BED RM. 12-0 x 11-0

cl

BED RM. 10-10 x 11-0

cl

lin.

bath

walk-in closet

DINING 14-8 x 11-8

FOYER 6-4 x 11-8

cl

vaulted ceiling

BED RM./ STUDY 14-8 x 11-8

PORCH

attic storage

down

BONUS RM. 14-4 x 21-8

skylights

©1995 Donald A. Gardner Architects, Inc.

PLAN HPT750126

Square Footage: 2,192
Bonus Room: 390 square feet
Width: 74'-10" Depth: 55'-8"

Exciting volumes and nine-foot ceilings add elegance to this comfortable, open plan. There's also a tray ceiling in the front bedroom/study. Hosts whose guests always end up in the kitchen will enjoy entertaining here with only columns separating it from the great room. Children's bedrooms share a full bath that's complete with a linen closet. The master suite, located in a quiet wing, is highlighted by a tray ceiling and includes a skylit bath with a garden tub, private toilet, double-bowl vanity and spacious walk-in closet.

PLAN HPT750127

Square Footage: 2,136
Bonus Room: 405 square feet
Width: 76'-4" Depth: 64'-4"

An expansive front porch, three dormers and a score of windows all add to the charm and character of this country home. The spacious great room features built-in cabinets, a fireplace and a cathedral ceiling that continues into the adjoining screened porch. An island kitchen is conveniently grouped with the great room, the dining room and the skylit breakfast area for the cook who enjoys conversation while preparing meals. The master suite features a cathedral ceiling, a large walk-in closet and a relaxing private bath with a skylit whirlpool tub and separate shower. Two secondary bedrooms share a full bath.

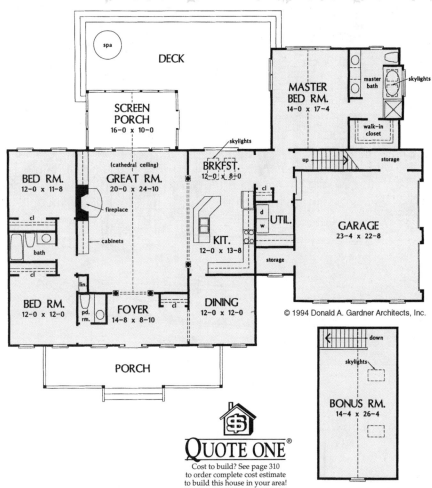

© 1994 Donald A. Gardner Architects, Inc.

QUOTE ONE®
Cost to build? See page 310
to order complete cost estimate
to build this house in your area!

© 1994 Donald A. Gardner Architects, Inc.   B. NATHAN.

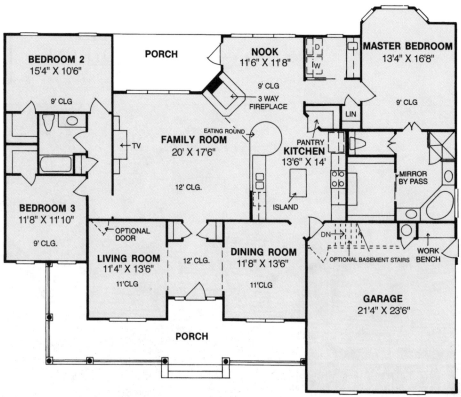

BEDROOM 2
15'4" X 10'6"

9' CLG

PORCH

NOOK
11'6" X 11'8"

9' CLG

3 WAY
FIREPLACE

MASTER BEDROOM
13'4" X 16'8"

9' CLG

EATING ROUND

FAMILY ROOM
20' X 17'6"

12' CLG.

PANTRY

KITCHEN
13'6" X 14'

LIN

TV

BEDROOM 3
11'8" X 11'10"

9' CLG.

ISLAND

MIRROR
BY PASS

OPTIONAL
DOOR

LIVING ROOM
11'4" X 13'6"

11'CLG

12' CLG.

DINING ROOM
11'8" X 13'6"

11'CLG

DN

OPTIONAL BASEMENT STAIRS

WORK
BENCH

GARAGE
21'4" X 23'6"

PORCH

PLAN HPT750128

Square Footage: 2,126
Width: 66'-0" Depth: 54'-0"

This country dream home excels in charm and efficiency. A traditional country porch entices you inside to the formal living and dining rooms flanking the foyer. A three-way fireplace warms the family room, island kitchen and breakfast nook. The secluded master bedroom offers its own bath with a corner soaking tub, two vanities, a separate shower, a compartmented toilet and a walk-in closet. Two additional bedrooms on the other side of the home share a hall bath. Please specify basement, slab or crawlspace foundation when ordering.

PLAN HPT750129

Square Footage: 1,727
Bonus Space: 563 square feet
Width: 52'-9" Depth: 66'-2"

This traditional country home features an array of family-friendly amenities. Triple dormers and a covered front porch enhance the exterior. The great room is warmed by a fireplace and is open to the dining area and kitchen. Three family bedrooms complete the main level, along with a rear porch and two-car garage. A bonus room is available for future use—perfect for a home office or fourth bedroom. Please specify basement, crawlspace or slab foundation when ordering.

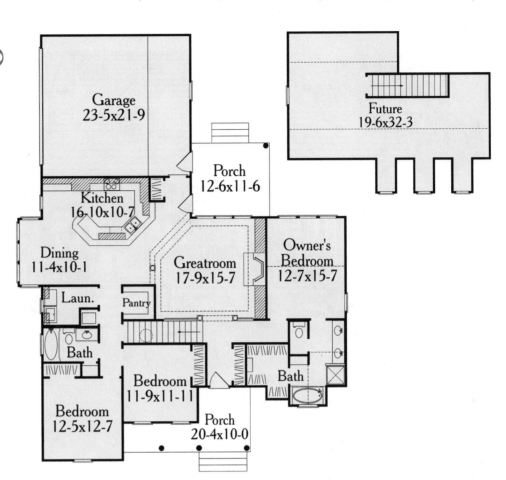

DECK

WOOD RAILING

PORCH
24' x 6'

STOR
8' x 6'

STOR
8' x 6'

GARAGE
22' x 22'

ATTIC
STAIRS

BREEZEWAY
22' x 8'

ENTRY

UTILITY

WASH | DRY

SINK

BATH

FREEZ.

BATH
VANITY

SHV'S

CLO.

SKYLIGHT

SLOPE CEILING

SHOWER

SEAT

SHV'S

LIN

STOR.

UP

CLO.

HEAT & A/C

MASTER SUITE
18' x 16'

FAMILY RM
25' x 15'

KITCHEN
COOK TOP
18' x 16'

PANT. OVEN

PANT. REF. D.W. SINK

BAR

SINK

SITTING

LIVING
15' x 14'

ENTRY

DINING
15' x 14'

EATING

PORCH
34' x 8'

WOOD RAILING

ATTIC

ATTIC

CLO.

CLO. LIN LIN

BATH

VANITY

CLO.

HEAT A/C

WH

BED RM.
16' x 12'

HALL

DOWN

BED RM.
14' x 12'

BED RM.
14' x 12'

CLO. CLO.

CLO. CLO.

PLAN HPT750130

First Floor: 2,008 square feet
Second Floor: 1,027 square feet
Total: 3,035 square feet
Width: 66'-0" Depth: 74'-0"

A porch with wood railings borders the facade of this plan, lending a farmhouse or country feel. The family room includes a fireplace and French doors to the porch, which opens further to the deck area. The master bedroom is filled with luxuries, from the walk-in closet with shelves, the full bath with a skylight, sloped ceiling and vanity, to the shower with a convenient seat. Three additional bedrooms upstairs share two full baths between them. A breezeway, placed between the garage and the house, leads easily to the deck area. Extras include a large utility room, pantry, half-bath downstairs and two storage areas. Please specify basement, crawl-space or slab foundation when ordering.

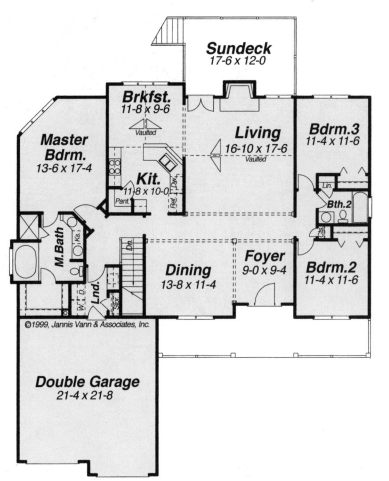

Sundeck
17-6 x 12-0

Brkfst.
11-8 x 9-6
Vaulted

Master
Bdrm.
13-6 x 17-4

Living
16-10 x 17-6
Vaulted

Bdrm.3
11-4 x 11-6

Kit.
11-8 x 10-0

Pant.

Lin.

Bth.2

M.Bath

Kls.

W.D.

Lnd.

Dn.

Dining
13-8 x 11-4

Foyer
9-0 x 9-4

Bdrm.2
11-4 x 11-6

©1999, Jannis Vann & Associates, Inc.

Double Garage
21-4 x 21-8

PLAN HPT750131

Square Footage: 1,865
Width: 56'-0" Depth: 58'-0"

Three dormers and a warming covered front porch would make anyone feel welcome in this country/ranch home. The vaulted ceiling in the living room definitely gives you a feeling of spaciousness along with the cozy fireplace. The elaborate kitchen features lots of counter space, a pantry and a breakfast area. On the far left side of the home, the master bedroom enjoys privacy. The home is completed with a double garage.

PLAN HPT750132

Square Footage: 2,450
Bonus Room: 423 square feet
Width: 79'-8" Depth: 68'-8"

A handsome display of columns frames the porch of this gracious Southern home. The foyer opens to the dining room and to a study, which could also be an additional bedroom. The open living room and family room are joined under a dramatic cathedral ceiling, divided with a showpiece fireplace that opens to both rooms. The efficient corner kitchen includes a handy breakfast nook that opens to a morning porch and a work island with a cooktop and curved snack bar. The master suite has a stylish tray ceiling, twin walk-in closets and a compartmented bath with an elegant bumped-out tub.

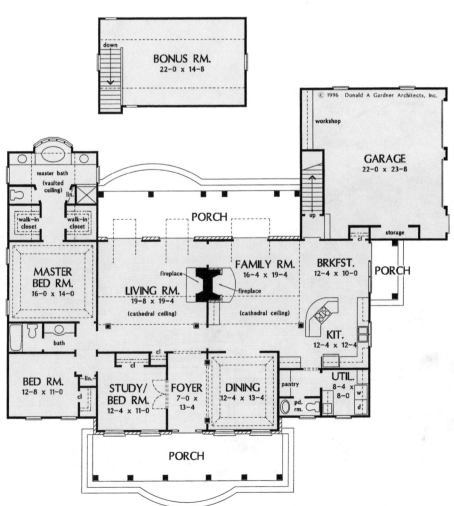

PLAN HPT750133

First Floor: 2,899 square feet
Second Floor: 1,519 square feet
Total: 4,418 square feet
Bonus Room: 540 square feet
Width: 108'-2" Depth: 62'-10"

Ⓛ

Horizontal siding and double-hung windows with muntins and shutters enhance the historic appeal of this 1½-story home. Two formal areas flank the foyer and include the living room to the left and the dining room to the right. Sleeping accommodations excel with a spacious master suite. Here, a private bath and two closets—one a walk-in—guarantee satisfaction. A bonus room further enhances this fabulous family home.

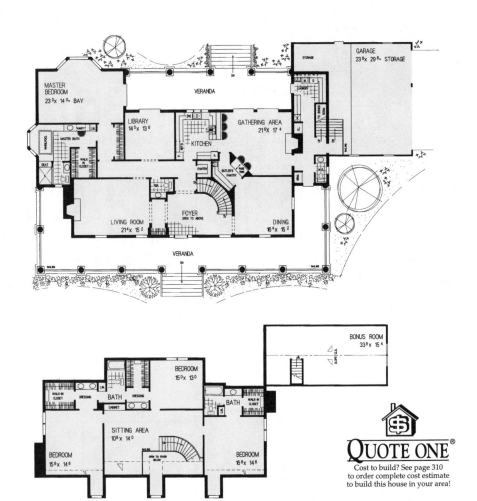

Quote One®
Cost to build? See page 310
to order complete cost estimate
to build this house in your area!

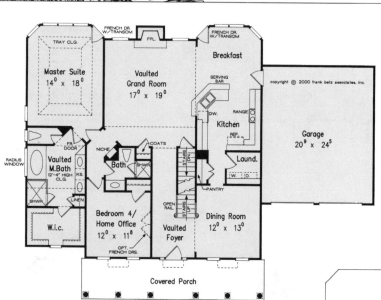

PLAN HPT750134

First Floor: 1,771 square feet
Second Floor: 627 square feet
Total: 2,398 square feet
Bonus Room: 285 square feet
Width: 65'-0" Depth: 49'-0"

Three dormers and a welcoming porch greet visitors to this four-bedroom home. The foyer—note the charming plant shelf above!—introduces a dining room to the right with easy access to the pantry and kitchen. This flexible design also offers an optional study with French doors opening to left of the foyer. The master suite and breakfast nook enjoy bay windows with French-door access to the backyard. The vaulted grand room features a fireplace and is open to the kitchen area. Two family bedrooms and an optional bonus room share a bath on the second level, while the master suite and one additional bedroom reside on the first floor. Please specify basement or crawlspace foundation when ordering.

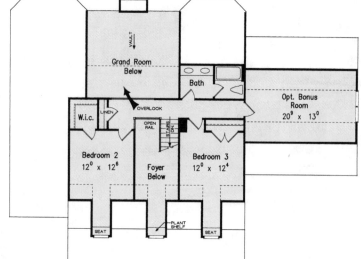

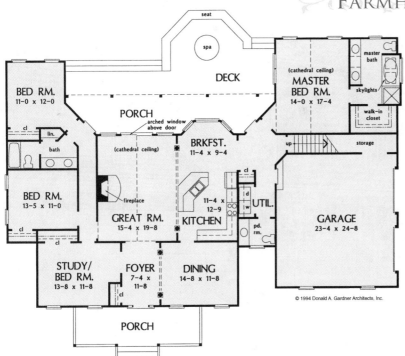

BONUS RM.
14-4 x 24-8

© 1994 Donald A. Gardner Architects, Inc.

Quote One®
Cost to build? See page 310
to order complete cost estimate
to build this house in your area!

PLAN HPT750135

Square Footage: 2,207
Bonus Room: 435 square feet
Width: 76'-1" Depth: 50'-0"

This quaint four-bedroom home with front and rear porches reinforces its beauty with arched windows and dormers. The pillared dining room opens on the right, while a study that could double as a guest room is available on the left. Straight ahead lies the massive great room with its cathedral ceiling, enchanting fireplace and access to the private rear porch. Within steps of the dining room is the efficient kitchen and the sunny breakfast nook. The master suite enjoys a cathedral ceiling, rear-deck access and a master bath with a skylit whirlpool tub. Three additional bedrooms located at the opposite end of the house share a full bath.

© 1994 Donald A. Gardner Architects, Inc.

B. NATHAN

PLAN HPT750136

Square Footage: 1,346
Width: 65'-0" Depth: 44'-2"

A great room that stretches into the dining room makes this design perfect for entertaining. A cozy fireplace, stylish built-ins and a cathedral ceiling further this casual yet elegant atmosphere. A rear deck extends living possibilities. The ample kitchen features an abundance of counter and cabinet space and an angled cooktop and serving bar that overlooks the great room. Two bedrooms, a hall bath and a handy laundry room make up the family sleeping wing while the master suite is privately located at the rear of the plan.

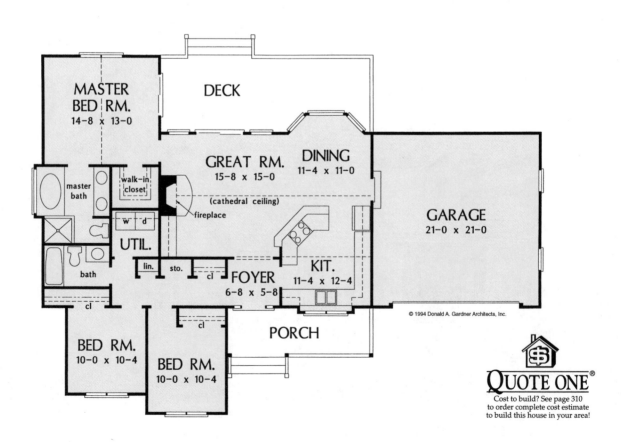

MASTER BED RM.
14-8 x 13-0

DECK

master bath

walk-in closet

GREAT RM.
15-8 x 15-0

DINING
11-4 x 11-0

(cathedral ceiling)
fireplace

GARAGE
21-0 x 21-0

w   d

UTIL.

bath

lin.   sto.   cl

FOYER
6-8 x 5-8

KIT.
11-4 x 12-4

cl

BED RM.
10-0 x 10-4

cl

BED RM.
10-0 x 10-4

PORCH

© 1994 Donald A. Gardner Architects, Inc.

Quote One®
Cost to build? See page 310
to order complete cost estimate
to build this house in your area!

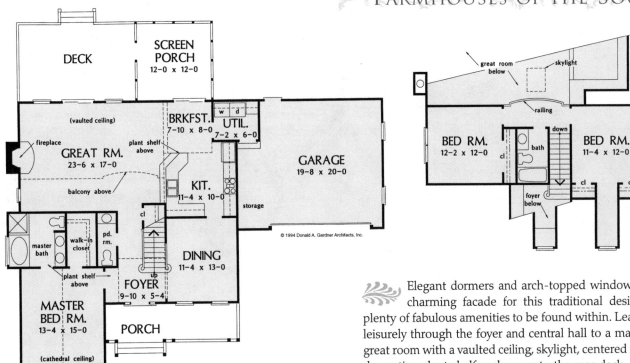

DECK

SCREEN PORCH
12-0 x 12-0

(vaulted ceiling)

fireplace

GREAT RM.
23-6 x 17-0

balcony above

plant shelf above

BRKFST.
7-10 x 8-0

UTIL.
7-2 x 6-0
w d

GARAGE
19-8 x 20-0

KIT.
11-4 x 10-0

storage

© 1994 Donald A. Gardner Architects, Inc.

master bath

walk-in closet

pd. rm.

cl

plant shelf above

MASTER BED RM.
13-4 x 15-0

FOYER
9-10 x 5-4

up

DINING
11-4 x 13-0

PORCH

(cathedral ceiling)

great room below

skylight

attic st

railing

BED RM.
12-2 x 12-0

cl

bath

down

BED RM.
11-4 x 12-0

cl   cl

foyer below

PLAN HPT750137

First Floor: 1,335 square feet
Second Floor: 488 square feet
Total: 1,823 square feet
Width: 61'-6" Depth: 54'-0"

QUOTE ONE®
Cost to build? See page 310
to order complete cost estimate
to build this house in your area!

Elegant dormers and arch-topped windows offer a charming facade for this traditional design, with plenty of fabulous amenities to be found within. Lead guests leisurely through the foyer and central hall to a magnificent great room with a vaulted ceiling, skylight, centered fireplace, decorative plant shelf and access to the rear deck. Attached to the nearby kitchen, a breakfast nook opens to a screened porch, perfect for informal alfresco dining. The well-appointed kitchen also serves the adjacent dining room for more formal occasions. A secluded main-floor master suite introduces high elegance with a cathedral ceiling and a Palladian-style window. Upstairs, a balcony hall connects two additional bedrooms that share a full bath.

© 1994 Donald A. Gardner Architects, Inc.

B. NATHAN

PLAN HPT750138

Square Footage: 1,322
Width: 56'-8" Depth: 63'-4"

 Small doesn't necessarily mean boring in this well-proportioned, three-bedroom country home. A gracious foyer leads to the great room through a set of elegant columns. In this living area, a cathedral ceiling works well with a fireplace and skylights to bring the utmost livability to the homeowner. Outside, an expansive deck includes room for a spa. A handsome master suite has a tray ceiling and a private bath. Two additional bedrooms sit to the left of the plan. Each enjoys ample closet space, and they share a hall bath.

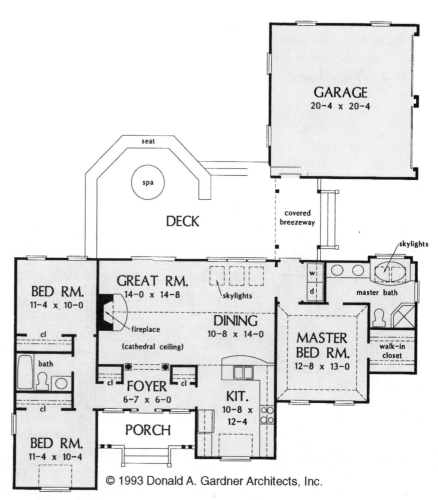

GARAGE
20-4 x 20-4

seat

spa

DECK

covered breezeway

skylights

GREAT RM.
14-0 x 14-8

skylights

fireplace

DINING
10-8 x 14-0

(cathedral ceiling)

master bath

w
d

BED RM.
11-4 x 10-0

cl

bath

cl

cl

FOYER
6-7 x 6-0

cl

KIT.
10-8 x 12-4

MASTER
BED RM.
12-8 x 13-0

walk-in
closet

PORCH

BED RM.
11-4 x 10-4

PLAN HPT750139

Square Footage: 1,633
Bonus Space: 595 square feet
Width: 65'-4" Depth: 55'-4"

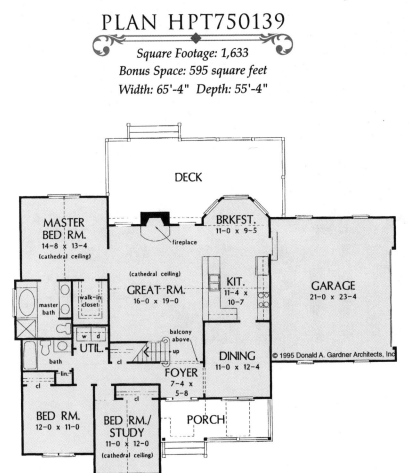

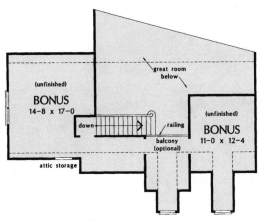

Stylish rooms and comfortable arrangements make this country home unique and inviting. The foyer opens from a quaint covered porch and leads to the expansive great room, which boasts a cathedral ceiling, an extended-hearth fireplace and access to the rear deck. The kitchen serves the formal dining room as well as the bayed breakfast nook, which offers windows that really bring in the outdoors. A secluded master suite nestles to the rear of the plan and features a walk-in closet, a garden tub and twin vanities. Two nearby bedrooms—or make one a study—share a full bath and a gallery hall that leads back to the foyer.

© 1995 Donald A. Gardner Architects, Inc.

S. NATHAN

©1991 Donald A. Gardner Architects, Inc.

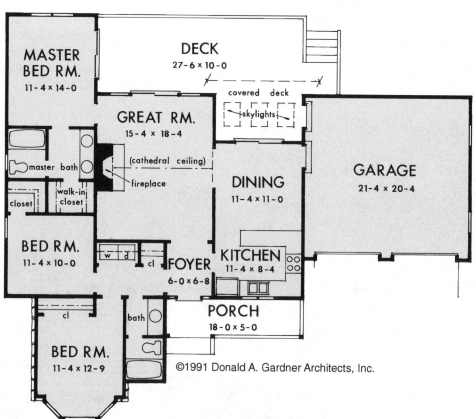

MASTER BED RM.
11-4 × 14-0

DECK
27-6 × 10-0

covered deck

skylights

GREAT RM.
15-4 × 18-4

(cathedral ceiling)

fireplace

master bath

closet

walk-in closet

GARAGE
21-4 × 20-4

DINING
11-4 × 11-0

BED RM.
11-4 × 10-0

w d

cl

FOYER
6-0 × 6-8

KITCHEN
11-4 × 8-4

cl

bath

PORCH
18-0 × 5-0

BED RM.
11-4 × 12-9

©1991 Donald A. Gardner Architects, Inc.

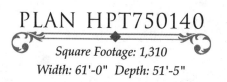

PLAN HPT750140

Square Footage: 1,310
Width: 61'-0" Depth: 51'-5"

A multi-pane bay window, decorative dormers and a covered porch dress up this one-story cottage. The foyer leads to an impressive great room with a cathedral ceiling and fireplace. The U-shaped kitchen, adjacent to the dining room, provides an ideal layout for food preparation. A large deck offers shelter while admitting cheery sunlight through skylights. The luxurious master bedroom, located to the rear of the house, takes advantage of the deck area and is assured privacy from two other bedrooms at the front of the house. These family bedrooms share a full bath.

PLAN HPT750141

Square Footage: 1,807
Bonus Room: 419 square feet
Width: 70'-8" Depth: 52'-8"

This comfortable country home begins with a front porch that opens to a columned foyer. To the right, enter the formal dining room. Decorative columns define the central great room, which boasts wide views of the outdoors. A nearby breakfast nook accommodates casual dining. The master suite and the great room both open to the rear porch. Family bedrooms share a full bath that includes double lavatories. Stairs next to the two-car garage lead upstairs to a skylit bonus room, which can be utilized as useful storage space.

Quote One®
Cost to build? See page 310
to order complete cost estimate
to build this house in your area!

© 1994 Donald A. Gardner Architects, Inc.

© 1994 Donald A. Gardner Architects, Inc.

PLAN HPT750142

First Floor: 990 square feet
Second Floor: 551 square feet
Total: 1,541 square feet
Width: 34'-8" Depth: 61'-10"

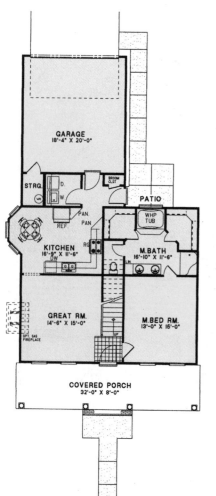

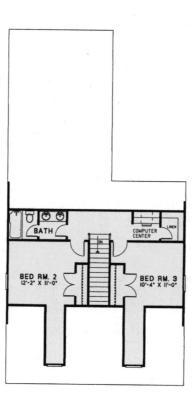

This plan would be ideal for a cottage by the lake or an urban neighborhood. Sit on the columned covered porch to look for signs of wildlife or check out the people going by. After you slave over the stove cooking that gourmet meal for eight, slip into a huge bubble bath in the whirlpool tub with a master bath as big as your kitchen. Two family bedrooms reside on the second floor where they share a full bath. Please specify crawlspace or slab foundation when ordering.

PLAN HPT750143

First Floor: 1,423 square feet
Second Floor: 871 square feet
Total: 2,294 square feet
Width: 47'-0" Depth: 57'-0"

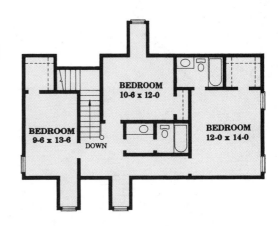

This delightful design blends the dormers, gables and shuttered windows of a farmhouse with the delicate porch trim and elegant oval window of a Victorian home. The foyer opens to the formal dining room, adjacent to a large island kitchen with ample counter space. The great room includes a fireplace flanked by double doors opening to the backyard and borders a sunlit breakfast area. The master suite provides a full bath with a corner garden tub and a large walk-in closet. The laundry area is conveniently nearby. Upstairs, each of three bedrooms has special features—one offers a walk-in closet and a private bath, another enjoys a dormer alcove, and the third provides both a walk-in closet and a dormer alcove.

A lovely spindled porch frames the living-room picture window, and a quaint cupola gives Victorian flavor to this ranch-style home. Inside, the family room has a dramatic vaulted ceiling with false beams. The fireplace is centered between two sets of long windows, one of which is actually a door to the rear patio. Three bedrooms occupy the right section of this plan. The master bedroom has a private bath, dressing room and walk-in closet. On the opposite side of the family room, the kitchen leads to an informal eating area and a formal dining room. Please specify crawlspace or slab foundation when ordering.

PLAN HPT750144

Square Footage: 1,898
Width: 72'-0" Depth: 42'-0"

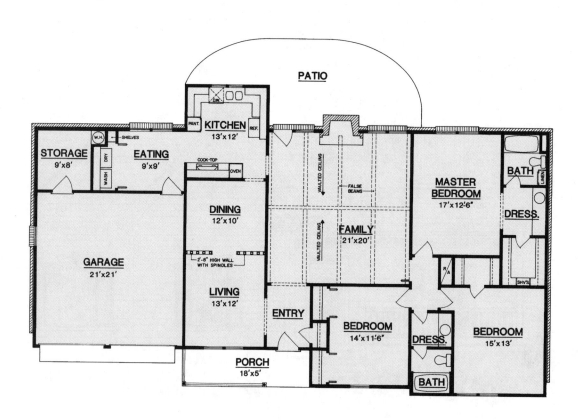

PLAN HPT750145

Square Footage: 1,395
Width: 73'-0" Depth: 37'-0"

This charming ranch-style home has much to offer in livability. The entry leads to the vaulted living room where the stone fireplace is easy to enjoy and provides a warm welcome on chilly evenings. There's an ingenious pass-through wood box so owners can replenish the fuel supply without venturing outside. The formal dining room adjoins the efficient kitchen with its convenient garage access. The pampering master suite boasts a dressing room and a full bath while two additional family bedrooms share a second full bath. Please specify crawlspace or slab foundation when ordering.

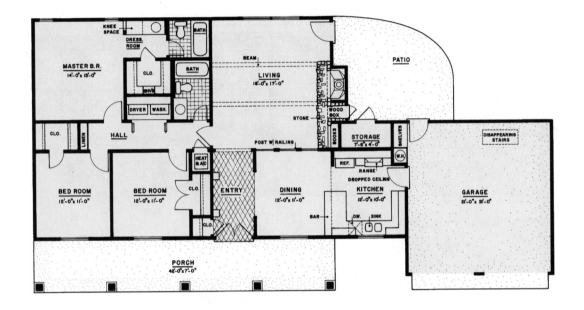

PLAN HPT750146

Square Footage: 1,606
Width: 62'-11" Depth: 52'-0"

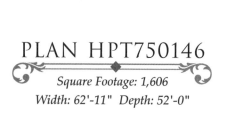 This ranch home enjoys a large covered front porch and a covered porch/patio in the rear, ready for the weekend barbecue. The great room sets the stage with a fireplace flanked by windows. The breakfast nook is illuminated by natural lighting via two skylights. The adjoining kitchen is generous with its allowance of counter space. A split-bedroom plan places the master suite on the far right for privacy with two family bedrooms sharing a full bath on the far left. Please specify basement, crawlspace or slab foundation when ordering.

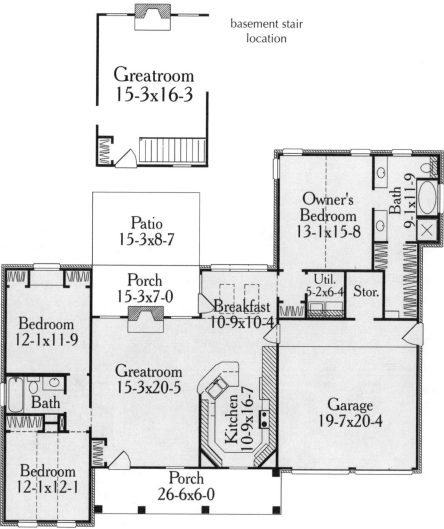

basement stair
location

Greatroom
15-3x16-3

Patio
15-3x8-7

Porch
15-3x7-0

Owner's
Bedroom
13-1x15-8

Bath
9-1x11-9

Util.
5-2x6-4

Stor.

Breakfast
10-9x10-4

Bedroom
12-1x11-9

Bath

Greatroom
15-3x20-5

Kitchen
10-9x16-7

Garage
19-7x20-4

Bedroom
12-1x12-1

Porch
26-6x6-0

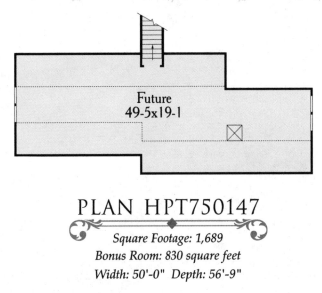

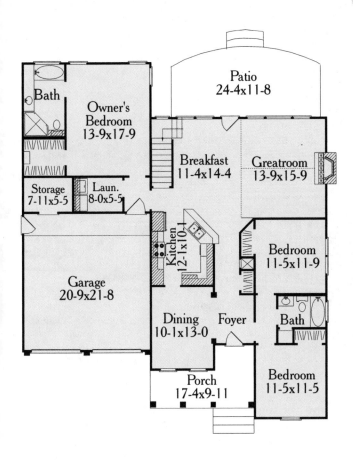

PLAN HPT750147

Square Footage: 1,689
Bonus Room: 830 square feet
Width: 50'-0" Depth: 56'-9"

Traditional accents and natural materials create an inviting home that's perfect for the countryside. A petite covered front porch introduces you to a foyer flanked by two family bedrooms and a dining room. The great room with a fireplace is open to the breakfast room, with the kitchen just a few steps away. The master bedroom is secluded behind the garage and laundry room, and includes a private bath, along with a walk-in closet. Please specify basement, crawlspace or slab foundation when ordering.

PLAN HPT750148

First Floor: 1,136 square feet
Second Floor: 464 square feet
Total: 1,600 square feet
Width: 58'-0" Depth: 42'-0"

Attractive yet very affordable, this three-bedroom home is perfect for every family. A raised porch purviews the front yard. The entry introduces the large living room with a warming fireplace and views of the front- and backyards. Stairs to the second floor are set privately between the living room and the dining area. The U-shaped kitchen opens to the dining area. A first-floor master suite features private access to the entry and a full bath. Tucked on the second floor, two family bedrooms share a full bath and attic access. Please specify crawlspace or slab foundation when ordering.

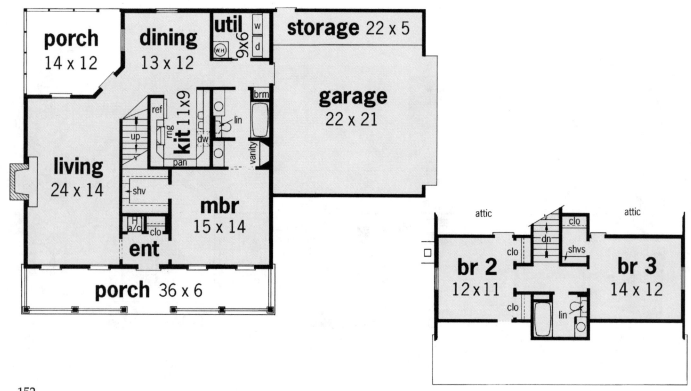

PLAN HPT750149

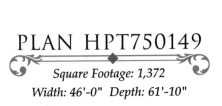

Square Footage: 1,372
Width: 46'-0" Depth: 61'-10"

This compact plan offers plenty of space for families just starting out or for empty-nesters scaling down. The great room's cathedral ceiling, combined with the openness of the adjoining dining room and kitchen, creates a sense of spaciousness beyond this plan's modest square footage. The dining room is enlarged by a bay window, while a picture window with an arched top allows light into the great room. The master bedroom features ample closet space and a skylit bath that boasts a double-sink vanity.

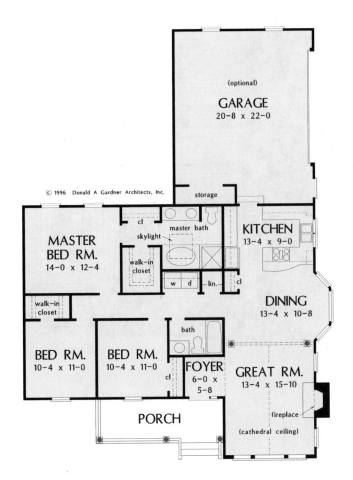

© 1996 Donald A Gardner Architects, Inc.

GARAGE
20-8 x 22-0
(optional)

storage

MASTER BED RM.
14-0 x 12-4

cl
skylight
master bath
walk-in closet
w d lin. cl

KITCHEN
13-4 x 9-0

walk-in closet

DINING
13-4 x 10-8

BED RM.
10-4 x 11-0

BED RM.
10-4 x 11-0

bath

FOYER
6-0 x 5-8
cl

GREAT RM.
13-4 x 15-10

fireplace

(cathedral ceiling)

PORCH

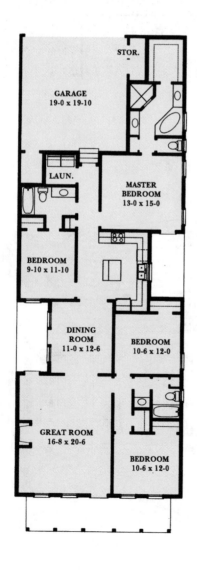

GARAGE
19-0 x 19-10

STOR.

LAUN.

MASTER
BEDROOM
13-0 x 15-0

BEDROOM
9-10 x 11-10

DINING
ROOM
11-0 x 12-6

BEDROOM
10-6 x 12-0

GREAT ROOM
16-8 x 20-6

BEDROOM
10-6 x 12-0

PLAN HPT750150

Square Footage: 1,816
Width: 30'-0" Depth: 86'-0"

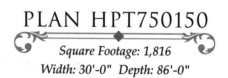 Perfect for a narrow lot, this charming Folk Victorian home presents a quaint facade that enjoys a delightful covered porch. Inside, the great room offers a warming fireplace and access to a side patio area. The formal dining room is just a step away where a pair of windows let in natural sunlight. The U-shaped island kitchen is large enough to accommodate the needs of any gourmet chef. Two bedrooms share a full bath at the front of the plan while a third bedroom sits opposite the kitchen. The master suite enjoys a bit of seclusion and privacy at the rear where a private bath leads to a generous walk-in closet.

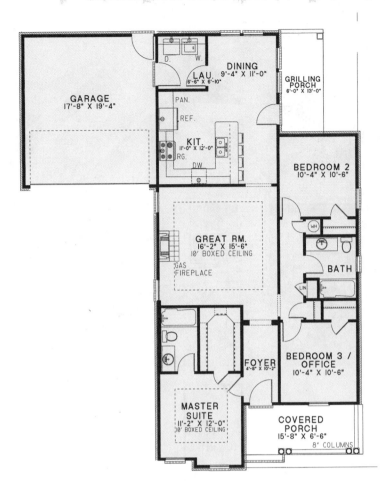

PLAN HPT750151

Square Footage: 1,289
Width: 45'-6" Depth: 56'-10"

Unusual rooflines, shuttered windows, double gables and a columned porch accent this home. The foyer leads to the great room, which features a boxed ceiling and a gas fireplace. The dining room is placed near the U-shaped kitchen with a snack bar. The private master suite is located at the front of the home with a walk-in closet and full bath. Two family bedrooms and a second bath complete this plan. Please specify basement, crawlspace or slab foundation when ordering.

Future
Storage
10-2x18-0

Future
21-0x14-7

Optional
Loft
22-2x20-3

←Open to Below→

Future
Storage
10-2x11-2

Rustic materials and simple style lend this traditional home efficiency. A covered front porch welcomes you inside to the combined living/dining area that overlooks a rear porch. The kitchen is central to the overall plan. Two family bedrooms are located at the front of the home, while the master suite is secluded at the rear for privacy. The master bedroom features a private bath with twin vanities and a walk-in closet. An optional loft and bonus area are available upstairs. Please specify crawlspace, slab or basement foundation when ordering.

PLAN HPT750152

Square Footage: 1,670
Bonus Space: 678 square feet
Width: 69'-2" Depth: 51'-3"

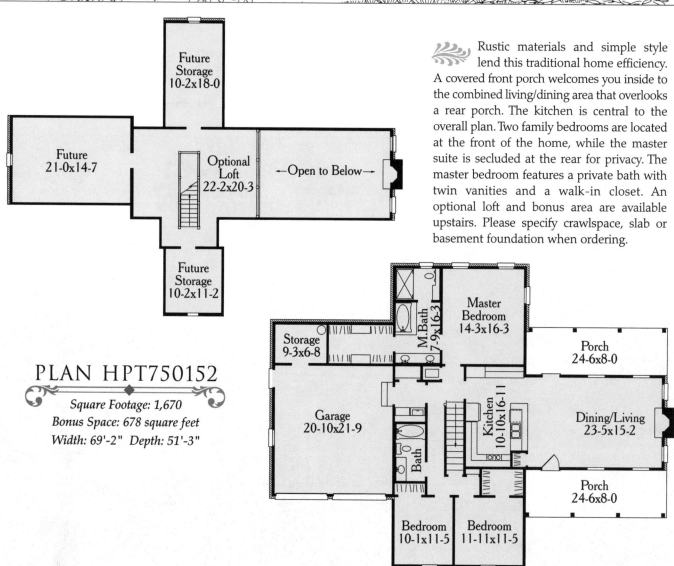

Storage
9-3x6-8

M.Bath
7-9x16-3

Master
Bedroom
14-3x16-3

Porch
24-6x8-0

Garage
20-10x21-9

Kitchen
10-10x16-11

Bath

Dining/Living
23-5x15-2

Porch
24-6x8-0

Bedroom
10-1x11-5

Bedroom
11-11x11-5

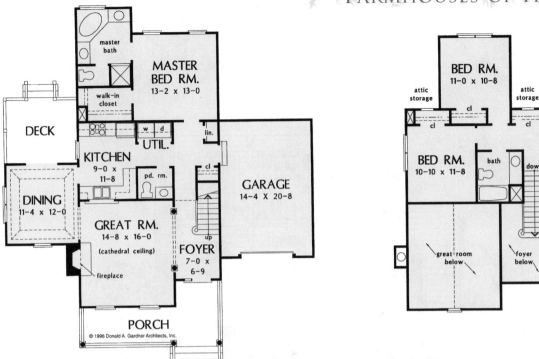

master bath

MASTER BED RM.
13-2 x 13-0

walk-in closet

DECK

w | d

UTIL.

lin.

KITCHEN
9-0 x 11-8

pd. rm.

cl

GARAGE
14-4 X 20-8

DINING
11-4 x 12-0

GREAT RM.
14-8 x 16-0
(cathedral ceiling)

up

FOYER
7-0 x 6-9

fireplace

PORCH

© 1996 Donald A. Gardner Architects, Inc.

BED RM.
11-0 x 10-8

attic storage

cl

attic storage

cl

cl

BED RM.
10-10 x 11-8

bath

down

great room below

foyer below

PLAN HPT750153

First Floor: 1,116 square feet
Second Floor: 442 square feet
Total: 1,558 square feet
Width: 49'-0" Depth: 52'-0"

This home is a great starter for a young family with plans to grow or for empty-nesters with a need for guest rooms. The two secondary bedrooms and shared bath on the second floor could also be used as office space. Additional attic storage is available as family needs expand. On the first floor, the front porch is perfect for relaxing. Inside, the foyer opens through a columned entrance to the large great room with its cathedral ceiling and fireplace. The master bedroom features a walk-in closet and a corner whirlpool tub.

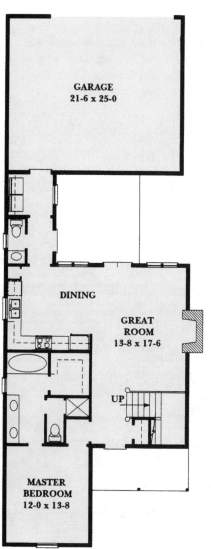

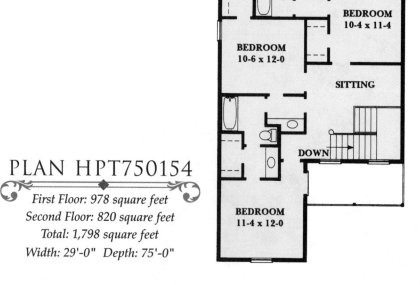

PLAN HPT750154

First Floor: 978 square feet
Second Floor: 820 square feet
Total: 1,798 square feet
Width: 29'-0" Depth: 75'-0"

The clapboard siding and double-stacked porches of this simple Victorian residence give warmth and appeal to this inviting design. Fish-scale shingles provide additional architectural ornamentation. Inside, an open-railed stairway rises from the foyer. The first-floor master suite is located off a vestibule adjacent to the foyer, providing privacy from family activities. The master suite has a roomy bath and a large walk-in closet. The L-shaped kitchen makes space for a dining table, which will be the center of family activities. The great room, with a wood-burning fireplace, opens to a large covered porch. Above, the open stairs rise to a sitting area, perfect for a computer or play center. Each of the three ample family bedrooms includes a walk-in closet. Additionally, each bedroom accesses its own private vanity.

PLAN HPT750155

First Floor: 1,274 square feet
Second Floor: 1,178 square feet
Total: 2,452 square feet
Width: 30'-0" Depth: 80'-0"

Adapted from George Barber's *The Cottage Souvenir #2*, published in 1890, this Victorian design possesses an irresistible charm and an updated floor plan. Elegant columns define the dining room, which adjoins a large great room with a fireplace. The nearby kitchen features a long angled work counter and opens to an expansive rear deck. A front bedroom serves as a guest suite with an adjacent bath. Three additional bedrooms, one a roomy master suite, are found upstairs. The master bedroom includes a dramatic bath with an angled tub, dual vanities and two walk-in closets. The two family bedrooms feature walk-in closets and private vanities.

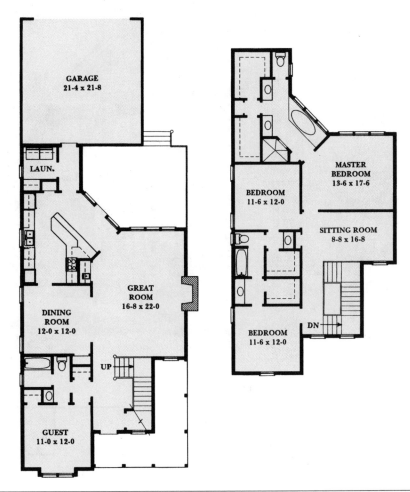

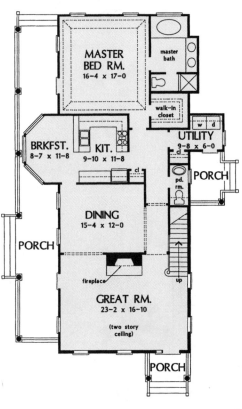

MASTER BED RM.
16-4 x 17-0

master bath

walk-in closet

BRKFST.
8-7 x 11-8

KIT.
9-10 x 11-8

UTILITY
9-8 x 6-0

w d

cl

PORCH

pd. rm.

DINING
15-4 x 12-0

PORCH

fireplace

up

GREAT RM.
23-2 x 16-10

(two story ceiling)

PORCH

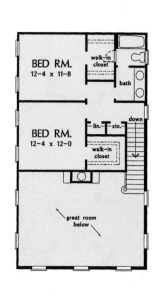

BED RM.
12-4 x 11-8

walk-in closet

bath

BED RM.
12-4 x 12-0

lin. sto. down

walk-in closet

great room below

GARAGE
22-4 x 25-4

PLAN HPT750156

First Floor: 1,545 square feet
Second Floor: 560 square feet
Total: 2,105 square feet
Width: 38'-0" Depth: 64'-4"

A graceful home with Old South charm, this two-story home offers a sleek design for narrow (or any!) lots. Enter to an impressive two-story great room with a fireplace followed by a spacious dining room. The U-shaped kitchen is designed for efficiency and serves both the dining room and the breakfast room well. The first-floor master suite is privately located and contains an elegant tray ceiling, walk-in closet and private bath. Two more bedrooms (each with a walk-in closet), a full bath and storage and linen space are located on the second floor. Note the detached two-car garage and the full-length covered porch that add much to the livability of this design.

PLAN HPT750157

First Floor: 1,350 square feet
Second Floor: 1,224 square feet
Total: 2,574 square feet
Width: 62'-0" Depth: 42'-0"

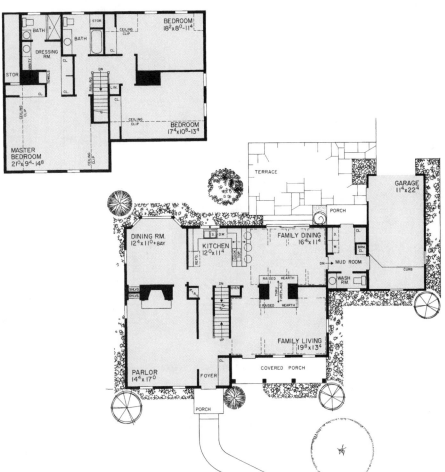

This Early American farmhouse features the simple gable rooflines, shuttered multi-pane windows and a pilastered front door of the era. While the front door welcomes guests to the foyer, the porch entrance will be enjoyed by family members, giving them immediate access to the casual living space of the house. A massive see-through, raised-hearth fireplace is the focal point of this area, providing warmth and fireglow to the family living and dining rooms. Beam ceilings add to the country atmosphere. The parlor enjoys special features that include fireplaces, a bay window and built-in bookcases. An efficient U-shaped kitchen easily serves both dining rooms and also provides a snack bar for meals on the go.

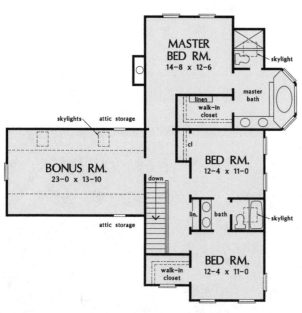

PLAN HPT750158

First Floor: 1,113 square feet
Second Floor: 960 square feet
Total: 2,073 square feet
Bonus Room: 338 square feet
Width: 49'-4" Depth: 58'-10"

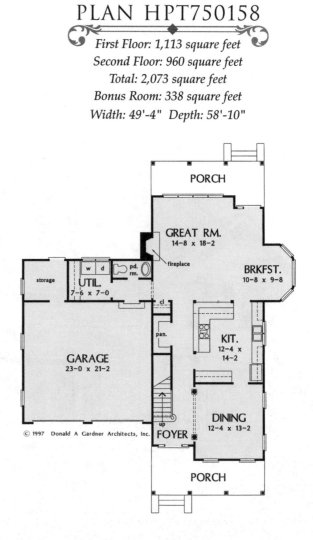

With a perfect blend of country and traditional, this family home fits nicely on a narrow lot. Columns define the entry to the dining room, while the kitchen, breakfast bay and great room remain open for a casual atmosphere. A half-bath and utility room are conveniently located nearby. Upstairs, the master suite has a luxurious bath with a sunny bay window. Two additional bedrooms share a skylit bath. A skylit bonus room over the garage allows the option of future expansion.

PLAN HPT750159

First Floor: 1,475 square feet
Second Floor: 730 square feet
Total: 2,205 square feet
Bonus Room: 430 square feet
Width: 71'-4" Depth: 76'-3"

With a bonus room over the garage and a full wrapping porch on the exterior, this farmhouse is a true crowd-pleaser. The central foyer opens on the right to a formal dining room and then leads back to the great room. The master suite is located on the first floor and features a walk-in closet and a bath with a garden tub. Family bedrooms are on the second floor, separated by a loft area. Each family bedroom includes its own bath.

1998 Donald A. Gardner, Inc.

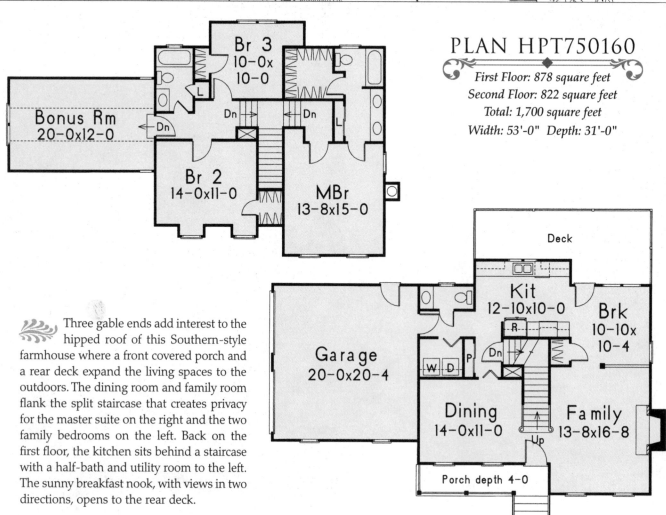

Bonus Rm
20-0x12-0

Br 3
10-0x
10-0

Br 2
14-0x11-0

MBr
13-8x15-0

Dn   Dn   Dn

PLAN HPT750160

First Floor: 878 square feet
Second Floor: 822 square feet
Total: 1,700 square feet
Width: 53'-0" Depth: 31'-0"

Deck

Kit
12-10x10-0

Brk
10-10x
10-4

Garage
20-0x20-4

W D P

R   Dn

Dining
14-0x11-0

Up

Family
13-8x16-8

Porch depth 4-0

Three gable ends add interest to the hipped roof of this Southern-style farmhouse where a front covered porch and a rear deck expand the living spaces to the outdoors. The dining room and family room flank the split staircase that creates privacy for the master suite on the right and the two family bedrooms on the left. Back on the first floor, the kitchen sits behind a staircase with a half-bath and utility room to the left. The sunny breakfast nook, with views in two directions, opens to the rear deck.

PLAN HPT750161

First Floor: 1,450 square feet
Second Floor: 1,517 square feet
Total: 2,967 square feet
Width: 69'-0" Depth: 37'-0"

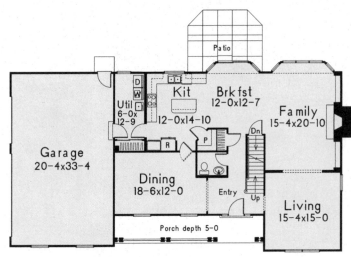

Patio

Kit

Brk fst
12-0x12-7

Util
6-0x
12-9

12-0x14-10

Family
15-4x20-10

Garage
20-4x33-4

Dn

Dining
18-6x12-0

Entry

Up

Living
15-4x15-0

Porch depth 5-0

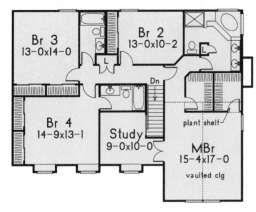

Br 3
13-0x14-0

Br 2
13-0x10-2

Dn

Br 4
14-9x13-1

Study
9-0x10-0

plant shelf

MBr
15-4x17-0

vaulted clg

The delightful farmhouse holds two family bedrooms, each with twin closets, and a master suite with a vaulted ceiling and a gorgeous arch-top window. The covered porch announces the entry that presents the stunning staircase. To the left, the spacious formal dining room accommodates large gatherings. A swinging door quiets the distractions of the adjoining island kitchen. A sunny bay, to the right, enlivens the breakfast nook which leads to the family room. To the right of the foyer, the living room opens to the family room via an elegant archway. Upstairs, the master suite includes twin walk-in closets and a study.

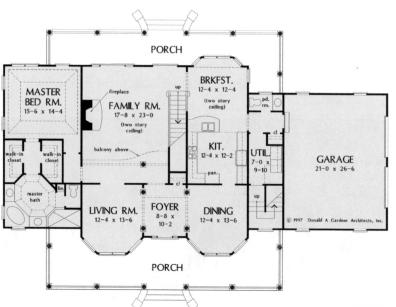

PORCH

MASTER
BED RM.
15-6 x 14-4

fireplace

FAMILY RM.
17-8 x 23-0
(two story ceiling)

BRKFST.
12-4 x 12-4
(two story ceiling)

up

pd. rm.

walk-in closet

walk-in closet

balcony above

KIT.
12-4 x 12-2

cl

UTIL.
7-0 x 9-10

GARAGE
21-0 x 26-6

lin.

master bath

pan.

LIVING RM.
12-4 x 13-6

FOYER
8-8 x 10-2

cl

DINING
12-4 x 13-6

up

PORCH

PLAN HPT750162

First Floor: 1,914 square feet
Second Floor: 597 square feet
Total: 2,511 square feet
Bonus Room: 487 square feet
Width: 79'-2" Depth: 51'-6"

Filled with charm, this design opens with a classic covered porch at the front. The entry leads to a foyer flanked by columns that separate the formal dining room on the right from the formal living room on the left. The family room boasts a two-story ceiling, a fireplace and sliding glass doors to the rear covered porch. The U-shaped kitchen separates the dining room from the bayed breakfast room. The first-floor master suite features a tray ceiling and a bath with a whirlpool tub, dual sinks and a separate shower.

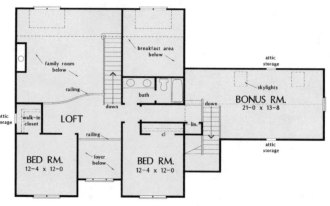

family room below

breakfast area below

attic storage

railing

bath

skylights

BONUS RM.
21-0 x 13-8

attic storage

walk-in closet

LOFT

down

down

lin.

attic storage

BED RM.
12-4 x 12-0

railing

cl

foyer below

BED RM.
12-4 x 12-0

attic storage

PLAN HPT750163

Square Footage: 1,903
Width: 65'-8" Depth: 55'-7"

This home combines the Victorian charm of yesteryear with a plan designed for today's families. Accented by columns, the great room with a fireplace is vaulted, while the foyer, dining room, kitchen, breakfast bay and bedroom/study boast impressive ten-foot ceilings. With a double-door entry, the secluded master suite features a tray ceiling, walk-in closet and private skylit bath. Two additional bedrooms share a full hall bath. The utility room sits next to the two-car garage entrance.

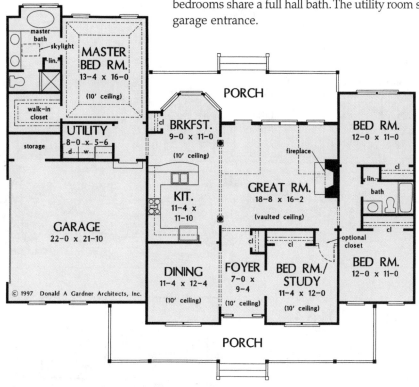

B. NATHAN

© 1997 Donald A. Gardner Architects, Inc.

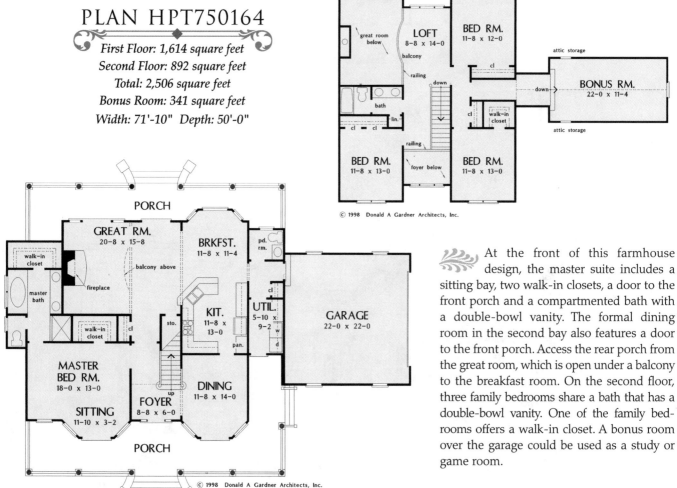

PLAN HPT750164

First Floor: 1,614 square feet

Second Floor: 892 square feet

Total: 2,506 square feet

Bonus Room: 341 square feet

Width: 71'-10" Depth: 50'-0"

At the front of this farmhouse design, the master suite includes a sitting bay, two walk-in closets, a door to the front porch and a compartmented bath with a double-bowl vanity. The formal dining room in the second bay also features a door to the front porch. Access the rear porch from the great room, which is open under a balcony to the breakfast room. On the second floor, three family bedrooms share a bath that has a double-bowl vanity. One of the family bedrooms offers a walk-in closet. A bonus room over the garage could be used as a study or game room.

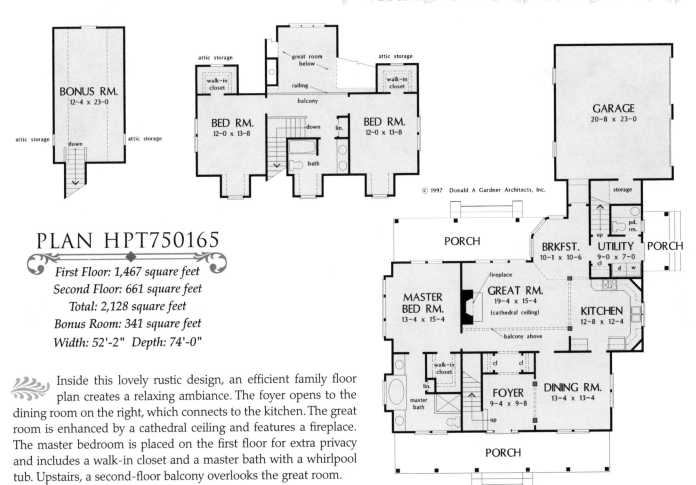

BONUS RM.
12-4 x 23-0

attic storage   attic storage

down

attic storage

great room below

attic storage

walk-in closet   walk-in closet

railing

balcony

BED RM.
12-0 x 13-8   down   lin.   BED RM.
12-0 x 13-8

bath

© 1997 Donald A Gardner Architects, Inc.

GARAGE
20-8 x 23-0

storage

up   pd. rm.

PORCH   BRKFST.
10-1 x 10-6   UTILITY
9-0 x 7-0   PORCH

cl   d   w

fireplace

MASTER
BED RM.
13-4 x 15-4   GREAT RM.
19-4 x 15-4
(cathedral ceiling)   KITCHEN
12-8 x 12-4

balcony above

walk-in closet   cl   cl

lin.   FOYER
9-4 x 9-8   DINING RM.
13-4 x 13-4

master bath   up

up

PORCH

PLAN HPT750165

First Floor: 1,467 square feet

Second Floor: 661 square feet

Total: 2,128 square feet

Bonus Room: 341 square feet

Width: 52'-2" Depth: 74'-0"

Inside this lovely rustic design, an efficient family floor plan creates a relaxing ambiance. The foyer opens to the dining room on the right, which connects to the kitchen. The great room is enhanced by a cathedral ceiling and features a fireplace. The master bedroom is placed on the first floor for extra privacy and includes a walk-in closet and a master bath with a whirlpool tub. Upstairs, a second-floor balcony overlooks the great room.

B. NATHAN

© 1997 Donald A. Gardner Architects, Inc.

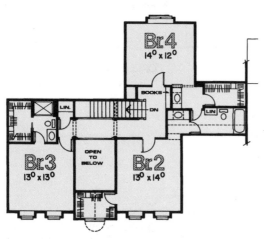

PLAN HPT750166

First Floor: 2,280 square feet
Second Floor: 1,014 square feet
Total: 3,294 square feet
Width: 67'-4" Depth: 64'-0"

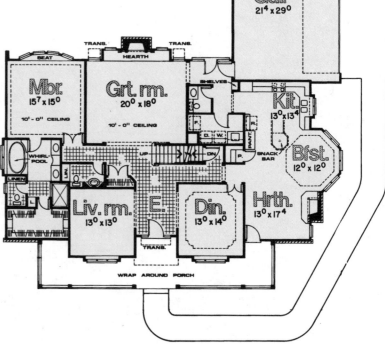

Bright windows and a wraparound porch enhance the elevation of this one-story home. A flush-hearth fireplace and transom windows highlight a volume great room planned for daily living. Nearby, a sunny bayed dinette is served by an island kitchen with a snack bar and two pantries. In the master bath, an oval whirlpool tub, dual vanities and a walk-in closet pamper the homeowners. Upstairs, Bedroom 3 includes a private bath while Bedrooms 2 and 4 share a Hollywood bath.

PLAN HPT750167

First Floor: 1,553 square feet
Second Floor: 1,587 square feet
Total: 3,140 square feet
Width: 58'-0" Depth: 40'-4"

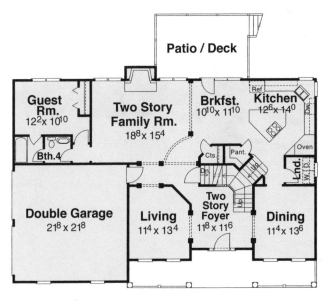

An elegant covered porch spans the front of this house and draws attention to the muntin windows and brick detailing. A two-story foyer is flanked by a dining room on the right and a living room on the left. A spacious kitchen—with plenty of counter space—leads into a cozy breakfast area, which opens to the rear sun deck. The two-story family room boasts a fireplace and an abundance of windows. A guest bedroom, with a full bath, completes the first level. A luxurious second-floor master bedroom includes a tray ceiling, a sitting area, His and Hers walk-in closets and an amenity-filled bath. Three additional bedrooms, two full baths and a balcony overlook to the family room and foyer round out this level.

Two Car
Garage
21³x21³

Deck

Great
Room
16⁰x17⁰

Kitchen
13³x16⁶

Breakfast
12⁶x12⁹

Dn

Up

Dining
Room
15⁰x12⁹

Foyer

Master
Bedroom
15⁶x16³

Porch

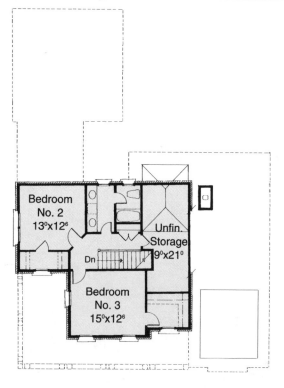

Bedroom
No. 2
13⁰x12⁶

Unfin.
Storage
9⁰x21⁰

Dn

Bedroom
No. 3
15⁰x12⁶

PLAN HPT750168

First Floor: 1,787 square feet

Second Floor: 851 square feet

Total: 2,638 square feet

Bonus Room: 189 square feet

Width: 51'-3"   Depth: 70'-6"

This beautiful brick design displays fine family livability in over 2,600 square feet. The wraparound porch welcomes family and friends to inside living areas. The great room sports an elegant ceiling, a fireplace and built-ins. The kitchen displays good traffic patterning. An island cooktop will please the house gourmet. The dining room features double doors that open to the porch. In the master bedroom, a pampering bath includes a whirlpool tub and separate vanities. A walk-in closet is located at the back of the bath. Two family bedrooms upstairs enjoy peace and quiet and a full hall bath with natural illumination. This home is designed with a walkout basement foundation.

The brick quoins draw attention to the cabin feeling of this home's facade, making it a perfect home for wooded areas. The covered front porch extends to the middle of the home, allowing for plenty of space to lounge outside. The open family room features a fireplace and connects to the breakfast nook where French doors lead to the rear patio. Upstairs, a deluxe raised tub and an immense walk-in closet grace the master suite. Two secondary bedrooms share a full hall bath with dual vanities and a compartmented toilet and tub.

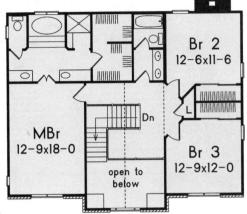

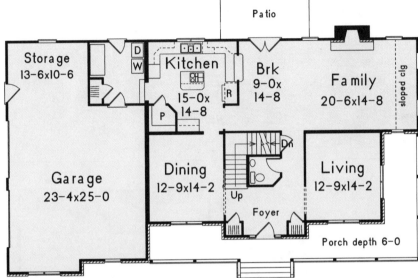

PLAN HPT750169

First Floor: 1,436 square feet
Second Floor: 1,069 square feet
Total: 2,505 square feet
Width: 70'-0" Depth: 40'-0"

© 1996 Donald A. Gardner Architects, Inc.

PLAN HPT750170

First Floor: 1,395 square feet
Second Floor: 502 square feet
Total: 1,897 square feet
Bonus Room: 316 square feet
Width: 53'-4" Depth: 51'-4"

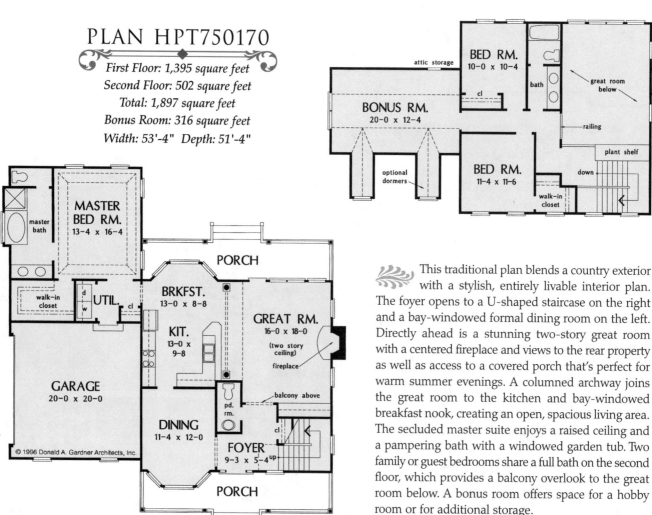

This traditional plan blends a country exterior with a stylish, entirely livable interior plan. The foyer opens to a U-shaped staircase on the right and a bay-windowed formal dining room on the left. Directly ahead is a stunning two-story great room with a centered fireplace and views to the rear property as well as access to a covered porch that's perfect for warm summer evenings. A columned archway joins the great room to the kitchen and bay-windowed breakfast nook, creating an open, spacious living area. The secluded master suite enjoys a raised ceiling and a pampering bath with a windowed garden tub. Two family or guest bedrooms share a full bath on the second floor, which provides a balcony overlook to the great room below. A bonus room offers space for a hobby room or for additional storage.

PLAN HPT750171

First Floor: 1,041 square feet
Second Floor: 998 square feet
Total: 2,039 square feet
Width: 44'-10" Depth: 84'-6"

This sweet facade pays homage to the architectural symmetry of simpler times. A deep front porch welcomes guests and complements a triplet of charming windows. Inside, formal rooms frame the foyer, which provides a discreet staircase. The kitchen is enhanced by an island snack bar and access to the rear breezeway. The family room is open to the kitchen and is warmed by a central fireplace. Upstairs, two secondary bedrooms have plenty of closet space and share a full bath. The master suite features two walk-in closets, a double-bowl vanity, and a separate shower and tub. A garage is placed to the rear of the plan.

This home, as shown in the photograph, may differ from the actual blueprints. For more detailed information, please check the floor plans carefully.

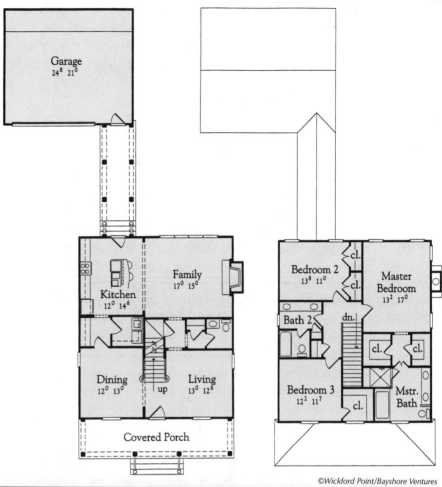

©Wickford Point/Bayshore Ventures

GARAGE
21-6 x 22-0

STOR.

UP TO BONUS

BREAKFAST

BEDROOM
12-0 x 15-0

DOWN

BEDROOM
12-0 x 15-2

UP

GREAT ROOM
18-6 x 22-0

MASTER BEDROOM
16-0 x 18-0

DINING ROOM
12-0 x 16-0

GUEST/STUDY
12-0 x 16-0

PLAN HPT750172

First Floor: 2,203 square feet
Second Floor: 698 square feet
Total: 2,901 square feet
Width: 74'-0" Depth: 71'-0"

This two-story farmhouse features a traditional exterior and a comfortable modernized interior. The formal dining room sits to the left of the entry, conveniently near the kitchen. The kitchen includes an island workstation, a pantry and a breakfast nook with its own porch. At the center of the design is a sunny and hearth-warmed great room. The master suite enjoys His and Hers walk-in closets, private access to the rear porch, and a soaking tub set in a bay window. A guest room or study has a view of the front porch. Upstairs, two family bedrooms share a full bath that includes a two-sink vanity.

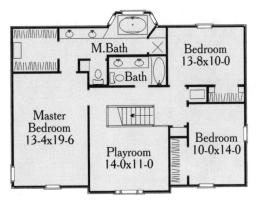

This classic farmhouse design enjoys an expansive covered porch that wraps all four sides of the first floor. This floor boasts open planning focused around the split-descending staircase that is accessed from both the kitchen/breakfast area and the foyer. The formal dining room abuts the island kitchen for convenience. On the right, the sunny study offers a quiet retreat while the great room delights with a window wall and an elegant fireplace. The second floor opens with a playroom that acts as a barrier between the two family bedrooms and the lavish master suite. Please specify basement, crawlspace or slab foundation when ordering.

PLAN HPT750173

First Floor: 1,370 square feet
Second Floor: 1,212 square feet
Total: 2,582 square feet
Width: 74'-0" Depth: 44'-0"

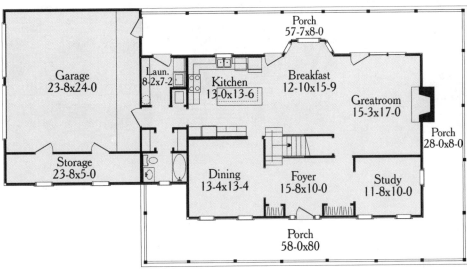

PLAN HPT750174

First Floor: 1,368 square feet
Second Floor: 1,246 square feet
Total: 2,614 square feet
Width: 43'-0" Depth: 68'-0"

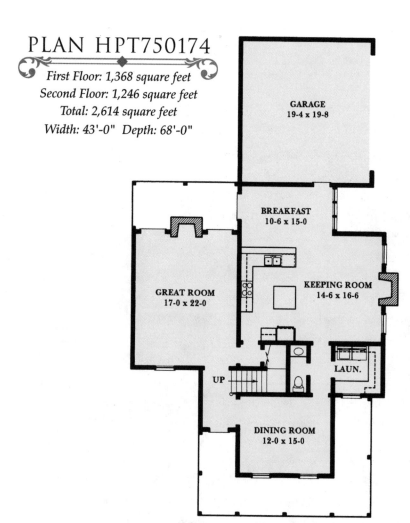

GARAGE
19-4 x 19-8

BREAKFAST
10-6 x 15-0

GREAT ROOM
17-0 x 22-0

KEEPING ROOM
14-6 x 16-6

UP

LAUN.

DINING ROOM
12-0 x 15-0

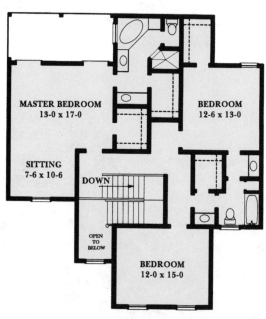

MASTER BEDROOM
13-0 x 17-0

BEDROOM
12-6 x 13-0

SITTING
7-6 x 10-6

DOWN

OPEN
TO
BELOW

BEDROOM
12-0 x 15-0

Precious Victorian detail and a wraparound porch with a railing add charm and class to this two-story home. Inside, two fireplaces can be enjoyed in either the great room or the keeping room. The L-shaped kitchen is complete with an island, snack bar and breakfast room. Plenty of counter space is provided in the laundry room directly across from the powder room. Three bedrooms, one the master bedroom, reside on the upper level. A luxurious private bath, two walk-in closets and a sitting area pamper in the master suite. Two additional bedrooms share a full bath that includes two separate vanities.

Br.#1
10/13

Stoop

Kitchen
13x12/4

Dining

Family Room
13x16

up

Porch
13/6x8

The front-facing fireplace and sloping roof create drama and privacy in this three-bedroom home. Relax on the front porch with a book or enjoy a family gathering inside. The angled front door opens to a spacious family room, complete with a cheerful fireplace. A good-sized kitchen/dining area lets the cook socialize with family or guests while preparing meals. A large bedroom and nearby full bath with an attached laundry area complete the first floor. Either of the two upstairs bedrooms could also serve as a study or recreation room.

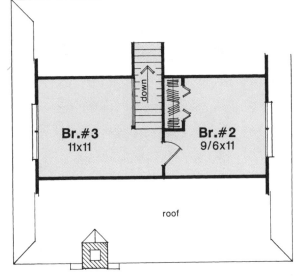

Br.#3
11x11

down

Br.#2
9/6x11

roof

PLAN HPT750175

First Floor: 728 square feet
Second Floor: 300 square feet
Total: 1,028 square feet
Width: 28'-0" Depth: 32'-0"

PLAN HPT750176

First Floor: 2,658 square feet

Second Floor: 1,429 square feet

Total: 4,087 square feet

Width: 98'-0" Depth: 66'-0"

L D

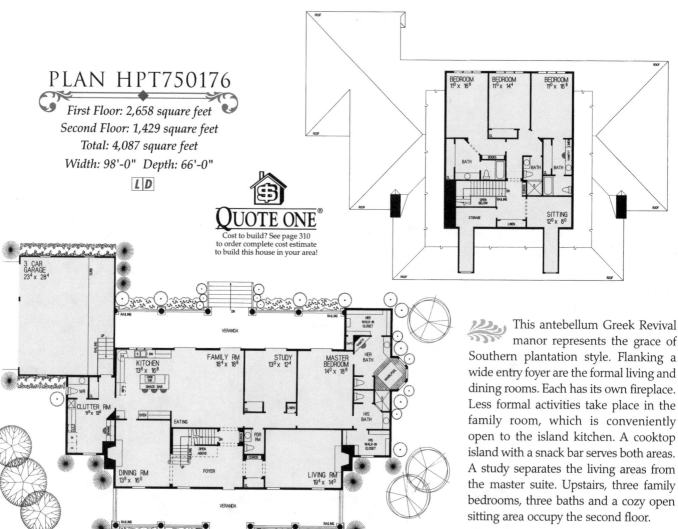

Quote One®

Cost to build? See page 310
to order complete cost estimate
to build this house in your area!

This antebellum Greek Revival manor represents the grace of Southern plantation style. Flanking a wide entry foyer are the formal living and dining rooms. Each has its own fireplace. Less formal activities take place in the family room, which is conveniently open to the island kitchen. A cooktop island with a snack bar serves both areas. A study separates the living areas from the master suite. Upstairs, three family bedrooms, three baths and a cozy open sitting area occupy the second floor.

PLAN HPT750177

Square Footage: 1,792
Width: 32'-0" Depth: 82'-0"

A blend of Southern comfort and Gulf Coast style sets this home apart. Inside, decorative arches and columns mark the grand entrance to the living and dining areas, while the gourmet kitchen provides a pass-through to the dining room. On cold nights, a fireplace warms the great room, and on warm evenings, French doors to the covered porch let in cool breezes. At the rear of the plan, the master suite privately accesses a sun deck, and French doors open to the covered porch. Two walk-in closets, a garden tub and a bayed sitting area add to the comfort of this suite.

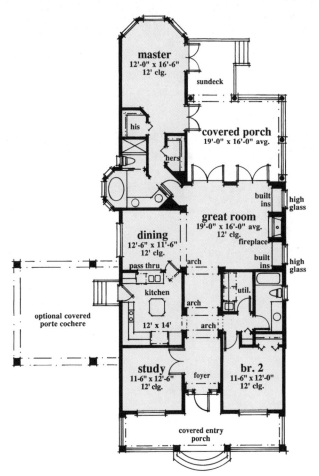

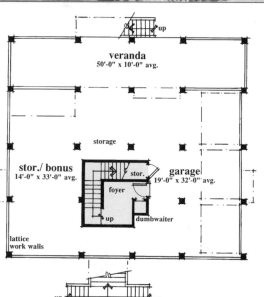

veranda
50'-0" x 10'-0" avg.

storage

stor./ bonus
14'-0" x 33'-0" avg.

stor.

foyer

garage
19'-0" x 32'-0" avg.

up

dumbwaiter

lattice
work walls

up   up

PLAN HPT750178

First Floor: 1,586 square feet
Second Floor: 601 square feet
Total: 2,187 square feet
Width: 50'-0" Depth: 44'-0"

Lattice walls, pickets and horizontal siding complement a relaxed Key West design that's perfect for waterfront properties. The grand room with a fireplace, the dining room and Bedroom 2 open through French doors to the veranda. The master suite occupies the entire second floor and features access to a private balcony through double doors. This pampering suite also includes a spacious walk-in closet and a full bath with a whirlpool tub. Enclosed storage/bonus space and a garage are available on the lower level. This home is designed with a pier foundation.

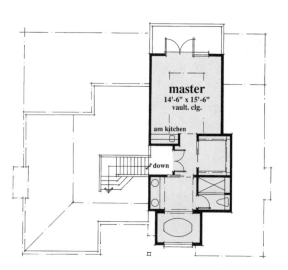

master
14'-6" x 15'-6"
vault. clg.

am kitchen

down

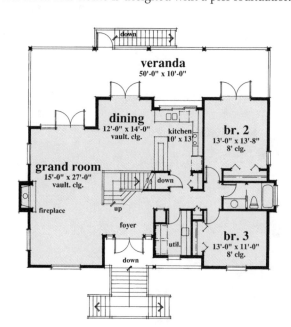

down

veranda
50'-0" x 10'-0"

dining
12'-0" x 14'-0"
vault. clg.

kitchen
10' x 13'

br. 2
13'-0" x 13'-8"
8' clg.

grand room
15'-0" x 27'-0"
vault. clg.

down

up

fireplace

foyer

util.

down

br. 3
13'-0" x 11'-0"
8' clg.

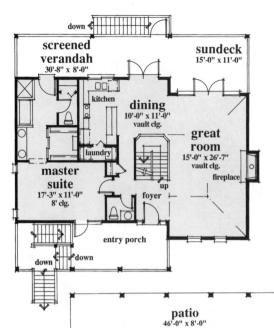

screened
verandah
30'-8" x 8'-0"

sundeck
15'-0" x 11'-0"

down

kitchen

dining
10'-0" x 11'-0"
vault clg.

great
room
15'-0" x 26'-7"
vault clg.

fireplace

laundry

master
suite
17'-3" x 11'-0"
8' clg.

up

foyer

entry porch

down   down

SOUTHERN COASTAL

PLAN HPT750179

First Floor: 1,189 square feet
Second Floor: 575 square feet
Total: 1,764 square feet
Width: 46'-0" Depth: 44'-6"

L

An abundance of porches and a deck encourage year-round indoor/outdoor relationships in this classic two-story home. The spacious great room, with its cozy fireplace, and the adjacent dining room both offer access to the screened porch/deck area through French doors. The private master suite accesses both front and rear porches and leads into a relaxing private bath complete with dual vanities and a walk-in closet. An additional family bedroom and a loft/bedroom are also available.

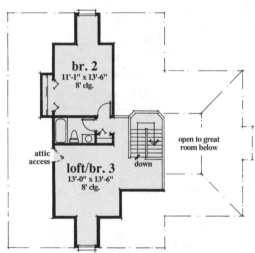

patio
46'-0" x 8'-0"

garage
24'-0" x 28'-0"

storage/bonus

up

br. 2
11'-1" x 13'-6"
8' clg.

attic
access

loft/br. 3
13'-0" x 13'-6"
8' clg.

down

open to great
room below

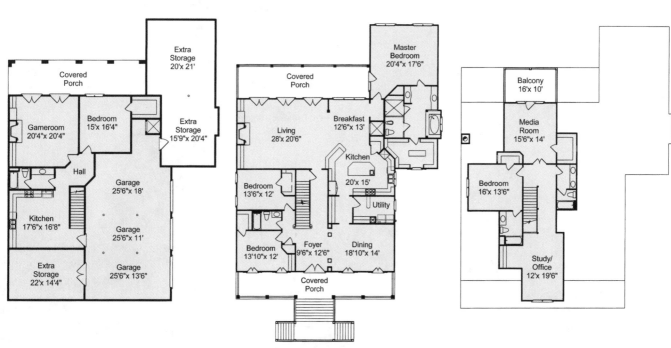

Extra Storage 20'x 21'

Covered Porch

Gameroom 20'4"x 20'4"

Bedroom 15'x 16'4"

Extra Storage 15'9"x 20'4"

Hall

Kitchen 17'6"x 16'8"

Garage 25'6"x 18'

Garage 25'6"x 11'

Extra Storage 22'x 14'4"

Garage 25'6"x 13'6"

Master Bedroom 20'4"x 17'6"

Covered Porch

Breakfast 12'6"x 13'

Living 28'x 20'6"

Kitchen 20'x 15'

Bedroom 13'6"x 12'

Utility

Bedroom 13'10"x 12'

Foyer 9'6"x 12'6"

Dining 18'10"x 14'

Covered Porch

Balcony 16'x 10'

Media Room 15'6"x 14'

Bedroom 16'x 13'6"

Study/ Office 12'x 19'6"

PLAN HPT750180

First Floor: 3,294 square feet
Second Floor: 1,202 square feet
Total: 4,496 square feet
Finished Basement: 1,366 square feet
Width: 63'-0" Depth: 82'-0"

Suited for a golf resort or lakeview site, this two-story, five-bedroom home includes room for plenty of guests. French doors open from the large front porch to the foyer, dining room and a family bedroom. French doors also lead from the hearth-warmed living room to the rear porch. The island kitchen features a breakfast area, walk-in pantry and convenient butler's pantry near the dining room. The master suite enjoys many luxuries, including private access to the rear porch. The second floor contains a family bedroom, media room with a balcony, a private study and two full baths. A kitchen, family bedroom, game room and plenty of extra storage adjoin a three-car garage in the walkout basement.

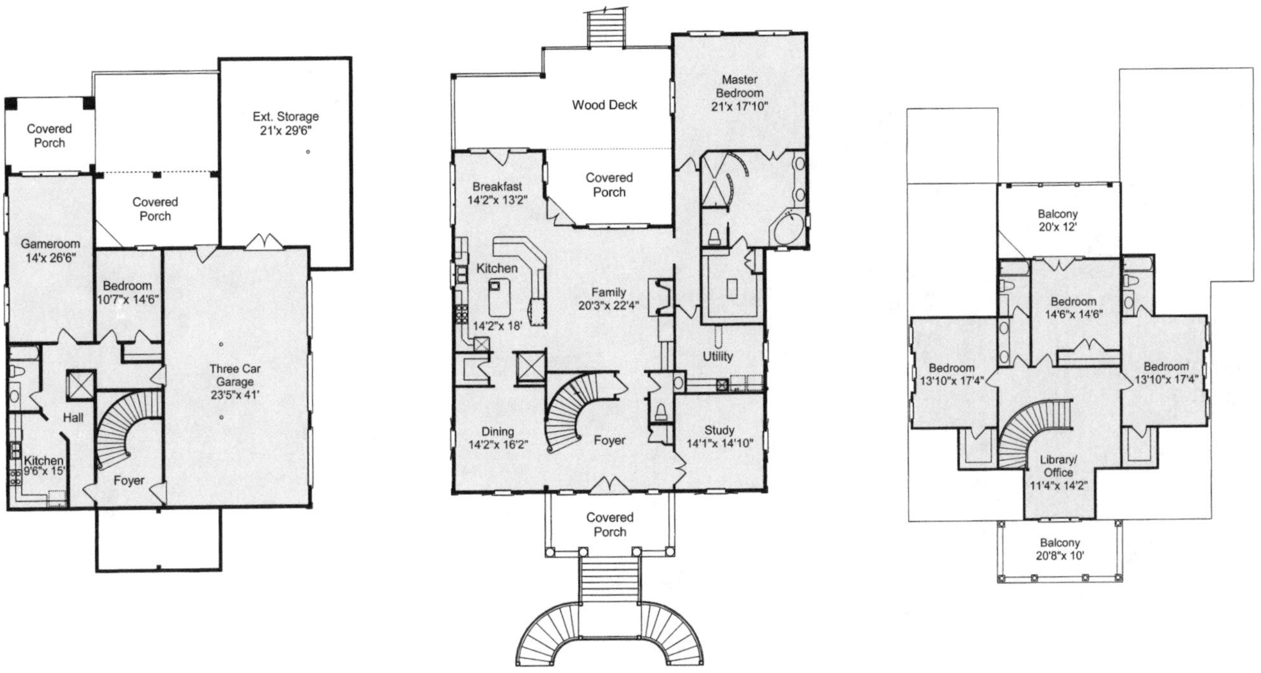
Covered Porch
Ext. Storage 21'x 29'6"
Covered Porch
Gameroom 14'x 26'6"
Bedroom 10'7"x 14'6"
Three Car Garage 23'5"x 41'
Hall
Kitchen 9'6"x 15'
Foyer
Wood Deck
Master Bedroom 21'x 17'10"
Breakfast 14'2"x 13'2"
Covered Porch
Kitchen 14'2"x 18'
Family 20'3"x 22'4"
Utility
Dining 14'2"x 16'2"
Foyer
Study 14'1"x 14'10"
Covered Porch
Balcony 20'x 12'
Bedroom 14'6"x 14'6"
Bedroom 13'10"x 17'4"
Bedroom 13'10"x 17'4"
Library/ Office 11'4"x 14'2"
Balcony 20'8"x 10'

PLAN HPT750181

First Floor: 2,974 square feet
Second Floor: 1,406 square feet
Total: 4,380 square feet
Finiahed Basement: 1,275 square feet
Width: 57'-0" Depth: 82'-0"

This two-story home with a finished basement is designed to pamper with a second kitchen on the lower level and an elevator that serves the lower and first floors. The sweeping staircase is the focal point of the grand foyer that is flanked by the dining room and the study. The well-equipped first-floor island kitchen serves the breakfast nook and the dining room with ease. The master suite, on the right, boasts a lavish bath and a magnificent walk-in closet. Three bedrooms sit on the second floor with two full baths and a library/office. The lower level holds the three-car garage, a large game room and final fifth bedroom along with the ancillary kitchen and a full bath.

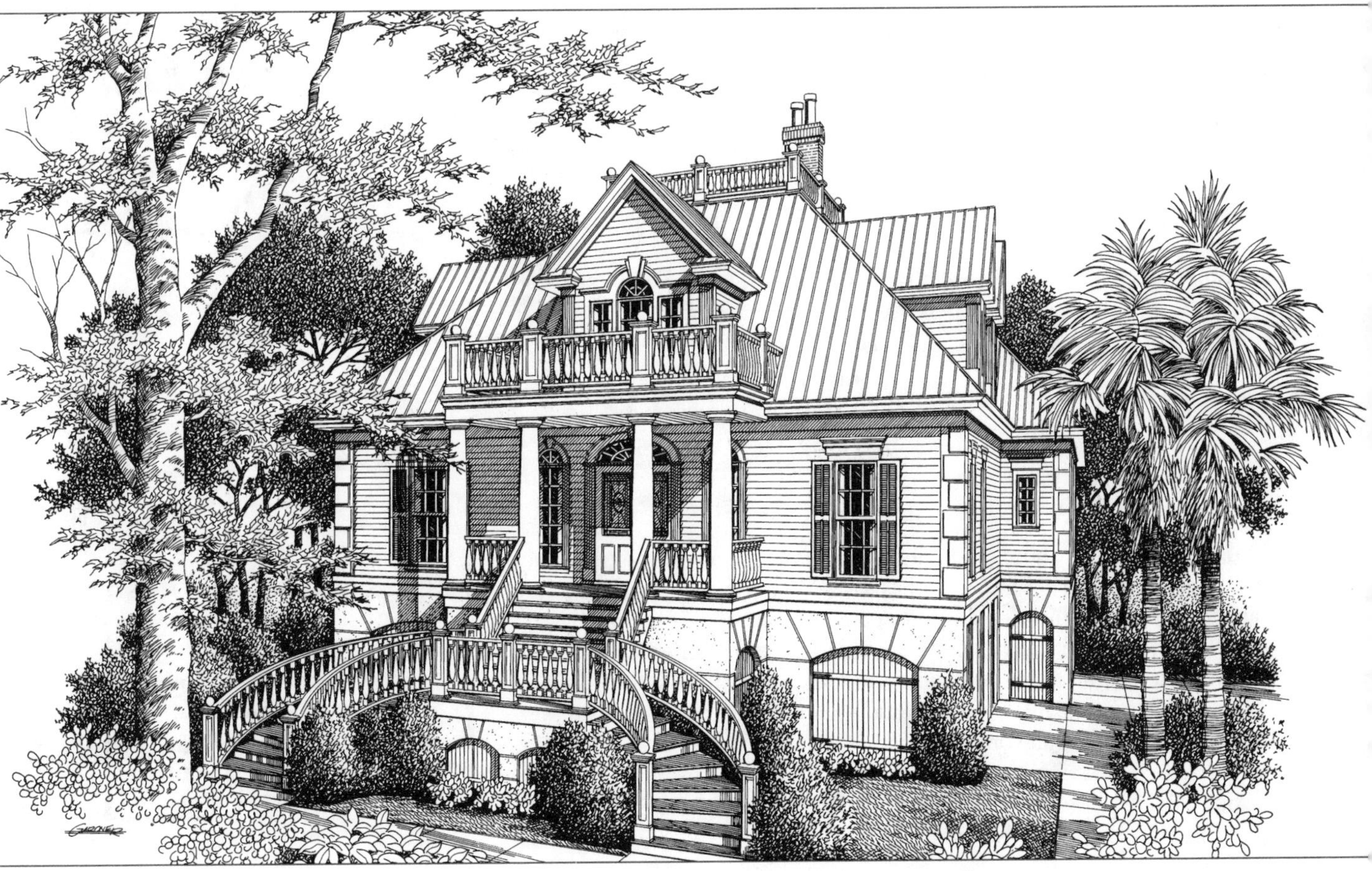

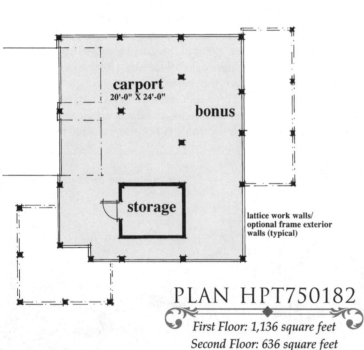

carport
20'-0" X 24'-0"

bonus

storage

lattice work walls/
optional frame exterior
walls (typical)

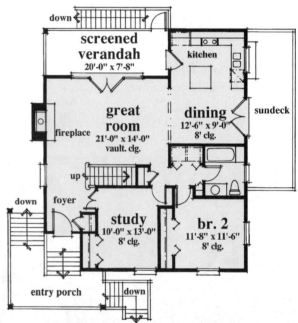

down

screened verandah
20'-0" x 7'-8"

kitchen

great room
21'-0" x 14'-0"
vault. clg.

fireplace

dining
12'-6" x 9'-0"
8' clg.

sundeck

up

foyer

down

study
10'-0" x 13'-0"
8' clg.

br. 2
11'-8" x 11'-6"
8' clg.

entry porch

down

PLAN HPT750182

First Floor: 1,136 square feet
Second Floor: 636 square feet
Total: 1,772 square feet
Width: 41'-9" Depth: 45'-0"

L

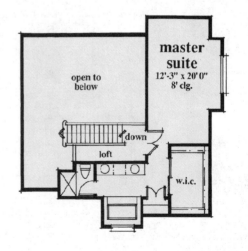

open to below

master suite
12'-3" x 20'0"
8' clg.

down

loft

w.i.c.

This two-story home's pleasing exterior is complemented by its warm character and decorative "widow's walk." The covered entry—with its dramatic transom window—leads to a spacious great room highlighted by a warming fireplace. To the right, the dining room and kitchen combine to provide a delightful place for mealtimes, with access to a side sun deck through double doors. Two bedrooms and a full bath complete the first floor. The luxurious master suite on the second floor features an oversized walk-in closet and a separate dressing area. The pampering master bath enjoys a relaxing whirlpool tub, double-bowl vanity and compartmented toilet. Please specify slab or pier foundation when ordering.

Symmetry and the perfect blend of past and future comprise this home. A steeply pitched roof caps a collection of Prairie-style windows and elegant columns. The portico leads to a mid-level foyer, which rises to the grand salon. A wide-open leisure room hosts a corner fireplace that's ultra cozy. The master wing sprawls from the front portico to the rear covered porch, rich with luxury amenities and plenty of secluded space.

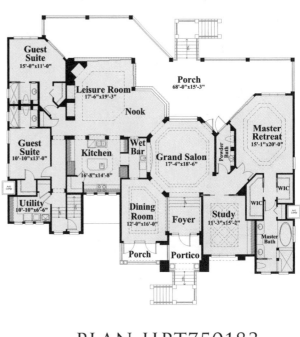

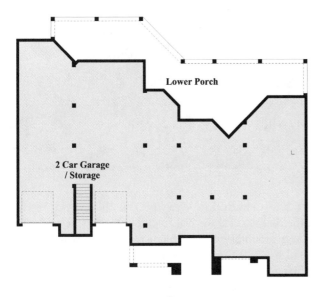

PLAN HPT750183

Square Footage: 3,074
Width: 77'-0" Depth: 66'-8"

PLAN HPT750184

First Floor: 1,642 square feet
Second Floor: 1,165 square feet
Total: 2,807 square feet
Width: 44'-6" Depth: 58'-0"

Inspired by 19th-Century Key West designs, the exterior of this plan is in the Neoclassical Revival tradition. Inside, the mid-level foyer eases the trip from ground level to the living and dining areas. Two sets of French doors lead out to the gallery and the sun deck. The master bedroom is on the first floor, with four family bedrooms upstairs. This home is designed with a pier foundation.

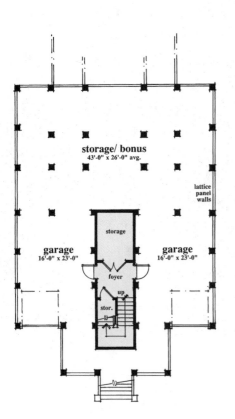

storage/ bonus
43'-0" x 26'-0" avg.

lattice panel walls

garage
16'-0" x 23'-0"

garage
16'-0" x 23'-0"

storage

foyer

stor.

up

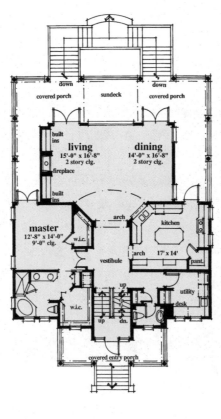

down

covered porch   sundeck   covered porch

built ins

living
15'-0" x 16'-8"
2 story clg.

dining
14'-0" x 16'-8"
2 story clg.

fireplace

built ins

arch

kitchen

master
12'-8" x 14'-0"
9'-0" clg.

w.i.c.

arch   17' x 14'

vestibule

pant.

w.i.c.

up

up   dn.

utility

desk

covered entry porch

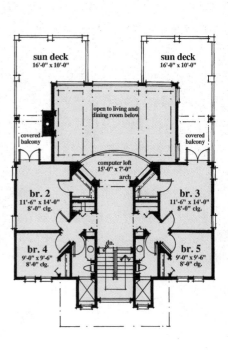

sun deck
16'-0" x 10'-0"

sun deck
16'-0" x 10'-0"

open to living and dining room below

covered balcony

covered balcony

computer loft
15'-0" x 10'-0"

arch

br. 2
11'-6" x 14'-0"
8'-0" clg.

br. 3
11'-6" x 14'-0"
8'-0" clg.

br. 4
9'-0" x 9'-6"
8'-0" clg.

dn.

br. 5
9'-0" x 9'-6"
8'-0" clg.

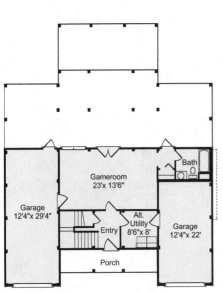

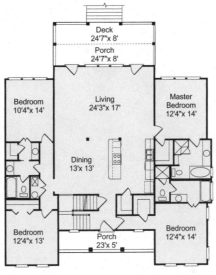

PLAN HPT750185

Main Level: 2,061 square feet
Upper Level: 464 square feet
Total: 2,525 square feet
Finished Basement: 452 square feet
Width: 50'-0" Depth: 63'-0"

This waterfront home offers classic seaboard details with louvered shutters, covered porches and an open floor plan. The lower level is comprised of two single-car garages, a game room with an accompanying full bath and a utility room. The U-shaped staircase leads to the main living areas where the island kitchen is open to the dining room. The living room offers a wall of windows with access to the rear porch and deck. Two bedrooms lie to the left and share a full bath. On the right are the master suite and a fourth bedroom—each with a private bath. Upstairs, a fifth bedroom with a bath completes the plan.

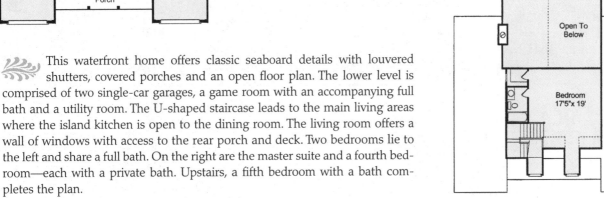

PLAN HPT750186

First Floor: 1,362 square feet
Second Floor: 481 square feet
Total: 1,843 square feet
Width: 49'-4" Depth: 44'-10"

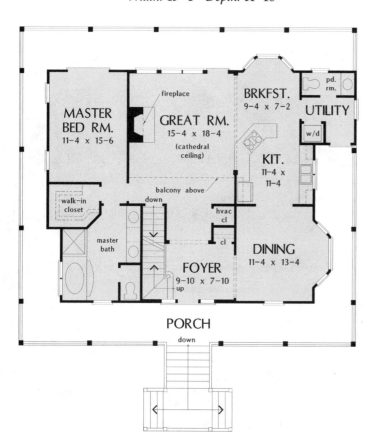

MASTER BED RM.
11-4 x 15-6

fireplace

GREAT RM.
15-4 x 18-4
(cathedral ceiling)

BRKFST.
9-4 x 7-2

UTILITY

pd. rm.

w/d

KIT.
11-4 x 11-4

walk-in closet

balcony above

down

hvac cl

cl

master bath

DINING
11-4 x 13-4

FOYER
9-10 x 7-10

up

PORCH

down

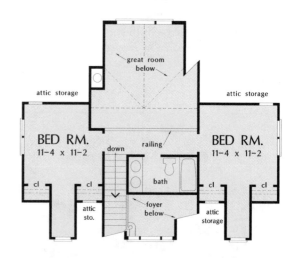

great room below

attic storage

attic storage

BED RM.
11-4 x 11-2

railing

BED RM.
11-4 x 11-2

cl

cl

down

bath

cl

cl

attic sto.

foyer below

attic storage

An enchanting wraparound porch, delightful dormers and bright bay windows create excitement inside and out for this coastal home. The large center dormer brightens the vaulted foyer, while the great room enjoys added light from a trio of rear clerestory windows. A balcony dividing the second-floor bedrooms overlooks the great room and visually connects the two floors. The master suite is located on the first floor and features back-porch access, a walk-in closet and a private bath with a garden tub and separate shower. The second-floor bedrooms, each with a dormer alcove, share a hall bath that includes a dual-sink vanity. ©1998 Donald A. Gardner Inc.

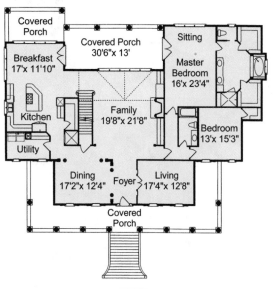

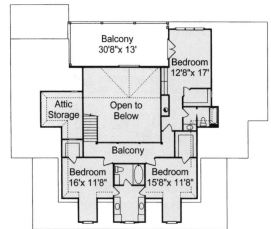

PLAN HPT750187

First Floor: 3,143 square feet
Second Floor: 901 square feet
Total: 4,944 square feet
Finished Basement: 1,818 square feet
Width: 80'-3" Depth: 66'-0"

This stunning seaside luxury home expresses the regional flavor of the Carolina coast. A wrapping covered front porch welcomes you into the main level. Inside, formal living and dining rooms flank the foyer. A fireplace and built-ins are featured in the family room, which views the rear covered porch. The gourmet island kitchen offers pantry storage and a breakfast nook. The main-level master bedroom provides a sitting area, private bath and two walk-in closets. A second bedroom is also located on this level, while three additional bedrooms and attic storage reside upstairs. The basement level provides a spacious garage, second kitchen, game room, guest bedroom, second utility room and a workshop.

PLAN HPT750188

First Floor: 1,642 square feet
Second Floor: 1,165 square feet
Total: 2,807 square feet
Width: 44'-6" Depth: 58'-0"

Hurricane shutters let fresh air in, while five decks make the outside easily accessible. Inside, the open living and dining area is defined by two pairs of French doors that frame a two-story wall of glass, while built-ins flank the living room fireplace. The efficient kitchen features a walk-in pantry, a work island and a door to the covered porch. Split sleeping quarters offer privacy to the first-floor master suite. Upstairs, a gallery loft leads to a computer area with a built-in desk and a balcony overlook. This home is designed with a pier foundation.

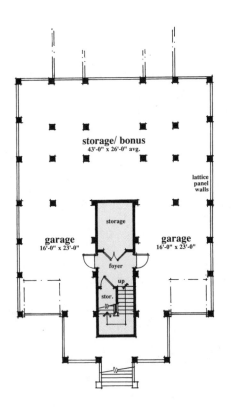

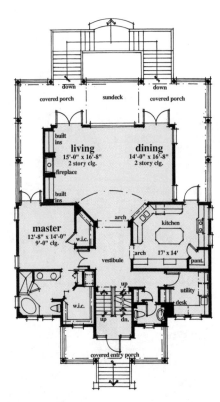

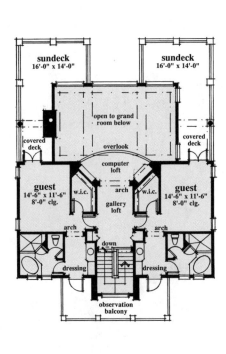

PLAN HPT750189

First Floor: 2,390 square feet

Second Floor: 1,200 square feet

Total: 3,590 square feet

Width: 61'-0" Depth: 64'-4"

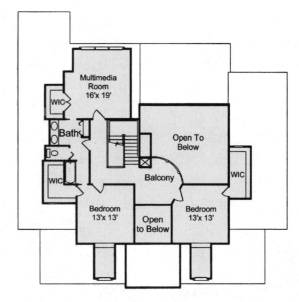

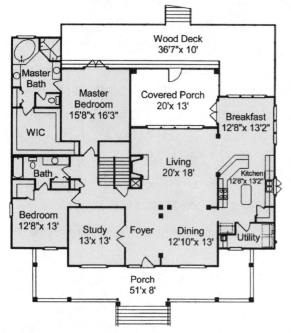

This luxurious waterfront design sings of Southern island influences. A front covered porch opens into a foyer, flanked on either side by a study and dining room. The living room warmed by a fireplace—safe from off-season ocean breezes—overlooks the rear covered porch. The island kitchen extends into a breakfast room. Beyond the covered porch, the wood deck is also accessed privately from the master suite. The suite includes a private whirlpool bath and huge walk-in closet. A guest suite is located on the first floor, while two additional bedrooms and a multimedia room are located on the second level.

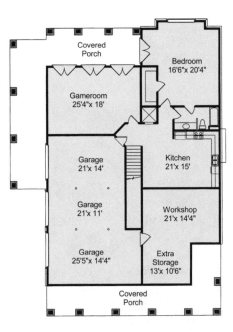

Covered Porch

Bedroom
16'6"x 20'4"

Gameroom
25'4"x 18'

Garage
21'x 14'

Kitchen
21'x 15'

Garage
21'x 11'

Workshop
21'x 14'4"

Garage
25'5"x 14'4"

Extra Storage
13'x 10'6"

Covered Porch

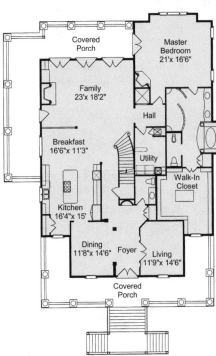

Covered Porch

Master Bedroom
21'x 16'6"

Family
23'x 18'2"

Hall

Breakfast
16'6"x 11'3"

Utility

Walk-In Closet

Kitchen
16'4"x 15'

Dining
11'8"x 14'6"

Foyer

Living
11'9"x 14'6"

Covered Porch

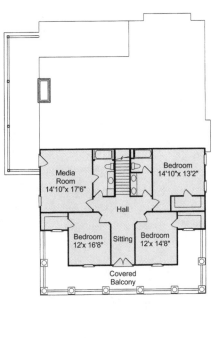

Media Room
14'10"x 17'6"

Bedroom
14'10"x 13'2"

Hall

Bedroom
12'x 16'8"

Sitting

Bedroom
12'x 14'8"

Covered Balcony

PLAN HPT750190

First Floor: 2,917 square feet
Second Floor: 1,407 square feet
Total: 4,324 square feet
Finished Basement: 1,481 square feet
Width: 59'-9" Depth: 79'-0"

This grand Southern home offers an impressive exterior dominated by the colonnaded porch with a full second-floor balcony. The foyer is flanked by the living room on the right and the dining room that conveniently adjoins the island kitchen on the left. The breakfast nook opens to the family room, which leads out to the rear covered porch. The master suite is found on the right with a lavish bath and a large walk-in closet. The second floor holds three family bedrooms, two baths and a media room. The centered sitting area accesses the front balcony.

PLAN HPT750191

First Floor: 1,855 square feet
Second Floor: 901 square feet
Total: 2,756 square feet
Width: 66'-0" *Depth:* 50'-0"

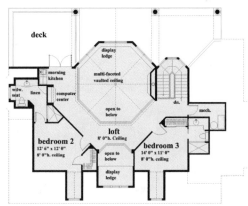

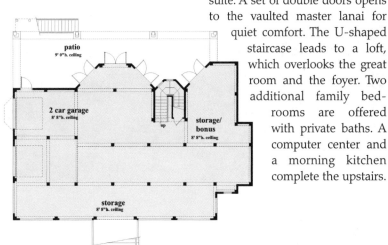

This Southern tidewater cottage is the perfect vacation hideaway. An octagonal great room with a multi-faceted vaulted ceiling illuminates the interior. The island kitchen is brightened by a bumped-out window and a pass-through to the lanai. Two walk-in closets and a whirlpool bath await to indulge the homeowner in the master suite. A set of double doors opens to the vaulted master lanai for quiet comfort. The U-shaped staircase leads to a loft, which overlooks the great room and the foyer. Two additional family bedrooms are offered with private baths. A computer center and a morning kitchen complete the upstairs.

PLAN HPT750192

First Floor: 1,742 square feet
Second Floor: 1,624 square feet
Total: 3,366 square feet
Width: 42'-10" Depth: 77'-6"

Porches abound on this grand two-story home—perfect for nature enthusiasts. The first floor holds the entertaining spaces, with the island kitchen acting as a hub around which all activity revolves. The den, with a cozy corner fireplace, and the breakfast nook are ideal for more intimate situations. For more elaborate entertaining, the living room offers a great deal of space and beautiful views. On the second floor, the master suite pampers with a luxurious bath and a private porch. Two additional bedrooms share a full bath on this floor while the first-floor bedroom works well as a guest bedroom.

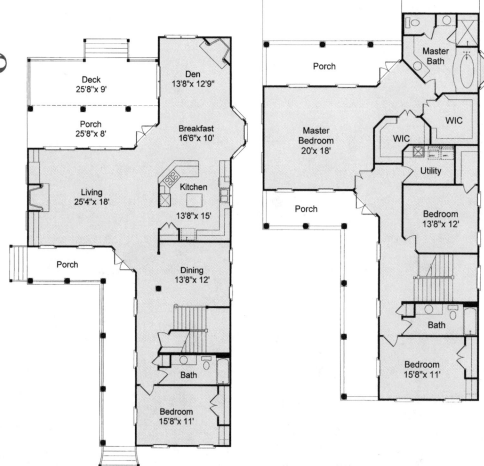

PLAN HPT750193

First Floor: 2,782 square feet
Second Floor: 1,767 square feet
Total: 4,549 square feet
Finished Basement: 1,418 square feet
Width: 55'-0" Depth: 73'-0"

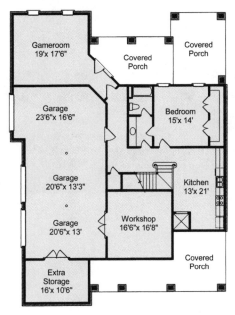

Gameroom 19'x 17'6"
Covered Porch
Covered Porch
Garage 23'6"x 16'6"
Bedroom 15'x 14'
Garage 20'6"x 13'3"
Kitchen 13'x 21'
Garage 20'6"x 13'
Workshop 16'6"x 16'8"
Covered Porch
Extra Storage 16'x 10'6"

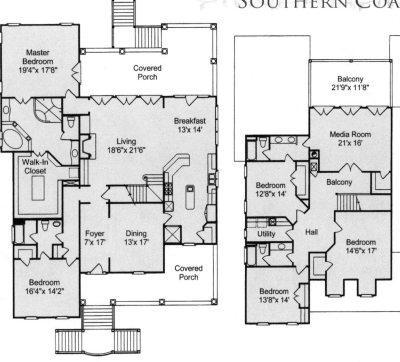

Master Bedroom 19'4"x 17'8"
Covered Porch
Breakfast 13'x 14'
Living 18'6"x 21'6"
Walk-In Closet
Foyer 7'x 17'
Dining 13'x 17'
Covered Porch
Bedroom 16'4"x 14'2"

Balcony 21'9"x 11'8"
Media Room 21'x 16'
Bedroom 12'8"x 14'
Balcony
Utility
Hall
Bedroom 14'6"x 17'
Bedroom 13'8"x 14'

This charming two-story home offers covered porches both front and back. The foyer opens on the right to the dining room that adjoins the galley kitchen with its island, pantry and snack bar. The breakfast nook sits in a sunny corner at the rear with the living room on its left. Here three sets of French doors open to the covered rear porch. The master suite is secluded on the far left with a lavish bath and an enormous walk-in closet. A second bedroom is at the front with private access to the hall bath. The second floor holds three additional bedrooms, two baths and a media room with a French door leading to the rear balcony.

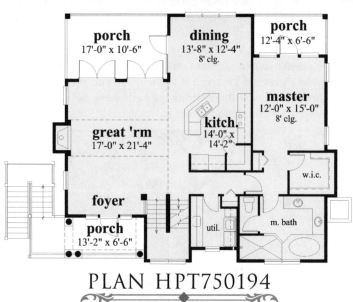

PLAN HPT750194

First Floor: 1,342 square feet

Second Floor: 511 square feet

Total: 1,853 square feet

Width: 44'-0" Depth: 40'-0"

porch 17'-0" x 10'-6"

dining 13'-8" x 12'-4" 8' clg.

porch 12'-4" x 6'-6"

great 'rm 17'-0" x 21'-4"

kitch. 14'-0" x 14'-2"

master 12'-0" x 15'-0" 8' clg.

w.i.c.

foyer

util.

m. bath

porch 13'-2" x 6'-6"

open deck 17'-0" x 10'-6"

bedroom 13'-8" x 12'-0" 12' clg.

open

loft

bath

bedroom 10'-0" x 13'-2" 12' clg.

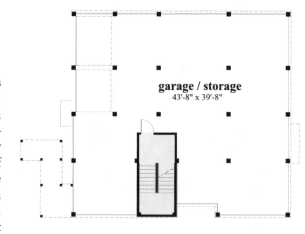

garage / storage 43'-8" x 39'-8"

Detailed fretwork complements a standing-seam roof on this tropical cottage. An arch-top transom provides an absolutely perfect highlight to the classic clapboard facade. An unrestrained floor plan offers cool digs for kicking back, and a sensational retreat for guests—whether the occasion is formal or casual. French doors open to a rear porch from the great room letting in fresh air and the sights and sounds of the great outdoors. Inside, the master bedroom leads to a dressing space with linen storage and a walk-in closet. The lavish bath includes a garden tub, an oversized shower and a wraparound vanity with two lavatories. Two secondary bedrooms on the upper level share a spacious loft that overlooks the great room. One of the bedrooms opens to a private deck.

198

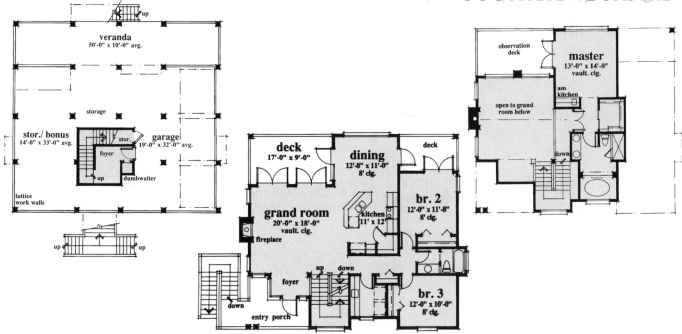

veranda
50'-0" x 10'-0" avg.

up

storage

stor./ bonus
14'-0" x 33'-0" avg.

stor.

foyer

garage
19'-0" x 32'-0" avg.

dumbwaiter

up

up

up

lattice
work walls

deck
17'-0" x 9'-0"

dining
12'-8" x 11'-0"
8' clg.

deck

grand room
20'-0" x 18'-0"
vault. clg.

kitchen
11' x 12'

br. 2
12'-0" x 11'-8"
8' clg.

fireplace

foyer

up

down

br. 3
12'-0" x 10'-0"
8' clg.

down

entry porch

observation
deck

master
13'-0" x 14'-0"
vault. clg.

open to grand
room below

am
kitchen

down

Amenities abound in this delightful two-story home. The foyer opens directly to the fantastic grand room, which offers a warming fireplace and two sets of double doors to the rear deck. The dining room also accesses this deck and a second deck shared with Bedroom 2. A convenient kitchen and another bedroom also reside on this level. Upstairs, the master bedroom reigns supreme. Entered through double doors, it pampers with a luxurious bath, walk-in closet, morning kitchen and private observation deck. This home is designed with a pier foundation.

PLAN HPT750195

First Floor: 1,342 square feet
Second Floor: 511 square feet
Total: 1,853 square feet
Width: 44'-0" Depth: 40'-0"

PLAN HPT750196

First Floor: 2,350 square feet
Second Floor: 1,338 square feet
Total: 3,688 square feet
Finished Basement: 1,509 square feet
Width: 63'-0" Depth: 72'-10"

Get away to this island of luxury—two to three family bedrooms and one enormous master suite should provide plenty of room for the entire crew. Enter the foyer via French doors to gain easy access to all levels. The basement level accesses a covered patio and allows future space for a summer kitchen, game room, home office, media room and a guest suite with an adjacent bath. Entertaining will be easy with the gathering room, dining area and Florida room that are open to one another and adjoin the rear covered patio. The master suite and a hobby room occupy the second level. An enormous walk-in closet, sumptuous bath and roomy private deck enhance the master bedroom.

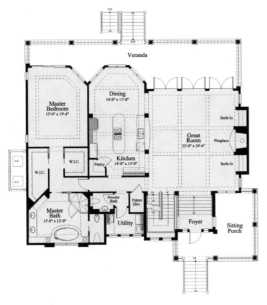

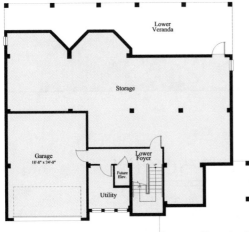

PLAN HPT750197

First Floor: 2,096 square feet
Second Floor: 892 square feet
Total: 2,988 square feet
Width: 58'-0" Depth: 54'-0"

The variety in the rooflines of this striking waterfront home will certainly make it the envy of the neighborhood. The two-story great room, with its fireplace and built-ins, is a short flight down from the foyer. The three sets of French doors give access to the covered lanai. The huge well-equipped kitchen will easily serve the gourmet who loves to entertain. The step ceiling and bay window of the dining room will add style to every meal. The master suite completes the first level. Two bedrooms and two full baths, along with an expansive loft, constitute the second level. Bedroom 3 enjoys an attached sun deck.

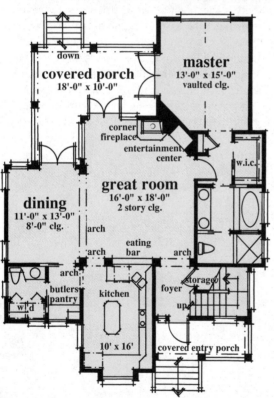

master
13'-0" x 15'-0"
vaulted clg.

covered porch
18'-0" x 10'-0"

down

corner
fireplace

entertainment
center

w.i.c.

great room
16'-0" x 18'-0"
2 story clg.

dining
11'-0" x 13'-0"
8'-0" clg.

arch

arch

arch

eating
bar

arch

**butlers
pantry**

w d

kitchen

10' x 16'

storage

foyer

up

covered entry porch

PLAN HPT750198

First Floor: 1,290 square feet
Second Floor: 548 square feet
Total: 1,838 square feet
Width: 38'-0" Depth: 51'-0"

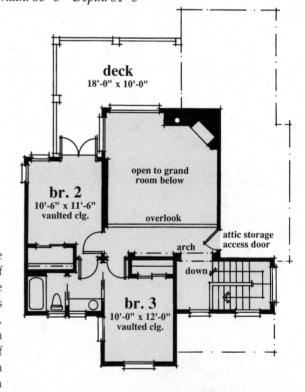

deck
18'-0" x 10'-0"

open to grand
room below

br. 2
10'-6" x 11'-6"
vaulted clg.

overlook

attic storage
access door

arch

down

br. 3
10'-0" x 12'-0"
vaulted clg.

Welcome home to casual, unstuffy living with this comfortable tidewater design. Asymmetrical lines celebrate the turn of the new century, and blend a current Gulf Coast style with vintage panache brought forward from its regional past. The heart of this home is the great room, where a put-your-feet-up atmosphere prevails, and the dusky hues of sunset can mingle with the sounds of ocean breakers. French doors open the master bedroom to a private area off the covered porch, where sunlight and sea breezes mingle with a spirit of bon vivant. Please specify basement or crawlspace foundation when ordering.

PLAN HPT750199

Square Footage: 2,136
Bonus Space: 1,428 square feet
Width: 44'-0" Depth: 63'-0"

This raised Tidewater design is well suited for many building situations, with comfortable outdoor areas that encourage year-round living. Horizontal siding and a steeply pitched roof call up a sense of the past, while a smart-space interior redefines the luxury of comfort with up-to-the-minute amenities. A vaulted ceiling highlights the great room, made comfy by a centered fireplace, extensive built-ins and French doors that let in fresh air and sunlight. The formal dining room opens from the entry hall and features a triple-window view of the side property. A secluded sitting area in the master suite features a wide window and a door to a private area of the rear porch. Two secondary bedrooms share a full bath.

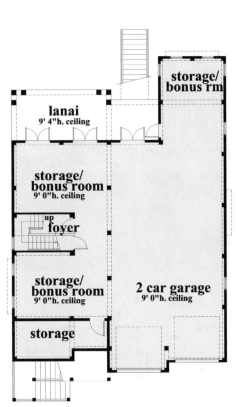

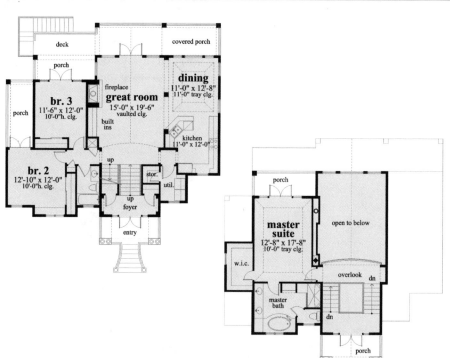

PLAN HPT750200

First Floor: 1,383 square feet
Second Floor: 595 square feet
Total: 1,978 square feet
Bonus Space: 617 square feet
Width: 48'-0" Depth: 42'-0"

This fabulous Key West home blends interior space with the great outdoors. This home boasts expansive porches and decks—with outside access from every area of the home. A sun-dappled foyer leads via a stately mid-level staircase to a splendid great room, which features a warming fireplace tucked in beside beautiful built-in cabinetry. Highlighted by a wall of glass that opens to the rear porch, this two-story living space serves as the stunning heart of the home and opens to the formal dining room and a well-appointed kitchen. Spacious secondary bedrooms on the main level open to outside spaces and share a full bath. Upstairs, a ten-foot tray ceiling highlights a very private master suite, which provides French doors to an upper-level porch. The master bath includes dual vanities, a whirlpool tub, compartmented toilet and oversized shower.

PLAN HPT750201

First Floor: 1,492 square feet

Second Floor: 854 square feet

Total: 2,346 square feet

Bonus Space: 810 square feet

Width: 44'-0" Depth: 48'-0"

The staircase leading to a columned front porch lends a touch of grandeur to this residence. The great room is made inviting with a fireplace and twin sets of double doors opening to a wraparound porch. The master suite also accesses the rear porch and features luxurious extras like His and Hers sinks, a separate garden tub and a huge walk-in closet. The kitchen provides plenty of counter space and overlooks the formal dining room. Upstairs, two additional bedrooms open up to a second-floor porch and have their own private baths and walk-in closets.

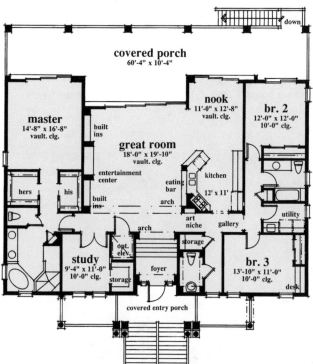

covered porch
60'-4" x 10'-4"

down

master
14'-8" x 16'-8"
vault. clg.

built ins

nook
11'-0" x 12'-8"
vault. clg.

br. 2
12'-0" x 12'-0"
10'-0" clg.

great room
18'-0" x 19'-10"
vault. clg.

entertainment center

kitchen

eating bar

12' x 11'

built ins

hers

his

art niche

arch

gallery

utility

arch

opt. elev.

storage

study
9'-4" x 11'-0"
10'-0" clg.

foyer

storage

br. 3
13'-10" x 11'-0"
10'-0" clg.

desk

covered entry porch

PLAN HPT750202

Square Footage: 2,385
Finished Basement: 1,271 square feet
Width: 60'-4"   Depth: 59'-4"

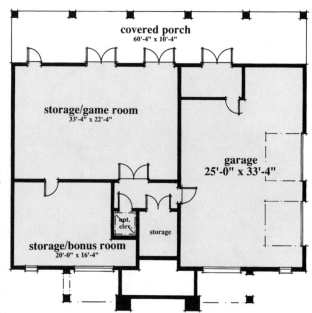

covered porch
60'-4" x 10'-4"

storage/game room
33'-4" x 22'-4"

garage
25'-0" x 33'-4"

opt. elev.

storage

storage/bonus room
20'-0" x 16'-4"

A classic pediment and low-pitched roof are topped by a cupola on this gorgeous coastal design, influenced by 19th-Century Caribbean plantation houses. Savory style blended with a contemporary seaside spirit invites entertaining as well as year-round living—plus room to grow. The beauty and warmth of natural light splash the spacious living area with a sense of the outdoors and a touch of joie de vivre. The great room features a wall of built-ins designed for even the most technology-savvy entertainment buff. Dazzling views through walls of glass are enlivened by the presence of a breezy portico. The master suite features a luxurious bath, a dressing area and two walk-in closets. Glass doors open to the portico and provide generous views of the seascape, while a nearby study offers an indoor retreat. Please specify pier or block foundation when ordering.

PLAN HPT750203

Square Footage: 2,385
Lower Foyer: 109 square feet
Width: 60'-0" Depth: 52'-0"

Floor plan labels:

- Deck
- Deck
- Deck
- Master Suite 16'-8" x 13'-6" 10'-0" Ceiling
- Nook 11'-3" x 11'-4" Vaulted
- Guest Suite #1 12'-0" x 12'-0" 10'-0" Ceiling
- Great Room 18'-6" x 18'-10" Vaulted
- Kitchen 12'-4" x 13'-3" Vaulted
- W.I.C.
- W.I.C.
- A/C
- A/C
- M. Bath
- Study 11'-0" x 13'-2" Vaulted Ceiling
- Foyer
- UP
- DN
- Utility
- Guest Suite #2 11'-0" x 13'-2" Vaulted
- Balcony
- Entry
- Balcony
- UP

Cottage accommodations are provided with th[is] vacation dream home. Once inside, the foyer steps [up] to the formal living areas on the main floor. To the left, a stud[y] enhanced by a vaulted ceiling and double doors that open to a fro[nt] balcony. Vaulted ceilings create a lofty feel throughout the home, especially in the central great room, which overlooks the rear deck. The island kitchen is open to an adjacent breakfast nook. Guest quarters reside on the right side of the plan—one boasts a private bath. The master suite is secluded on the left for privacy and features two walk-in closets and a pampering whirlpool master bath. Downstairs, storage space abounds alongside the two-car garage.

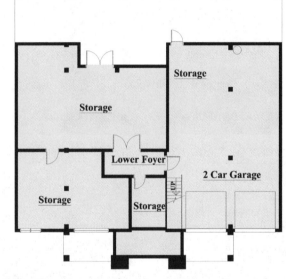

Floor plan labels:

- Storage
- Storage
- Storage
- Lower Foyer
- Storage
- 2 Car Garage
- UP

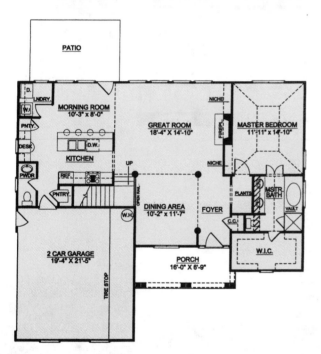

PLAN HPT750204

First Floor: 1,234 square feet
Second Floor: 458 square feet
Total: 1,692 square feet
Bonus Space: 236 square feet
Width: 48'-6" Depth: 42'-4"

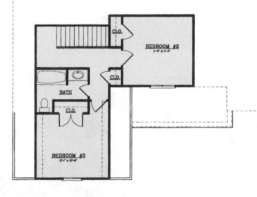

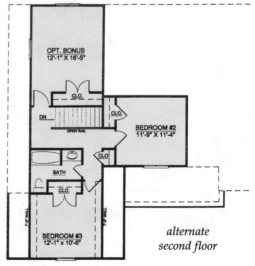

alternate
second floor

This early American Cape Cod home is a quaint haven for any family. Enter from the porch to the foyer, which opens to the dining area and great room. The great room is illuminated by a wall of windows and features a fireplace with two built-in niches on either side. An efficient kitchen is brightened by the morning room, which accesses an outdoor patio. The opposite side of the home is dedicated to the master suite, which includes a vaulted master bath and a spacious walk-in closet. A two-car garage completes this level. Two secondary bedrooms reside upstairs and share a full hall bath. An optional bonus room can be used as a fourth bedroom, a playroom or a home office.

PLAN HPT750205

First Floor: 1,760 square feet
Second Floor: 853 square feet
Total: 2,613 square feet
Width: 56'-0" Depth: 46'-6"

Rustic details shape the exterior of this unique country cottage. A covered front porch opens to a foyer that leads directly to the spacious great room, warmed by a country fireplace. A curved wall of windows invites nature indoors and overlooks the rear porch. The island kitchen is open to the formal dining room, also great for casual occasions. The first-floor master bedroom features a twin-vanity dressing area and a walk-in closet. Upstairs, a balcony overlooks the two-story great room. Two family bedrooms—each with a private bath—share the second-floor study that opens to a petite front porch. Please specify basement, crawlspace or slab foundation when ordering.

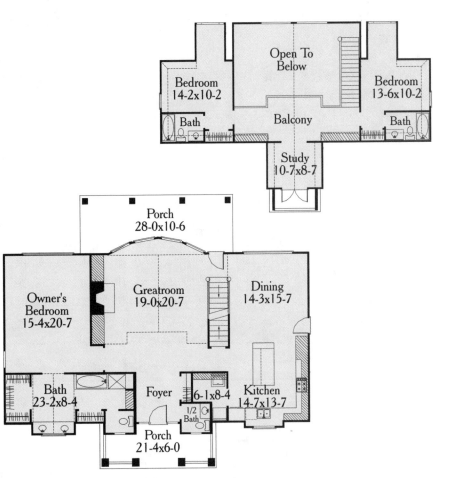

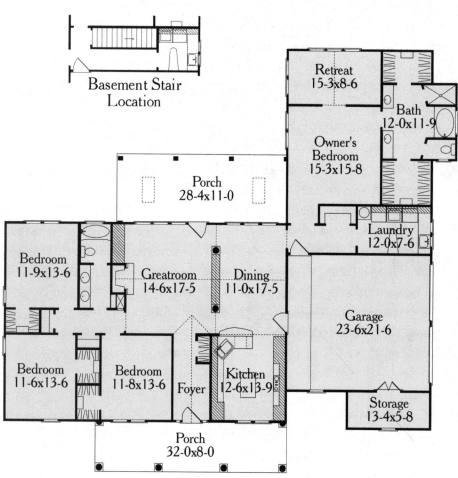

Basement Stair Location

Porch
28-4x11-0

Retreat
15-3x8-6

Bath
12-0x11-9

Owner's
Bedroom
15-3x15-8

Laundry
12-0x7-6

Bedroom
11-9x13-6

Greatroom
14-6x17-5

Dining
11-0x17-5

Garage
23-6x21-6

Bedroom
11-6x13-6

Bedroom
11-8x13-6

Foyer

Kitchen
12-6x13-9

Storage
13-4x5-8

Porch
32-0x8-0

PLAN HPT750206

Square Footage: 2,360
Width: 75'-2" Depth: 68'-0"

Columns, transoms and a clerestory lend this house stylish country charm. Inside, a built-in media center, a fireplace and columns add to the wonderful livability of this home. The modified galley kitchen features a serving bar and an island workstation. Escape to the relaxing master suite featuring a private sitting room and a luxurious bath set between His and Hers walk-in closets. Three bedrooms share a bath on the other side of the plan, ensuring privacy. Note the handy storage area in the two-car, side-entry garage. Please specify basement, crawlspace or slab foundation when ordering.

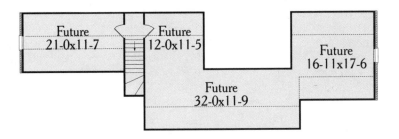

Future
21-0x11-7

Future
12-0x11-5

Future
16-11x17-6

Future
32-0x11-9

PLAN HPT750207

Square Footage: 2,636
Bonus Space: 1,132 square feet
Width: 74'-5" Depth: 64'-5"

This 1½-story, Colonial Revival home adds a pedimented porch from the Georgian era for a stately effect. The side-loading garage keeps the facade fresh and symmetrical. Columns define the formal dining room while a butler's pantry connects it to the expansive kitchen. The sunny sitting/breakfast nook lies at the opposite end of the kitchen. The generous great room delights with a window wall, a fireplace and built-ins. The master suite sits at the back with twin walk-in closets leading to the lavish bath. A wealth of undeveloped space is available on the second floor for future use. Please specify basement, crawlspace or slab foundation when ordering.

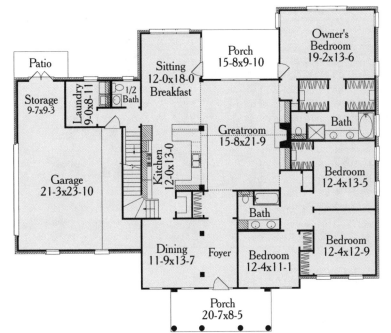

Patio

Storage
9-7x9-3

Laundry
9-0x8-11

1/2 Bath

Sitting
12-0x18-0
Breakfast

Porch
15-8x9-10

Owner's
Bedroom
19-2x13-6

Bath

Greatroom
15-8x21-9

Garage
21-3x23-10

Kitchen
12-0x13-0

Bedroom
12-4x13-5

Bath

Bath

Dining
11-9x13-7

Foyer

Bedroom
12-4x11-1

Bedroom
12-4x12-9

Porch
20-7x8-5

PLAN HPT750208

Square Footage: 2,555
Width: 66'-1" Depth: 77'-7"

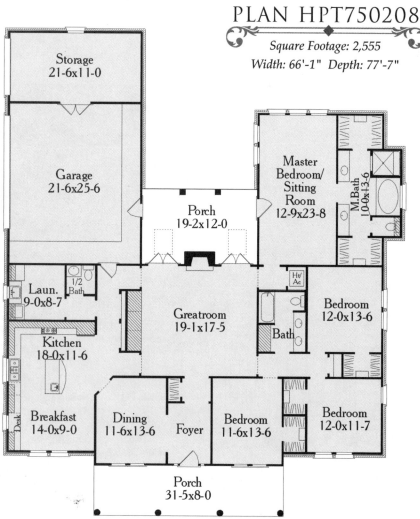

Storage
21-6x11-0

Garage
21-6x25-6

Porch
19-2x12-0

Master Bedroom/Sitting Room
12-9x23-8

M.Bath
10-0x13-6

Laun.
9-0x8-7

1/2 Bath

Kitchen
18-0x11-6

Greatroom
19-1x17-5

Bath

Ht/Ac

Bedroom
12-0x13-6

Breakfast
14-0x9-0

Dining
11-6x13-6

Foyer

Bedroom
11-6x13-6

Bedroom
12-0x11-7

Porch
31-5x8-0

Basement Stair Location

1/2 Bath

Greatroom

Kitchen

Dining

A steeply pitched roof and transoms over multi-pane windows give this house great curb appeal. To the left of the foyer is the formal dining room with through access to the kitchen and breakfast area. A large island/snack bar adds plenty of counter space for food preparation. Double French doors frame the fireplace in the great room, leading to the skylit covered porch at the rear of the home. The master suite has a light-filled sitting room and a luxurious bath with two walk-in closets, a garden tub and separate shower. At the front, three secondary bedrooms all have walk-in closets. Please specify basement, crawlspace or slab foundation when ordering.

Storage
17-4x5-8

Garage
20-4x21-4

Master
Bedroom
12-0x17-1

Bath

Porch
17-4x10-0

Laundry
7-4x6-3

1/2
Bath

Bedroom
11-4x10-0

Bath

Greatroom
17-4x17-4

Pantry

Bedroom
11-4x11-4

Bedroom
11-3x10-1

Foyer

Dining
11-3x13-4

Kitchen/
Breakfast
11-4x20-5

©Larry James Designs

Porch
31-0x8-0

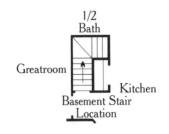

1/2
Bath

Greatroom

Kitchen

Basement Stair
Location

PLAN HPT750209

Square Footage: 1,997
Width: 56'-4" Depth: 67'-4"

The wide front steps, columned porch and symmetrical layout give this charming home a Georgian appeal. The central great room offers radiant French doors on both sides of the fireplace. Outside those doors is a comfortable covered porch with two skylights, expanding the livable space to the outdoors. The large kitchen with its walk-in pantry, island/snack bar and breakfast nook will gratify any cook. To the left of the great room reside four bedrooms—three secondary bedrooms and a master suite. The master suite enjoys a walk-in closet, twin vanity sinks, a separate shower and tub, and private access to the rear porch. Please specify basement, crawlspace or slab foundation when ordering.

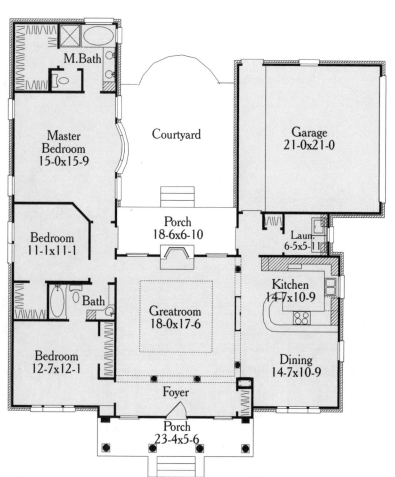

M.Bath

Master
Bedroom
15-0x15-9

Courtyard

Garage
21-0x21-0

Bedroom
11-1x11-1

Porch
18-6x6-10

Laun.
6-5x5-1

Bath

Greatroom
18-0x17-6

Kitchen
14-7x10-9

Bedroom
12-7x12-1

Dining
14-7x10-9

Foyer

Porch
23-4x5-6

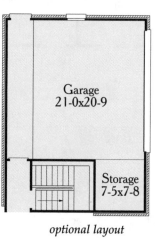

Garage
21-0x20-9

Storage
7-5x7-8

optional layout

PLAN HPT750210

Square Footage: 1,792
Width: 56'-0" Depth: 62'-10"

The classic style of this family home provides timeless elegance and symmetry. The covered front porch opens to a foyer leading to the spacious great room. Family bedrooms are found to the left, while the kitchen/dining room area is found to the right. The master suite features its own private bath and walk-in closet. The two family bedrooms share a full hall bath. The rear porch expands to a courtyard, overlooked by the master suite. A garage with optional storage and a laundry room complete this floor plan. Please specify basement, crawlspace or slab foundation when ordering.

PLAN HPT750211

Square Footage: 1,675
Width: 63'-11" Depth: 54'-8"

A full porch of columns gives a relaxing emphasis to this country home. Inside, the great room includes a cozy fireplace framed by windows. An open floor plan connects the great room, dining room and kitchen. The island/snack bar adds to the available work space in the kitchen. Walk-in closets dominate this plan, with one in each of three bedrooms and one by the laundry room as well. The two-car garage contains a storage area for family treasures. The master bedroom boasts a wonderful view of the rear yard and a private bath. Please specify basement, crawlspace or slab foundation when ordering.

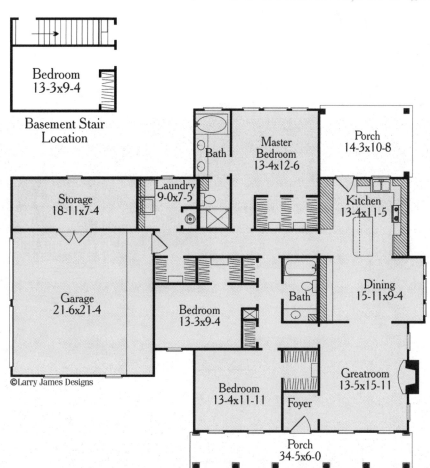

Bedroom
13-3x9-4

Basement Stair
Location

Storage
18-11x7-4

Laundry
9-0x7-5

Bath

Master
Bedroom
13-4x12-6

Porch
14-3x10-8

Kitchen
13-4x11-5

Garage
21-6x21-4

Bedroom
13-3x9-4

Bath

Dining
15-11x9-4

Greatroom
13-5x15-11

Bedroom
13-4x11-11

Foyer

©Larry James Designs

Porch
34-5x6-0

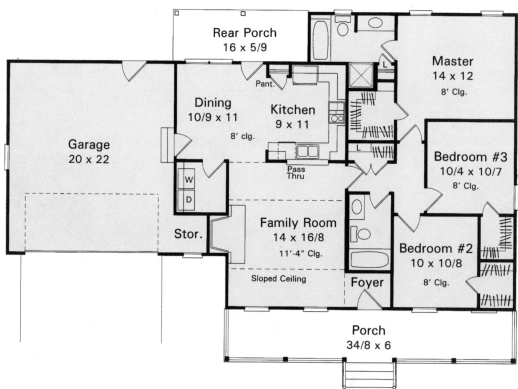

Rear Porch
16 x 5/9

Pant.

Dining
10/9 x 11
8' clg.

Kitchen
9 x 11

Master
14 x 12
8' Clg.

Garage
20 x 22

W
D

Stor.

Pass
Thru

Bedroom #3
10/4 x 10/7
8' Clg.

Family Room
14 x 16/8
11'-4" Clg.

Foyer

Bedroom #2
10 x 10/8
8' Clg.

Sloped Ceiling

Porch
34/8 x 6

PLAN HPT750212

Square Footage: 1,253
Width: 61'-3" Depth: 40'-6"

This petite ranch-style home is perfect for a young family. A covered front porch welcomes you inside to a cozy family room warmed by a fireplace. The efficient U-shaped kitchen opens to a dining area that accesses the rear porch. A laundry room is placed just outside of the garage. Family sleeping quarters are situated to the right side of the home. The master bedroom offers its own bath and walk-in closet, while Bedrooms 2 and 3 share a hall bath.

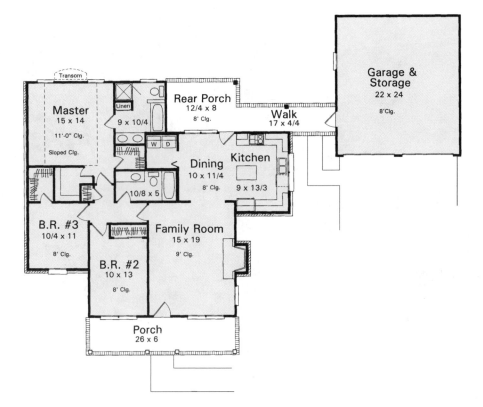

PLAN HPT750213

Square Footage: 1,406
Width: 76'-6" Depth: 57'-1"

A country flavor runs rampant through the design and facade of this home. The covered porch provides shelter from the hot sun and breezy evenings and leads to the family room where a warming fireplace awaits. The dining room is just left of the kitchen for serving convenience. The U-shaped kitchen also offers an island. A well-designed walkway leads from the garage to the rear porch with access to the home through the dining area. Two family bedrooms enjoy abundant closet space. The stepped-ceiling master bedroom features transoms and a private bath.

217

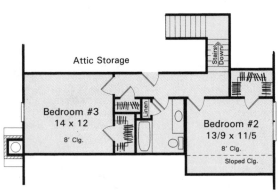

PLAN HPT750214

First Floor: 1,409 square feet
Second Floor: 557 square feet
Total: 1,966 square feet
Width: 48'-2" Depth: 67'-5"

This plan offers you country with a touch of class. The thoughtful stair location directs kid traffic away from the front of the house. A beautiful kitchen provides an island that's perfect for casual living. However, the formal dining room is great for entertaining. A large laundry room makes it easy to take care of the family's wash. Huge bedrooms and closets appeal to the whole family. There are porches to the front and rear of this great home.

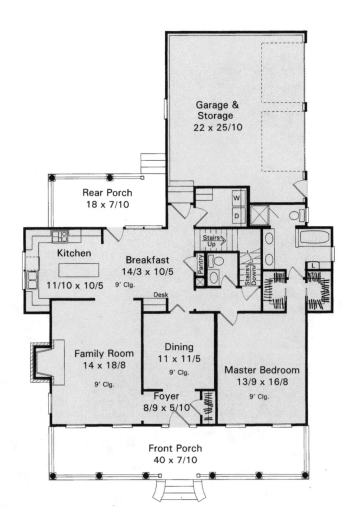

Attic Storage

Bedroom #3
14 x 12
8' Clg.

Linen

Bedroom #2
13/9 x 11/5
8' Clg.
Sloped Clg.

Stairs Down

Garage & Storage
22 x 25/10

Rear Porch
18 x 7/10

Kitchen
11/10 x 10/5

Breakfast
14/3 x 10/5
9' Clg.

Pantry

W
D

Stairs Up

Stairs Down

L

Desk

Family Room
14 x 18/8
9' Clg.

Dining
11 x 11/5
9' Clg.

Master Bedroom
13/9 x 16/8
9' Clg.

Foyer
8/9 x 5/10

Front Porch
40 x 7/10

PLAN HPT750215

Square Footage: 1,333
Width: 55'-6" Depth: 64'-3"

This country home sports a cozy cottage look with its covered porch and chimney. The fireplace resides in the roomy family room, awaiting guests. The open dining room and kitchen area provide plenty of casual dining space and access the rear porch. An island offers even more counter space. Two family bedrooms and a master bedroom are located on the left of the plan. The master bedroom enjoys a spacious private bath.

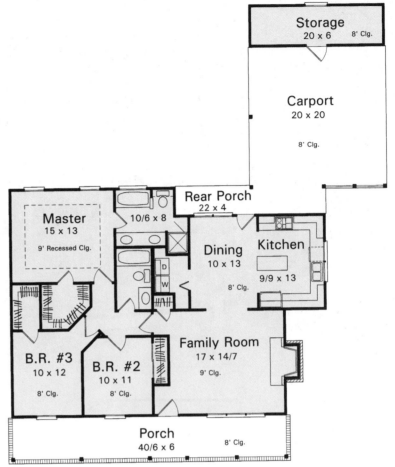

Storage
20 x 6   8' Clg.

Carport
20 x 20

8' Clg.

Rear Porch
22 x 4

Master
15 x 13
9' Recessed Clg.

10/6 x 8

Dining
10 x 13
8' Clg.

Kitchen
9/9 x 13

B.R. #3
10 x 12
8' Clg.

B.R. #2
10 x 11
8' Clg.

Family Room
17 x 14/7
9' Clg.

Porch
40/6 x 6   8' Clg.

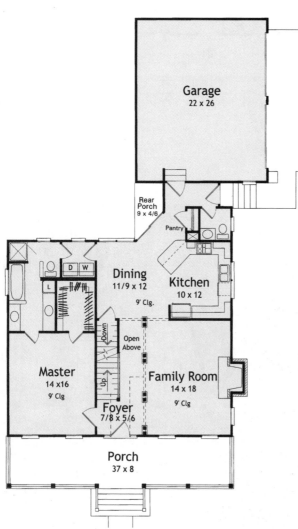

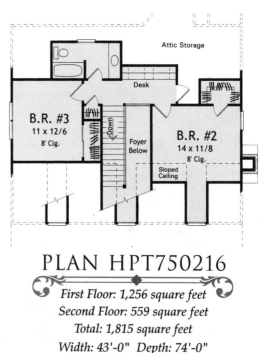

PLAN HPT750216

First Floor: 1,256 square feet
Second Floor: 559 square feet
Total: 1,815 square feet
Width: 43'-0" Depth: 74'-0"

This country home presents a large welcoming front porch. Walk through the front door into the magnificent foyer with a dormer above. There's a desk at the top of the stairs that overlooks the foyer. Two family bedrooms share a full bath on the second floor, while the master bedroom is on the first level. The master suite includes a walk-in closet and private bathroom. Note the laundry room situated conveniently near the master bath. The spacious kitchen features a serving bar and pantry.

PLAN HPT750217

Square Footage: 3,566
Width: 88'-0" Depth: 70'-8"

Symmetrically grand, this home features large windows which flood the interior with natural light. The massive sunken great room with a vaulted ceiling includes an exciting balcony overlook of the towering atrium window wall. The open breakfast nook and hearth room adjoin the kitchen. Four fireplaces throughout the house create an overall sense of warmth. A colonnade, a private entrance to the rear deck, and a sunken tub with a fireplace complement the master suite. Two family bedrooms share a dual-vanity bath between them.

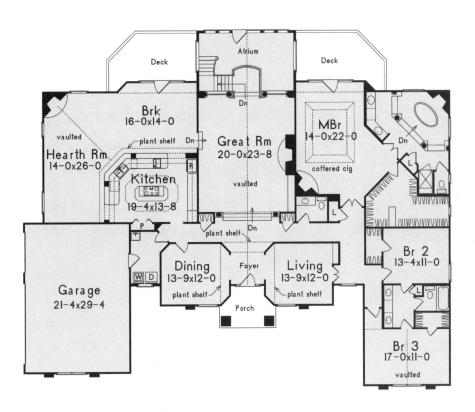

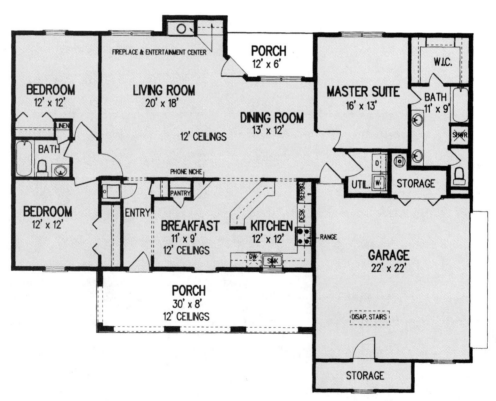

FIREPLACE & ENTERTAINMENT CENTER

PORCH
12' x 6'

BEDROOM
12' x 12'

LIVING ROOM
20' x 18'

DINING ROOM
13' x 12'

MASTER SUITE
16' x 13'

W.I.C.

BATH
11' x 9'

12' CEILINGS

LINEN

BATH

PHONE NICHE

PANTRY

ENTRY

SHWR

UTIL.

STORAGE

BEDROOM
12' x 12'

BREAKFAST
11' x 9'
12' CEILINGS

KITCHEN
12' x 12'

DESK

REFER.

RANGE

DW

SINK

PORCH
30' x 8'
12' CEILINGS

GARAGE
22' x 22'

DISAP. STAIRS

STORAGE

PLAN HPT750218

Square Footage: 1,770

Width: 64'-0" Depth: 48'-0"

Keystones and segmental arches draw attention to this beautifully covered porch. Quoins accenting the stucco and shutters that outline the windows create a versatile facade. A conveniently placed kitchen and breakfast area greet the homeowner or guest upon entry—no more carrying groceries through the house! A living room and dining room are open to each other. A fireplace and entertainment center are built-in, creating the focal point. The well-built master suite includes dual vanities and a spacious walk-in closet. Two additional bedrooms share a bath to the left of the plan. Please specify crawlspace or slab foundation when ordering.

PLAN HPT750219

Square Footage: 2,660
Width: 66'-4" Depth: 74'-4"

The time-honored popularity of the Palladian window is beautifully showcased in this magnificent home. The double-door entry leads into the foyer and welcomes guests into a formal living and dining room area, with wonderful views. As you approach the entrance to the master suite, you pass the den/study, which can easily become a guest or bedroom suite. A gently bowed soffit and stepped-ceiling treatments add excitement to the master bedroom, with floor-length windows framing the bed. The master bath comes complete with a double vanity and make-up area and a soaking tub, balanced by the large shower and private toilet chamber. The walk-in closet caps off this well-appointed space with ample hanging and built-in areas.

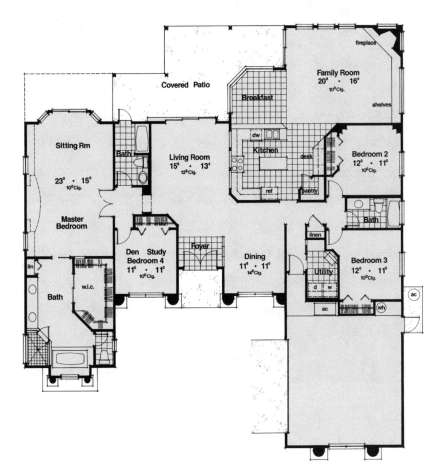

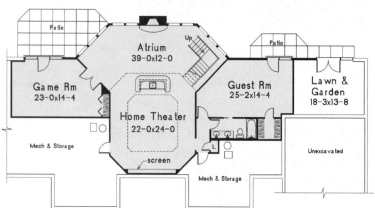

Patio

Atrium
39-0x12-0

Up

Patio

Game Rm
23-0x14-4

Guest Rm
25-2x14-4

Lawn &
Garden
18-3x13-8

Home Theater
22-0x24-0

screen

Mech & Storage

Unexcavated

Mech & Storage

L

PLAN HPT750220

Square Footage: 3,050
Finshed Basement: 1,776 square feet
Width: 109'-0" Depth: 57'-6"

The grand facade on this home is accented by the large window details. Sunbursts, keystones and lintels decorate the arches of the windows. The brightly lit entry connects to the great room with a balcony and a massive bay-shaped atrium. The kitchen features an island snack bar, walk-in pantry, computer area and atrium overlook. The master suite includes a sitting area, two walk-in closets, an atrium overlook and a luxury bath with a private courtyard. The family room/atrium, home theater, game room and guest bedroom comprise the lower level.

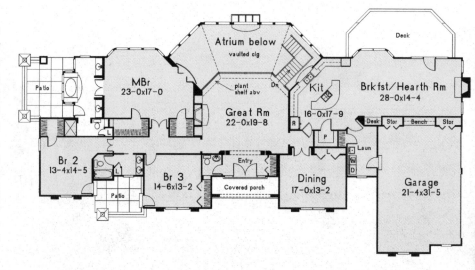

Deck

Patio

MBr
23-0x17-0

Atrium below
vaulted clg

plant
shelf abv

Dn

Kit
16-0x17-9

Brkfst/Hearth Rm
28-0x14-4

Desk Stor Bench Stor

Great Rm
22-0x19-8

R

Br 2
13-4x14-5

P

Laun
W D

Br 3
14-6x13-2

Entry

Dining
17-0x13-2

Garage
21-4x31-5

Covered porch

Patio

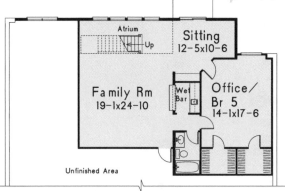

Atrium

Up

Sitting
12-5x10-6

Family Rm
19-1x24-10

Wet Bar

Office/ Br 5
14-1x17-6

Unfinished Area

PLAN HPT750221

Square Footage: 2,408
Finished Basement: 1,100 square feet
Width: 75'-8" Depth: 52'-6"

Contemporary and Mediterranean influences shape the spirit and inner spaces of this new-age home. An arched entrance and front covered porch welcome you inside to the formal dining room and great room. The relaxing kitchen/breakfast area is reserved for more intimate and casual occasions. The master suite provides a walk-in closet and private bath. Bedrooms 2 and 3 share a hall bath. Bedroom 4 makes the perfect guest suite. A family room, sitting area, wet bar, office and additional bath reside in the baesement.

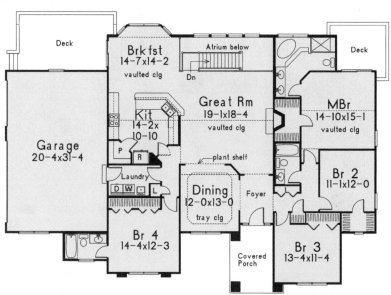

Deck

Brkfst
14-7x14-2
vaulted clg

Atrium below

Dn

Deck

Great Rm
19-1x18-4
vaulted clg

MBr
14-10x15-1
vaulted clg

Kit
14-2x
10-10

Garage
20-4x31-4

P

R

plant shelf

Br 2
11-1x12-0

Laundry

D W L

Dining
12-0x13-0
tray clg

Foyer

Br 4
14-4x12-3

Br 3
13-4x11-4

Covered Porch

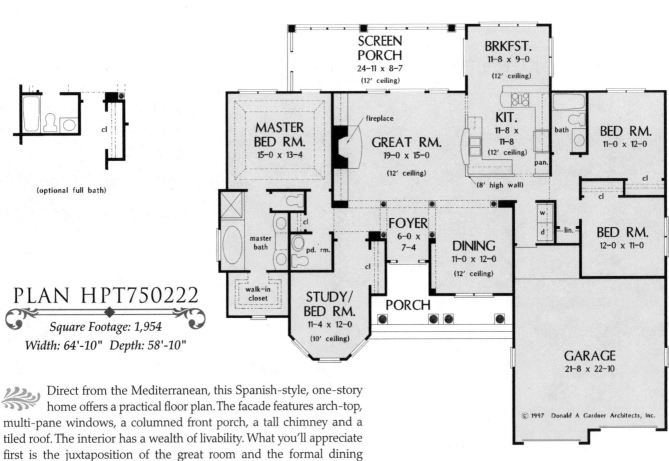

SCREEN
PORCH
24-11 x 8-7
(12' ceiling)

BRKFST.
11-8 x 9-0
(12' ceiling)

KIT.
11-8 x
11-8
(12' ceiling)

BED RM.
11-0 x 12-0

MASTER
BED RM.
15-0 x 13-4

fireplace

GREAT RM.
19-0 x 15-0
(12' ceiling)

bath

pan.

(8' high wall)

cl

cl

master
bath

cl

pd. rm.

FOYER
6-0 x
7-4

DINING
11-0 x 12-0
(12' ceiling)

w

d

lin.

BED RM.
12-0 x 11-0

walk-in
closet

cl

STUDY/
BED RM.
11-4 x 12-0
(10' ceiling)

PORCH

GARAGE
21-8 x 22-10

© 1997 Donald A Gardner Architects, Inc.

cl

(optional full bath)

PLAN HPT750222

Square Footage: 1,954
Width: 64'-10" Depth: 58'-10"

Direct from the Mediterranean, this Spanish-style, one-story home offers a practical floor plan. The facade features arch-top, multi-pane windows, a columned front porch, a tall chimney and a tiled roof. The interior has a wealth of livability. What you'll appreciate first is the juxtaposition of the great room and the formal dining room—both defined by columns. A more casual eating area is attached to the L-shaped kitchen and accesses a screened porch. Three bedrooms mean abundant sleeping space. The study could be a fourth bedroom—choose the full bath option in this case. A tray ceiling decorates the master suite, which is further enhanced by a bath with a separate shower and tub, walk-in closet and double sinks.

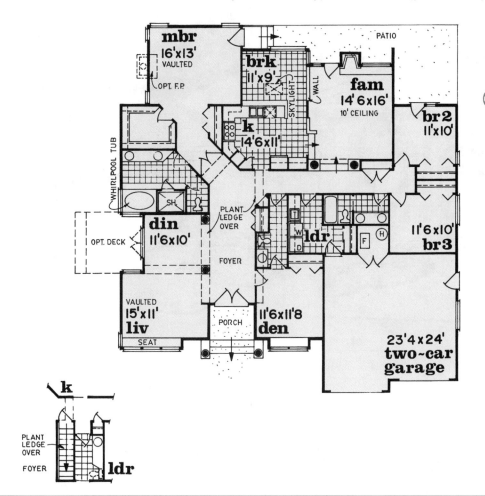

PLAN HPT750223

Square Footage: 2,471
Width: 60'-0" Depth: 63'-6"

Decorative columns with a plant ledge entablature define the living and dining room entrances. The den, tucked off the foyer, can double as a guest room or home office. The well-planned kitchen serves the eating bar and skylit breakfast room. Large walk-in and wall closets, a luxurious ensuite with a double vanity, whirlpool tub, oversized shower and patio access are just some of the master suite features. Two additional bedrooms share a main bath that includes a twin vanity. The large laundry area holds extra storage and a folding counter.

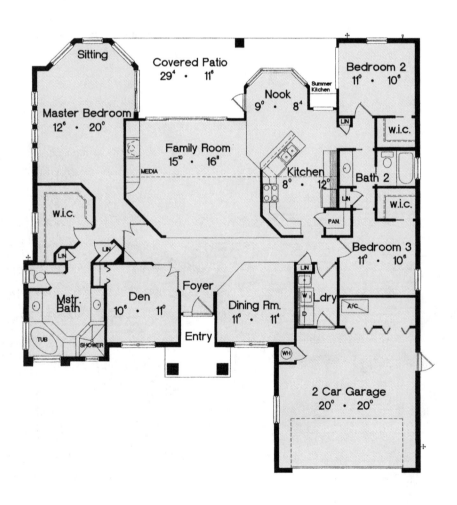

PLAN HPT750224

Square Footage: 2,118
Width: 58'-0" Depth: 62'-0"

The lavishness of the exterior of this home is continued inside, culminating with the expansive master suite. A wall of windows, a sitting area with a bay window, and a pampering bath with a garden tub combine to create a pampering suite. The large family room enjoys a built-in media center and double sets of sliding glass doors that open to the covered patio. The well-equipped kitchen is situated conveniently between the formal dining room and the sunny breakfast nook.

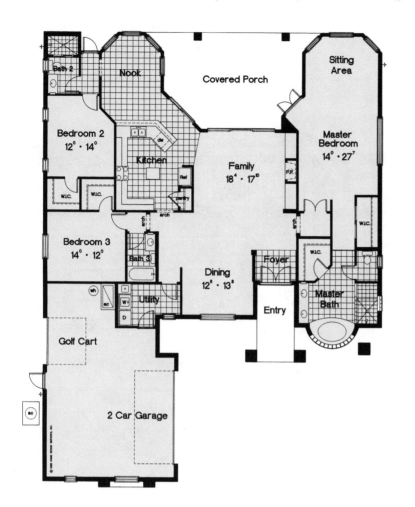

PLAN HPT750225

Square Footage: 2,503
Width: 60'-0" Depth: 78'-4"

Square pillars elegantly introduce the entry of this gracious three-bedroom home. Past the two-door entry, a Mediterranean-style family room impresses guests. The built-in entertainment center surrounding the fireplace enhances the spacious feel of the living room. To the right resides a master suite with a sunny sitting area, two walk-in closets, private access to the rear covered porch, and a master bath featuring a soaking tub set in a concave wall of glass. To the left of the design are the two family bedrooms—note the walk-in closets and private baths for each room!—a kitchen, bayed breakfast nook and handy utility room. This home would be perfect for placement on or near a golf course—the plan includes its own golf-cart garage door.

PLAN HPT750226

First Floor: 1,735 square feet
Second Floor: 674 square feet
Total: 2,409 square feet
Width: 59'-8" Depth: 45'-0"

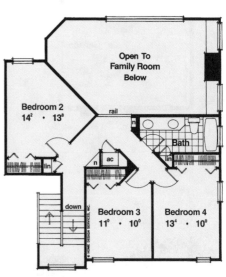

The vaulted and two-story ceilings of this plan belie the fact that it is, in fact, a two-story home. The excitement and openness was made possible by placing the majority of the second-floor bedrooms over the kitchen and garage areas. A decorative niche is the focal point of the master suite, which is complete with a windowed bed wall and sliding glass doors to the patio. The exceptional design of the master bath includes His and Hers vanities, a corner soaking tub and a thoughtful shower shower/toilet chamber. The kitchen views the family room and rear yard and the nook has a mitered glass wall. Three generously sized bedrooms share a hall bath.

PLAN HPT750227

Square Footage: 2,311
Bonus Room: 279 square feet
Width: 64'-4" Depth: 61'-8"

A niche becomes the focal point as the tiled foyer flows to the heart of the home. The gourmet kitchen invites all occasions—planned events and casual gatherings—with an island counter, a sizable pantry and angled counters. A wall of sliding glass doors in the living room offers wide views of the back property. Two walk-in closets introduce a spacious bath in the master suite. Tucked out of the way near the master suite's entry vestibule is a convenient powder room. Three family bedrooms and a full bath are placed at the opposite end of the plan. A cabana bath serves traffic from the back covered patio.

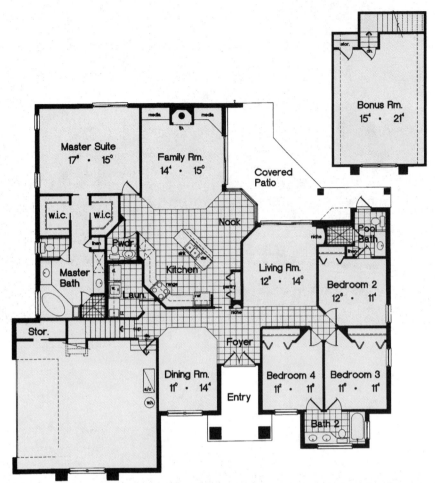

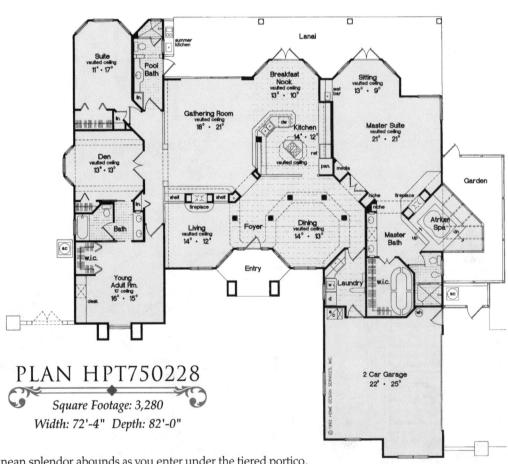

PLAN HPT750228

Square Footage: 3,280
Width: 72'-4" Depth: 82'-0"

Mediterranean splendor abounds as you enter under the tiered portico. The foyer opens to the living room on the left and the dining room on the right where attention to details—columns and soffits—creates elegance and excitement. The living and gathering rooms share a see-through fireplace, and beyond the sliding glass doors, the lanai offers a summer kitchen. The magnificent master suite offers a wet bar in the bayed sitting area. A solarium is, however, the focal point here with an African spa and a through-fireplace.

PLAN HPT750229

Square Footage: 3,424
Bonus Room: 507 square feet
Width: 82'-4" Depth: 83'-8"

This lovely five-bedroom home exudes the beauty and warmth of a Mediterranean villa. The foyer views explode in all directions with the dominant use of octagonal shapes throughout. Double doors lead to the master wing, which abounds with niches. The sitting area of the master bedroom has a commanding view of the rear gardens. A bedroom just off the master suite is perfect for a guest room or office. The formal living and dining rooms share expansive glass walls and marble or tile pathways. The mitered glass wall of the breakfast nook can be viewed fron the huge island kitchen. While two of the bedrooms on the right share a pullman-style bath, the rear bedroom is a complete suite.

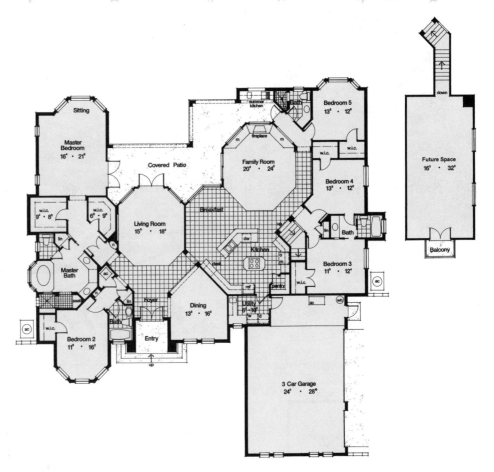

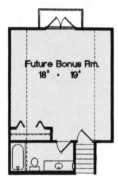

Future Bonus Rm.
18⁰ · 19⁴

PLAN HPT750230

Square Footage: 2,774
Bonus Room: 493 square feet
Width: 65'-4" Depth: 85'-10"

A very efficient plan that minimizes the use of enclosed hallways creates a very open feeling of space and orderliness. As you enter the foyer you have a clear view through the spacious living room to the covered patio beyond. The formal dining area is to the right and the master wing is to the left. The master bedroom boasts a sitting area, access to the patio, His and Hers walk-in closets, dual vanities, a walk-in shower and a compartmented toilet. A large island kitchen overlooks the nook and family room, which has a built-in media/fireplace wall. Three additional bedrooms and two full baths complete the plan.

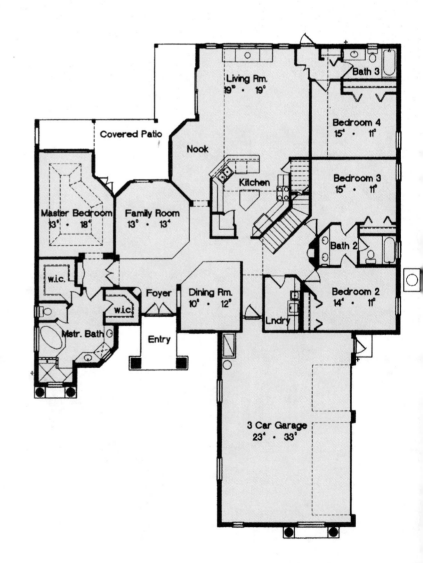

PLAN HPT750231

Square Footage: 4,222
Bonus Space: 590 square feet
Width: 83'-10" Depth: 112'-0"

The striking facade of this magnificent estate is just the beginning of the excitement you will encounter inside. The entry foyer passes the formal dining room to the columned gallery, which leads to all regions of the house, with the formal living room at the head. The living room opens to the rear patio and the showpiece pool lying flush against the dramatic rear windows of the house. A sunken wet bar serves the living room and the pool via a swim-up bar. The contemporary kitchen has a work island and all the amenities for gourmet preparation. The family sleeping wing begins with an octagonal vestibule and contains three bedrooms with private baths.

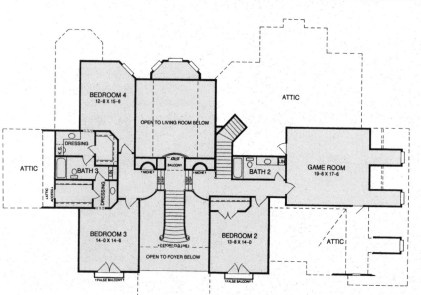

PLAN HPT750232

First Floor: 3,264 square feet
Second Floor: 1,671 square feet
Total: 4,935 square feet
Width: 96'-10" Depth: 65'-1"

An impressive entry, multi-pane windows and mock balconies combine to give this facade an elegance to be proud of. The grand foyer is flanked by a formal dining room to the right and a cozy study to the left. The sunken living room is graced by a fireplace, a wondrous piano bay and a vaulted ceiling. The sunny breakfast room and family room make casual entertaining a breeze. Located on the first floor, the master bedroom suite is lavish with its luxuries. Upstairs, three bedrooms share two full baths and access to a large game room. Please specify crawlspace or slab foundation when ordering.

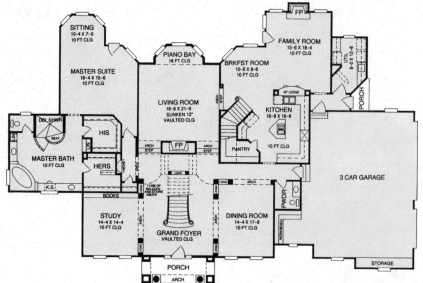

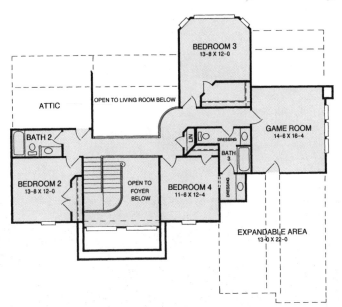

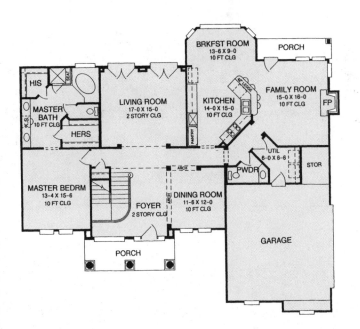

PLAN HPT750233

First Floor: 1,919 square feet
Second Floor: 1,190 square feet
Total: 3,109 square feet
Bonus Room: 286 square feet
Width: 64'-6" Depth: 55'-10"

Flower boxes, arches and multi-pane windows all combine to create the elegant facade of this four-bedroom home. Inside, the two-story foyer has a formal dining room to its right and leads to a two-story living room that is filled with light. An efficient kitchen opens to a bayed breakfast room and shares a snack bar with a cozy family room. Located on the first floor for privacy, the master suite is graced with a luxurious bath. Upstairs, three secondary bedrooms share two full baths and have access to a large game room. For future growth there is an expandable area accessed through the game room. Please specify basement, crawlspace or slab foundation when ordering.

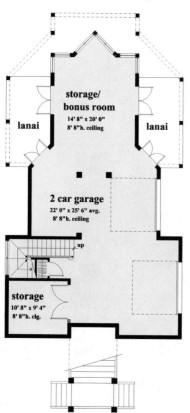

storage/
bonus room
14' 8" x 20' 0"
8' 8"h. ceiling

lanai

lanai

2 car garage
22' 0" x 25' 6" avg.
8' 8" ceiling

up

storage
10' 8" x 9' 4"
8' 8" clg.

deck

great room
15' 0" x 16' 0"
2-story clg.
fireplace

ver.

ver.

built-in
cabinetry

pass-thru

dining
9' 4" x 12' 8"
9' 4"h. clg.

kitchen
pantry
8' 8" x 14' 0"

up

foyer

bedroom 2
11' 0" x 11' 0"
9' 4"h. ceiling

ut.

p.

entry

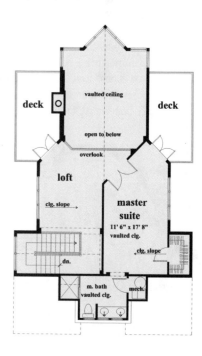

deck

vaulted ceiling

deck

open to below

overlook

loft

master
suite
11' 6" x 17' 8"
vaulted clg.

clg. slope

clg. slope

dn.

m. bath
vaulted clg.

mech.

PLAN HPT750234

First Floor: 1,143 square feet
Second Floor: 651 square feet
Total: 1,794 square feet
Bonus Space: 476 square feet
Width: 32'-0" Depth: 57'-0"

Italian country elegance graces the exterior of this casa bellisima, swept in Mediterranean enchantment. The covered entryway extends into the foyer, where straight ahead, the two-story great room spaciously enhances the interior. This room features a warming fireplace and offers built-in cabinetry. The open dining room extends through double doors to the veranda on the left side on the plan. The adjacent kitchen features efficient pantry space. A family bedroom with a bath, a powder room and a utility room also reside on this main floor. Upstairs, a vaulted master suite with a vaulted private bath and a deck share the floor with a loft area, which overlooks the great room.

This magnificent villa boasts a beautiful stucco exterior, Spanish-tiled roof and Old World details such as arches and accent columns framing the spectacular entry. Open rooms, French doors and vaulted ceilings add an air of spaciousness throughout the home. The heart of the home is served by a well-crafted kitchen with wrapping counter space and an island cooktop counter. The breakfast nook enjoys a view of the veranda and beyond. An open formal dining room provides dazzling views and an ambiance of elegance and comfort. On the upper level, the master suite features a sitting area and a private veranda.

PLAN HPT750235

First Floor: 1,671 square feet
Second Floor: 846 square feet
Total: 2,517 square feet
Vestibule: 140 square feet
Width: 44'-0" Depth: 55'-0"

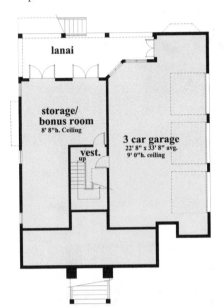

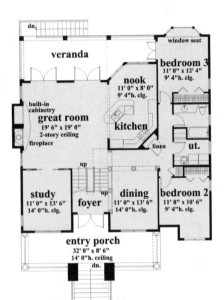

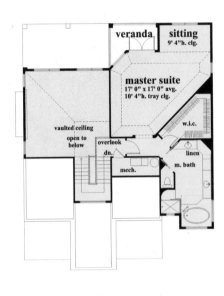

PLAN HPT750236

First Floor: 1,247 square feet
Second Floor: 1,221 square feet
Total: 2,468 square feet
Width: 24'-0" Depth: 86'-0"

The romantic character of the hacienda is captured in this appealing residence. The barrel-tile roof, smooth stucco exterior and rope columns are other characteristics of the Spanish Colonial style. The great room is generously sized, while a downstairs guest room can also double as a study or office. A sunny dining room opens to a spacious kitchen with a large island and breakfast bar. Above, there is a sitting area large enough for a computer and desk area. A luxurious master suite privately accesses an upstairs deck. The front bedroom also has walkout access to the front balcony. Please specify basement or crawlspace foundation when ordering.

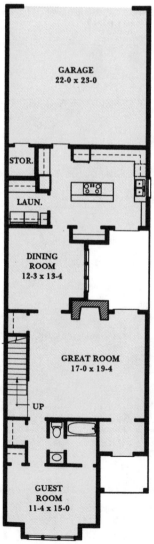

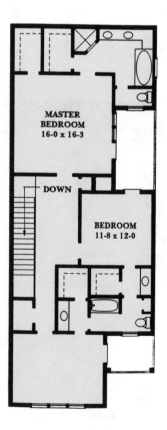

PLAN HPT750237

First Floor: 2,357 square feet
Second Floor: 1,021 square feet
Total: 3,378 square feet
Bonus Room: 168 square feet
Width: 70'-0" Depth: 62'-6"

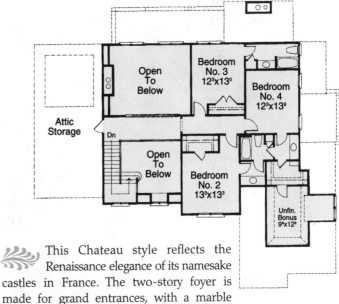

Attic Storage

Open To Below

Bedroom No. 3
12³x13⁰

Bedroom No. 4
12³x13⁹

Dn

Open To Below

Bedroom No. 2
13³x13³

Unfin. Bonus
9⁹x12⁸

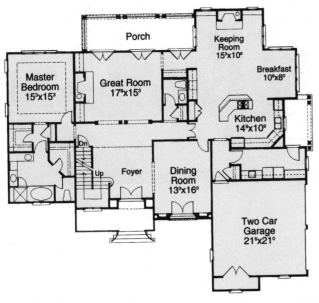

Porch

Keeping Room
15³x10⁶

Breakfast
10⁶x8⁰

Master Bedroom
15³x15³

Great Room
17⁹x15³

Kitchen
14⁹x10⁹

Dn

Up

Foyer

Dining Room
13³x16⁰

Two Car Garage
21⁶x21⁰

This Chateau style reflects the Renaissance elegance of its namesake castles in France. The two-story foyer is made for grand entrances, with a marble floor and a sweeping staircase. The foyer opens to the formal dining room and leads to the great room with its fireplace, vaulted ceiling and wet bar. Also located on the first floor is the master suite, which has twin walk-in closets. A quaint keeping room with a fireplace adjoins the kitchen and breakfast areas. Upstairs you will find three generous bedrooms and two baths, one private, plus a bonus room. This home is designed with a walkout basement foundation.

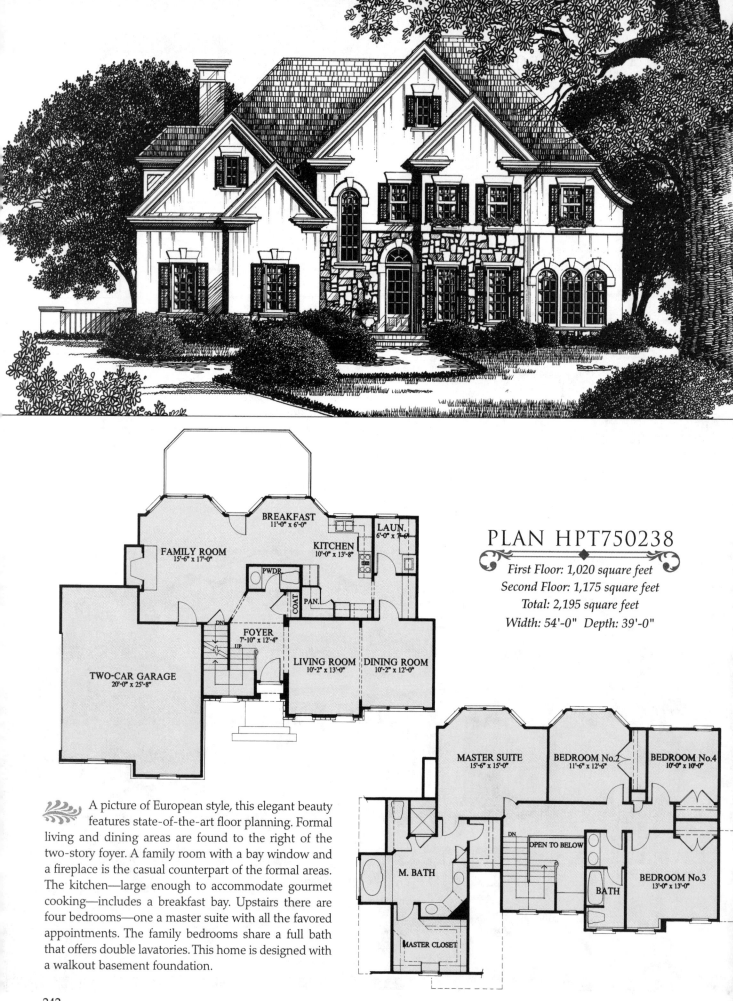

PLAN HPT750238

First Floor: 1,020 square feet
Second Floor: 1,175 square feet
Total: 2,195 square feet
Width: 54'-0" Depth: 39'-0"

First Floor

BREAKFAST
11'-0" x 6'-0"

LAUN.
6'-0" x 7'-6"

FAMILY ROOM
15'-6" x 17'-0"

KITCHEN
10'-0" x 13'-8"

PWDR.

COAT

PAN.

FOYER
7'-10" x 12'-4"

DN

UP

LIVING ROOM
10'-2" x 13'-0"

DINING ROOM
10'-2" x 12'-0"

TWO-CAR GARAGE
20'-0" x 25'-8"

Second Floor

MASTER SUITE
15'-6" x 15'-0"

BEDROOM No.2
11'-6" x 12'-6"

BEDROOM No.4
10'-0" x 10'-0"

DN

OPEN TO BELOW

M. BATH

BATH

BEDROOM No.3
13'-0" x 13'-0"

MASTER CLOSET

A picture of European style, this elegant beauty features state-of-the-art floor planning. Formal living and dining areas are found to the right of the two-story foyer. A family room with a bay window and a fireplace is the casual counterpart of the formal areas. The kitchen—large enough to accommodate gourmet cooking—includes a breakfast bay. Upstairs there are four bedrooms—one a master suite with all the favored appointments. The family bedrooms share a full bath that offers double lavatories. This home is designed with a walkout basement foundation.

PLAN HPT750239

First Floor: 1,395 square feet
Second Floor: 1,210 square feet
Total: 2,605 square feet
Bonus Room: 225 square feet
Width: 47'-0" Depth: 49'-6"

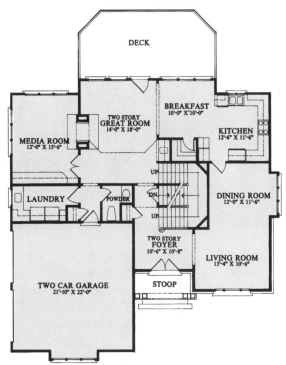

QUOTE ONE®
Cost to build? See page 310
to order complete cost estimate
to build this house in your area!

A gentle mix of stucco and stone, a box-bay window and a covered entry make this country home very inviting. The two-story foyer opens to formal living and dining rooms, bright with natural light. A spacious U-shaped kitchen adjoins a breakfast nook with views of the outdoors. This area flows to the two-story great room, which offers a through-fireplace shared with the media room. Upstairs, a plush retreat awaits the homeowner with a quiet sitting bay. The unfinished bonus room provides further storage space. This home is designed with a walkout basement foundation.

PLAN HPT750240

First Floor: 1,724 square feet
Second Floor: 700 square feet
Total: 2,424 square feet
Width: 47'-10" Depth: 63'-8"

QUOTE ONE®
Cost to build? See page 310
to order complete cost estimate
to build this house in your area!

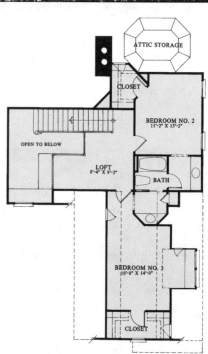

ATTIC STORAGE

CLOSET

OPEN TO BELOW

BEDROOM NO. 2
11'-2" X 13'-2"

LOFT
8'-4" X 9'-2"

BATH

BEDROOM NO. 3
10'-8" X 14'-0"

CLOSET

DECK

BREAKFAST
10'-4" X 10'-4"

MASTER SITTING
10'-4" x 6'-0"

GREAT ROOM
17'-0" X 17'-0"

MASTER BEDROOM
15'-4" X 13'-0"

KITCHEN
13'-4" X 17'-0"

DINING ROOM
12'-10" X 10'-6"

FOYER
5'-0" X 13'-6"

MASTER BATH
12'-2" X 12'-8"

POWDER

LAUNDRY
6'-0" X 6'-10"

W.I.C.

LIVING ROOM
11'-4" X 10'-8"

STOOP

TWO CAR GARAGE
21'-4" X 21'-4"

All the charm of gables, stonework and multi-level
rooflines combine to create this home. To the left
of the foyer, you will see the dining room highlighted by a
tray ceiling and expansive windows with transoms. This
room and the living room flow together to form one large
entertainment area. The gourmet kitchen holds a work
island, oversized pantry and adjoining octagonal breakfast
room. The great room features a pass-through wet bar, a
fireplace and bookcases. The master suite enjoys privacy at
the rear of the home. An open-rail loft above the foyer
leads to two additional bedrooms with walk-in closets, private
vanities and a shared bath. This home is designed with a
walkout basement foundation.

Deck

Breakfast
13³ x 10⁰

Kitchen

Master Bedroom
13³ x 17⁹

Great Room
14⁶ x 19⁰

13⁶ x 16⁰

Two Car Garage
21³ x 21⁶

Dining Room
12⁰ x 16⁰

Study
11³ x 15³

PLAN HPT750241

First Floor: 1,932 square feet

Second Floor: 807 square feet

Total: 2,739 square feet

Width: 63'-0" Depth: 51'-6"

To the left of the recessed entry foyer, the box-windowed formal dining room leads to a large L-shaped kitchen with a separate utility area, an island cooktop and a sunny breakfast bay with deck access. The great room features a fireplace and rear access through French doors. To the right of the foyer is a quiet study with another fireplace. The lavish master suite includes a bay-windowed sitting area, an elegant tray ceiling and a private bath with dual walk-in closets and vanities, a separate shower and a whirlpool tub. Two of the three second-floor bedrooms include walk-in closets. This home is designed with a walkout basement foundation.

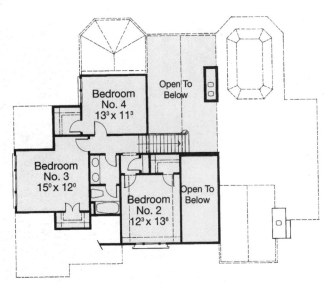

Bedroom No. 4
13³ x 11³

Open To Below

Bedroom No. 3
15⁰ x 12⁰

Bedroom No. 2
12³ x 13⁶

Open To Below

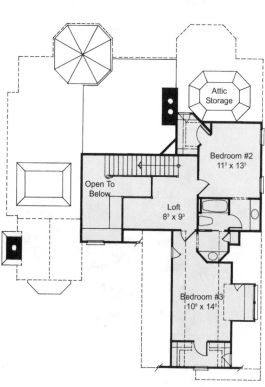

There's nowhere to go but up in this bright and airy three-bedroom home. Nearly every room provides a volume ceiling, including the living room and dining room, breakfast nook, master suite and T-shaped secondary bedroom on the second floor. Natural light fills the first floor via a ribbon of windows in the formal dining room and bay windows in the living room, breakfast nook and master bedroom. Fireplaces in the living room and great room will keep these spaces cozy and entertain the eye. A private master suite with a sumptuous bath resides on the first floor, while two family bedrooms share a full bath on the second floor. The upstairs loft overlooks the main floor below. This home is designed with a walkout basement foundation.

PLAN HPT750242

First Floor: 1,724 square feet
Second Floor: 700 square feet
Total: 2,424 square feet
Width: 47'-10" Depth: 63'-6"

PLAN HPT750243

Square Footage: 2,140
Width: 62'-0" Depth: 60'-6"

Imagine the luxurious living you'll enjoy in this beautiful home! The natural beauty of stone combined with sophisticated window detailing represents the good taste you'll find carried throughout the design. Common living areas occupy the center of the plan and include the great room with a fireplace, the sun room and the breakfast area, plus rear and side porches. A second fireplace is located in the front den. The master suite features private access to the rear porch and a wonderfully planned bath. This home is designed with a walkout basement foundation.

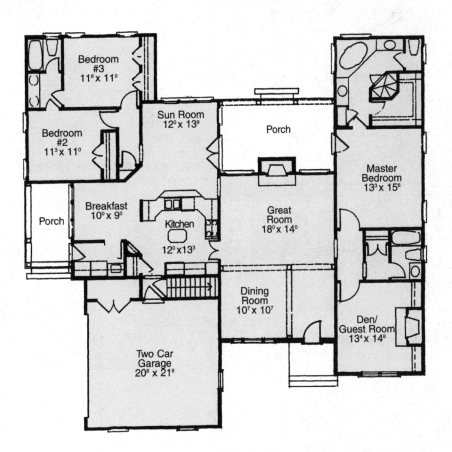

2-CAR GARAGE
21'-3" x 26'-0"

Quote One®
Cost to build? See page 310
to order complete cost estimate
to build this house in your area!

LAUN.

BREAKFAST
11'-6" x 12'-0"

KITCHEN
14'-0" x 16'-6"

PAN.

DN

GREAT ROOM
16'-0" x 20'-6"

M. BATH

SITTING

MASTER SUITE
15'-6" x 23'-3"

MASTER CLOSET

BEDROOM No.3
12'-0" x 13'-6"

DINING ROOM
13'-0" x 13'-6"

FOYER

STUDY/
BEDROOM No.2
13'-0" x 13'-6"

GUEST ROOM/
CHILDRENS
DEN
13'-6" x 16'-9"

PLAN HPT750244

Square Footage: 2,785
Width: 72'-0" Depth: 73'-0"

The balance and symmetry of this European home has an inviting quality about it. An entry foyer allows a grand view out of the back of the house and leads directly to the great room. Just off the great room, there is a convenient and functional gourmet kitchen and a bright adjoining bay-windowed breakfast room. The master suite enjoys privacy in its position at the rear of the home. Three other bedrooms—one which might serve as a guest room or children's den and one that might work well as a study—round out the sleeping accommodations. This home is designed with a walkout basement foundation.

PLAN HPT750245

Square Footage: 1,684
Finished Basement: 1,684 square feet
Width: 55'-6" Depth: 57'-6"

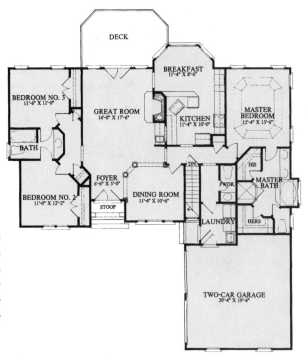

QUOTE ONE®

Cost to build? See page 310
to order complete cost estimate
to build this house in your area!

Charming and compact, this home is as beautiful as it is practical. The impressive arch over the double front door is repeated with an arched window in the formal dining room. This room opens to a spacious great room with a fireplace and sits near the kitchen and bayed breakfast area. Split sleeping arrangements put the master suite at the right of the plan and two family bedrooms at the left. This home is designed with a walkout basement foundation.

PLAN HPT750246

Square Footage: 3,032
Width: 73'-0" Depth: 87'-8"

This country estate is bedecked with all the details that pronounce its French origins. They include the study with built-in shelves, family room and keeping room with a cozy fireplace. Dine in one of two areas—the formal dining room or the casual breakfast room. A large porch to the rear can be reached through the breakfast room or the master suite's sitting area. All three bedrooms in the plan have walk-in closets. Bedrooms 2 and 3 share a full bath that includes private vanities.

PLAN HPT750247

Square Footage: 2,000
Width: 68'-0" Depth: 64'-0"

Steep rooflines and columns make this home one to remember. Starburst windows align along the exterior and offer a nice touch of sophistication. Extra amenities run rampant through this one-story home. The sun room can be enjoyed during every season. An eating nook right off the kitchen brightens the rear of the home well. A utility and storage area are also found at the rear of the home. A cozy study privately accesses the side porch. The master bedroom is complete with dual vanities and His and Hers closets. Two family bedrooms reside to the left of the plan. Please specify crawlspace or slab foundation when ordering.

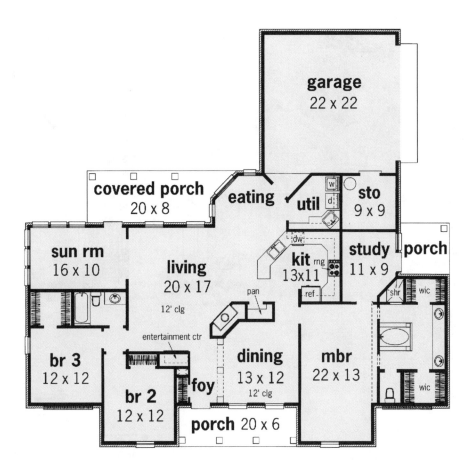

garage
22 x 22

covered porch
20 x 8

eating

util

sto
9 x 9

sun rm
16 x 10

living
20 x 17
12' clg

kit
13x11
rng

ref

study
11 x 9

porch

dw

pan

shr wic

entertainment ctr

br 3
12 x 12

foy

dining
13 x 12
12' clg

mbr
22 x 13

wic

br 2
12 x 12

porch 20 x 6

PLAN HPT750248

Square Footage: 1,891
Width: 49'-0" Depth: 64'-0"

The gated courtyard adds privacy and personality to this charming two-bedroom home. The open interior includes a sunken family room with a sloped ceiling, a gracious fireplace, built-ins and access to a rear porch. A brilliantly sunny dining room sits opposite an open and cleverly angled kitchen—allowing for ease of service between the dining room and the morning room. The living room could be replaced as a third bedroom or a study. The master suite includes a dual-bowl vanity, a separate bath and shower, and a large walk-in closet. Please specify crawlspace or slab foundation when ordering.

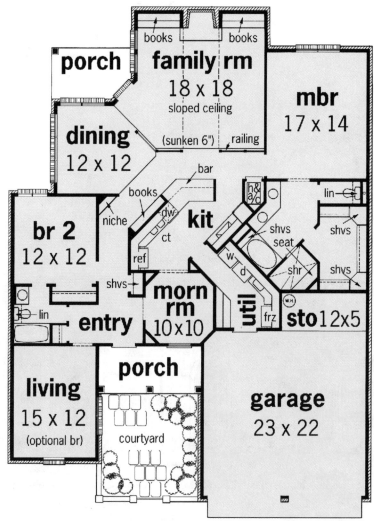

PLAN HPT750249

Square Footage: 3,960
Width: 96'-0" Depth: 90'-0"

A hipped roofline, with varying elevations, accents this stunning design and lends superb curb appeal. Double doors in the uniquely shaped family room open to the rear porch and deck. A large family room, complete with a corner fireplace, is accessible from all points of the house—the kitchen, deck, dining room, living room and the hallway leading to the sleeping quarters on the right side of the plan—creating a perfect hub of activity. The master suite features a private bath, a large walk-in closet and a sitting room with a fireplace. The three-car garage holds a convenient storage area. Please specify basement, crawlspace or slab foundation when ordering.

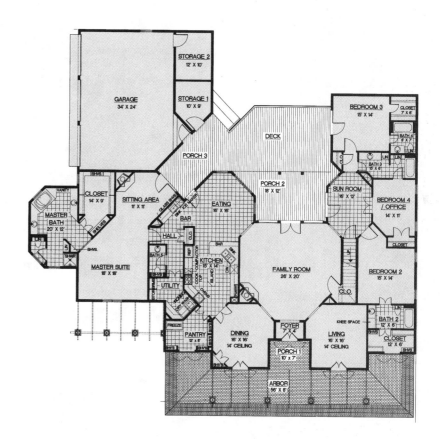

This home features capped, hipped rooflines that capture a French fairytale appeal. Inside, the formal dining room sits across the foyer from the hardworking kitchen. An eating nook is a perfect spot for casual meals. The living room boasts a built-in entertainment center, bookshelves, a wet bar and a warm and cozy fireplace. The master bedroom enjoys the rear right of the plan. Two walk-in closets, dual vanities, a separate tub and shower and a compartmented toilet pamper the homeowners. Three spacious family bedrooms—one with its own bath—complete the second floor.

porch 30 x 8

mbr 18 x 14

built in entertainment center and library

living 18 x 19

bar

up

a/c lin

clo

lin

clo

eating 13 x 10

ct

kit 13 x 12

pan

foy

shr

dining 19 x 13

desk

ref dw

frz wh

d/w

util

sto

garage 22 x 22

PLAN HPT750250

First Floor: 1,884 square feet
Second Floor: 1,034 square feet
Total: 2,918 square feet
Width: 49'-0" Depth: 79'-0"

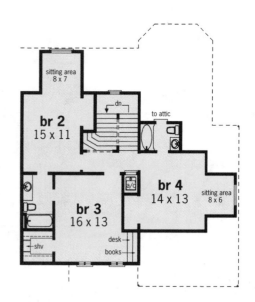

sitting area 8 x 7

br 2 15 x 11

dn

to attic

br 4 14 x 13

sitting area 8 x 6

br 3 16 x 13

a/c

shv

desk

books

PLAN HPT750251

First Floor: 1,802 square feet
Second Floor: 670 square feet
Total: 2,472 square feet
Width: 49'-0" Depth: 79'-0"

An appealing capped roof creates a very French design on this plan. A small porch leads to the foyer that opens to the dining room on the right. Across the hall, the convenient kitchen enjoys a casual eating nook and easy service to the rear living room. Built-ins, a fireplace, a wet bar and rear-porch access enhance the versatile living room. The master suite is found at the rear and luxuriates in comfort with two walk-in closets, dual vanities, a compartmented toilet and a separate bath and shower. On the second floor, two family bedrooms share a full bath that includes dual vanities.

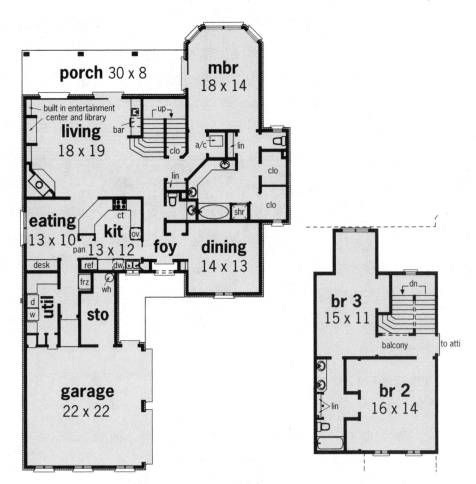

PLAN HPT750252

Square Footage: 2,791
Width: 84'-0" Depth: 54'-0"

This stately country home is a quaint mix of Colonial style and romantic French flavor. Inside, formal living and dining rooms flank the entry foyer. Two sets of double doors open from the family room to the rear patio. A romantic courtyard is placed to the far right of the plan, just beyond the family bedrooms. A three-car garage with an extra storage room offers plenty of space. The family game room is reserved for recreational fun. Please specify crawlspace or slab foundation when ordering.

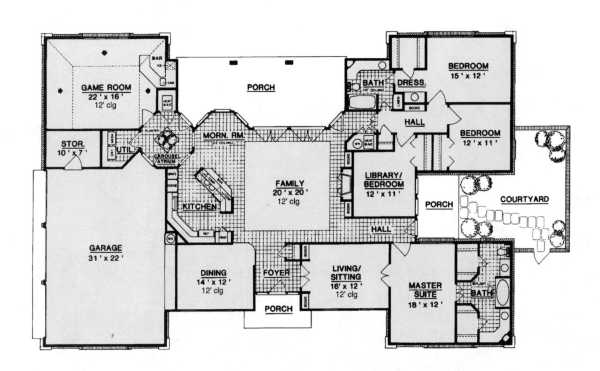

PLAN HPT750253

Square Footage: 1,994
Width: 49'-0" Depth: 68'-0"

French accents inspire this European-influenced creation. A quaint courtyard introduces guests to this family compound. Inside, the central kitchen opens to the morning room. A sunken family room with sloped ceilings features a fireplace and access to the rear porch. The master bedroom, with a private bath and walk-in closet, is placed on the right side of the plan. Two additional family bedrooms reside on the left and share a full bath. Please specify crawlspace or slab foundation when ordering.

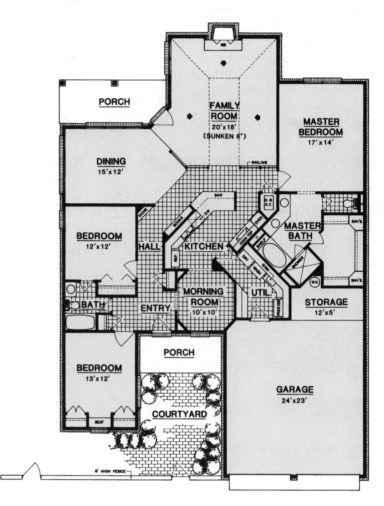

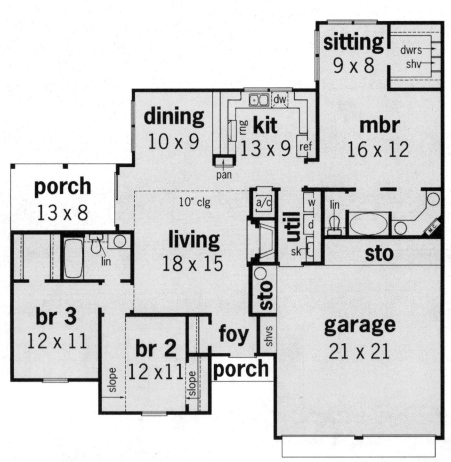

porch
13 x 8

br 3
12 x 11

br 2
12 x 11

foy

porch

dining
10 x 9

kit
13 x 9

mbr
16 x 12

sitting
9 x 8

dwrs
shv

pan

ref

rng

dw

10" clg

living
18 x 15

a/c

util

w
d

sk

lin

sto

lin

m.c.

sto

shvs

sto

garage
21 x 21

lin

slope

slope

PLAN HPT750254

Square Footage: 1,442
Width: 54'-0" Depth: 50'-0"

A French facade accentuates the cozy appeal of this home with corner quoins, shuttered windows, transoms and a stucco finish. The foyer introduces the spacious and open living room, which flows into the dining room and kitchen. A fireplace warms this area. The U-shaped kitchen features a window sink and a pantry. The kitchen is also within a few steps of the dining area. Two family bedrooms to the left of the plan share a full hall bath. The master bedroom sports a bright sitting bay, a walk-in closet with built-ins and a roomy bath. Please specify crawlspace or slab foundation when ordering.

PLAN HPT750255

Square Footage: 1,380
Width: 46'-0" Depth: 56'-0"

A Palladian window set in a stucco facade under a hipped roof lends gracious charm to this three-bedroom home. The welcoming front porch opens to a slope-ceilinged living room, featuring a corner fireplace. The U-shaped kitchen opens directly to the dining room and its patio access. A utility/storage room connects the two-car garage to the kitchen. This plan splits the master suite from the two family bedrooms on the left for added privacy. Note the dual vanity sinks in the master bath. Please specify crawlspace or slab foundation when ordering.

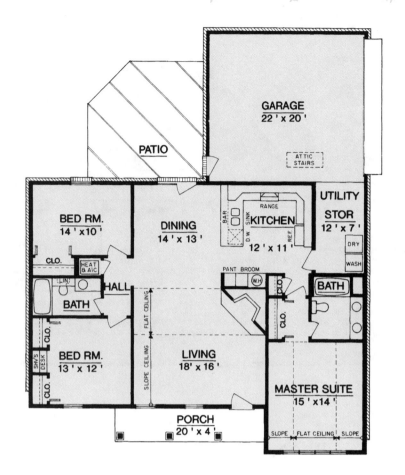

PLAN HPT750256

Square Footage: 1,964
Width: 38'-10" Depth: 90'-1"

Steeply pitched rooflines and a brick and stucco finish accentuate the country appeal of this French design. An entry stoop is welcomed by a set of double doors to the foyer. Two family bedrooms to the left of the entry share a full hall bath near the laundry facilities. To the right, a columned-accented dining room features double French doors to a garden courtyard. The kitchen provides plenty of countertops to work on and a cooktop island. A fireplace, built-ins and French doors to a rear porch make the family room ideal for casual relaxation. The master suite affords seclusion with an oversized walk-in closet and a sumptuous bath.

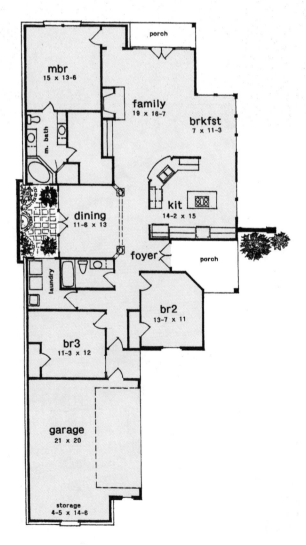

PLAN HPT750257

Square Footage: 2,007
Width: 40'-0" Depth: 94'-10"

An ornate stucco facade with brick highlights refines this French cottage. The double-door entrance sits to the side—perfect for a courtyard welcome. A dining and family room utlize an open layout for easy traffic flow. The circular kitchen space features an island and complementary breakfast bay. Bedrooms 2 and 3 share a hall bath. The master suite, apart from the main living areas, enjoys privacy and a full bath with a spacious walk-in closet.

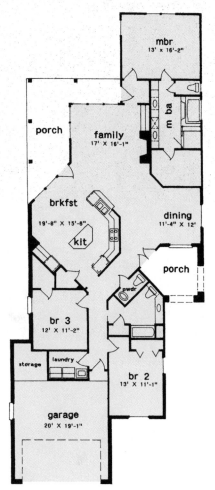

PLAN HPT750258

Square Footage: 1,923
Width: 40'-6" Depth: 89'-0"

 Subtle details make this home an elegant French country design. The entry foyer is found within a courtyard and opens to the dining room at the left. The kitchen, breakfast room and family room work together to form a casual gathering space. The family room also has double French doors to the rear porch while the breakfast area opens to a private courtyard. The master suite is found at the rear for privacy. Included in the suite are an amenity-filled bath and a spacious walk-in closet. Two family bedrooms share a full bath and are convenient to the laundry facilities.

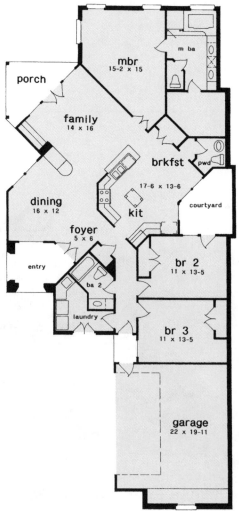

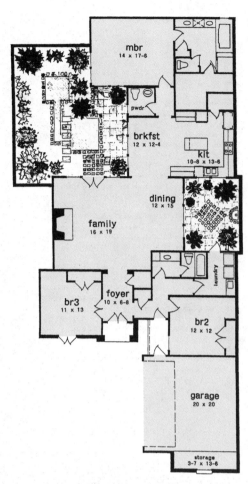

PLAN HPT750259

Square Footage: 2,133
Width: 43'-3" Depth: 95'-0"

 This charming French country cottage boasts all the romance of the old world and all the amenities of the modern age. French shutters, hipped rooflines, and stucco and brick detailing combine to give the exterior a distinct style. Double doors open to a foyer that is flanked on either side by two family bedrooms, which share a hall bath. The laundry room accesses a quiet garden. A huge fireplace warms the family room/dining area combination. The island kitchen opens to a breakfast room. The master suite is complemented by a private bath with a walk-in closet. The rear courtyard patio is accessed by double doors from the family room.

PLAN HPT750260

Square Footage: 1,868
Width: 40'-0" Depth: 81'-4"

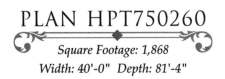 Dreaming of the French countryside or the courtyard grace of Louisiana French design? This one-story home is a picturesque addition to any neighborhood. A stucco and brick finish with transom windows and shutters creates a cozy look. Inside, the foyer opens to the dining room and a corridor with a wet bar. The family room is at the rear and works well with the kitchen and breakfast area. A porch off the breakfast room also connects to the master suite. Two family bedrooms share a hall bath.

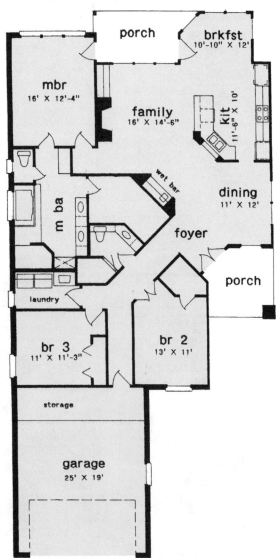

PLAN HPT750261

Square Footage: 1,823
Width: 38'-10" Depth: 94'-10"

This home's long, narrow footprint is ideal for an in-fill or slim lot. A beautiful facade using stucco, brick, shuttered windows and steepled rooftops is as inviting as the floor plan. A courtyard entrance is flanked by the open dining and family spaces. Two family bedrooms are split from the master suite, which fosters privacy. The master bedroom, at the rear of the home, enjoys simple luxuries in the dual-vanity bath. A two-car garage completes this plan.

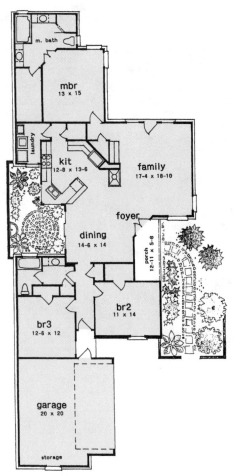

PLAN HPT750262

Square Footage: 2,163
Width: 44'-0" Depth: 83'-0"

 This cozy stucco design fits a shady lane in town or takes advantage of the views in the country. French doors open from an arched entryway with a transom window to the foyer. Two family bedrooms flank the foyer, while a hallway opens to the dining room. Across the hall, the kitchen and breakfast room serve up casual and formal meals. A loggia, just before the family room, accesses a garden courtyard. The family room sports a fireplace, built-ins and French doors to the rear yard. The master suite features a spacious walk-in closet and an amenity-filled bath.

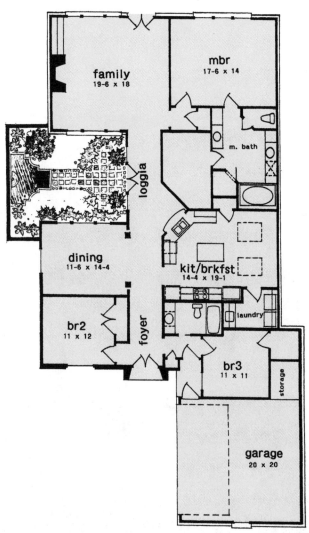

PLAN HPT750263

Square Footage: 1,823
Width: 38'-10" Depth: 94'-10"

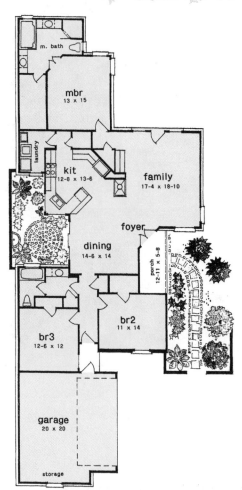

This splendid European cottage boasts the romantic influence of the French countryside. French shutters, stucco, and brick detailing highlight the eye-catching exterior. A covered front porch welcomes you inside to a foyer flanked on either side by a dining area and a family room. The laundry room is placed just behind the kitchen. The master suite is secluded to the rear of the plan for privacy and includes a private bath with a walk-in closet. Two additional bedrooms and a hall bath are located at the front of the plan. The two-car garage features extra storage space.

PLAN HPT750264

Square Footage: 1,964
Width: 38'-10" Depth: 90'-1"

 This narrow-lot plan possesses all the appeal and romance of a European cottage design. The front porch welcomes you to a charming set of front double doors. Two family bedrooms that share a hall bath, a laundry room and two-car garage with storage are located at the front of the plan. The island kitchen easily serves the dining room that accesses a private garden and the casual breakfast room. The spacious family room offers a warming fireplace, built-ins and back-porch access. The plan is completed by the master suite, which features a private bath and walk-in closet.

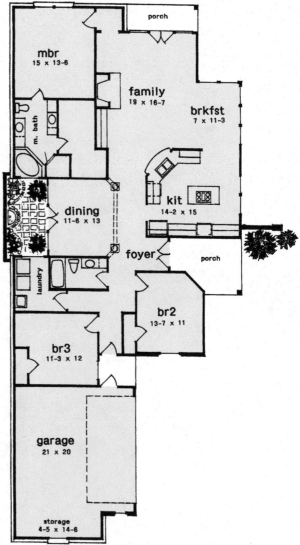

PLAN HPT750265

Square Footage: 1,804
Width: 49'-10" Depth: 74'-9"

Heavy European influences bring warmth and charm to this lovely cottage home. The family room—with an elaborate fireplace and built-ins—along with the dining room, is the heart of this home. Entertaining will be a snap with the convenience and efficiency of the well-equipped and easily accessible kitchen. An alternate to the formal dining room, the sunny breakfast area allows for more casual dining. A rear porch is accessed via the breakfast area and the family room. An exquisite master suite and two bedrooms with a shared bath complete the living spaces.

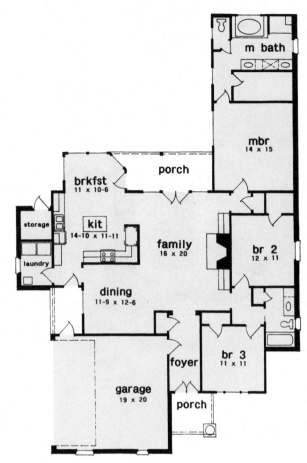

PLAN HPT750266

Square Footage: 2,300
Width: 58'-10" Depth: 83'-0"

This French Provincial charmer offers a stunning stucco and brick exterior and classic European style. At the heart of the home, the family room provides a fireplace and access to a rear covered porch. The island kitchen serves a breakfast bay that overlooks the backyard. The master suite is tucked away at the back of the plan with a fine bath and walk-in closet. Two family bedrooms—or make one a study—share a full bath and a hall that leads to the family room. An additional suite or guest quarters resides near the service entrance—a perfect arrangement for a live-in relative.

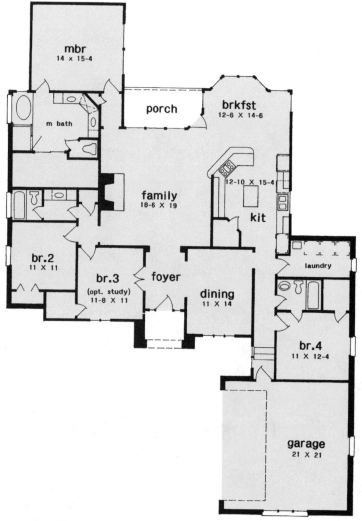

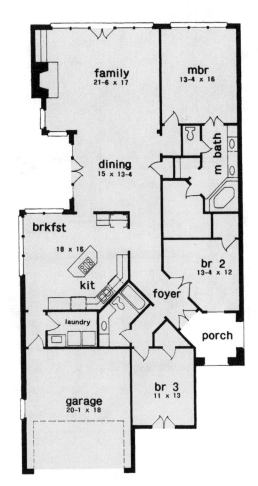

PLAN HPT750267

Square Footage: 2,048
Width: 38'-10" Depth: 75'-0"

 Presenting a narrow frontage, this plan provides spacious rooms for a family. Enter through a front corner porch or through a side courtyard that opens to the dining room. A fireplace warms the family room, which accesses the rear yard through French doors. A bright corner breakfast nook highlights the kitchen, which provides a cooktop island and laundry-room access. The master suite features a walk-in closet and separate vanities in the compartmented bath. Two family bedrooms share a full bath.

This chateau is packed with luxurious amenities, starting with an open foyer and a wide living space that opens to a private loggia. Walls of rear windows look out to this sumptuous area, which includes a fountain. A gourmet kitchen with a cooktop island counter serves the formal dining room. The plan offers three optional sets of doors to the flex room and an office/study, which could easily convert to a guest room. A sequestered master suite offers a garden tub and generous wardrobe space.

PLAN HPT750268

First Floor: 2,320 square feet
Second Floor: 601 square feet
Total: 2,921 square feet
Width: 59'-0" Depth: 98'-6"

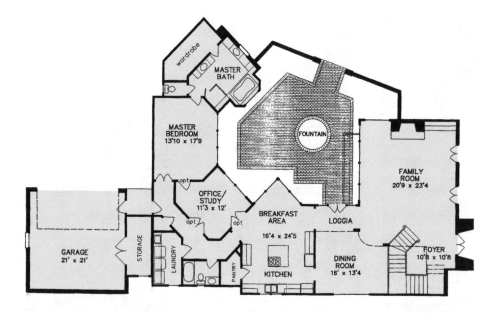

272

PLAN HPT750269

Square Footage: 2,678
Width: 69'-4" Depth: 84'-8"

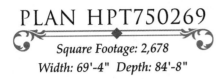

In true French country style, this home begins with a lovely terrace that announces the double-door entry. The main foyer separates formal living and dining areas and leads back to a large family room with a fireplace and built-ins. The breakfast room overlooks a wrapping porch and opens to the island kitchen. Three bedrooms are found on the left side of the plan—two family bedrooms sharing a full bath and a master suite with a sitting area. A fourth bedroom is tucked behind the two-car garage and features a private bath.

PLAN HPT750270

First Floor: 2,719 square feet
Second Floor: 618 square feet
Total: 3,337 square feet
Width: 47'-6" Depth: 119'-7"

Looks are deceiving in this narrow design that enjoys plenty of room despite its small appearance. The living room opens from the front portico and accesses a covered porch to the rear overlooking the courtyard. A staircase from the family room leads up to two family bedrooms that share a bath but have separate vanities. Open to the family room, the kitchen provides a walk-in pantry, cooktop island and window sink. The study and master bedroom are to the rear of the plan.

PLAN HPT750271

First Floor: 1,967 square feet
Second Floor: 1,572 square feet
Total: 3,539 square feet
Width: 39'-4" Depth: 89'-0"

A heaven-reaching facade uses short spires and hipped rooflines that melt over high windows. The entry loggia is accented by columns and a short set of stairs that lead to a spectacular gallery. The lengthy formal dining room connects to the kitchen for easy service. The kitchen features a large work island and a walk-in pantry. The family room is the hub of casual entertaining with warmth from the fireplace and rear-porch and gallery access for outdoor interaction. A first-floor bedroom makes an ideal guest suite or home office. Upstairs, three family bedrooms share two baths while the master suite relaxes in sumptuous splendor.

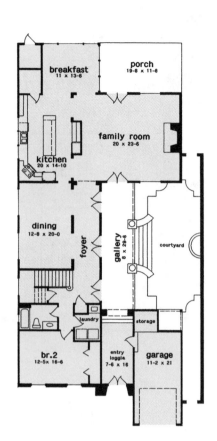

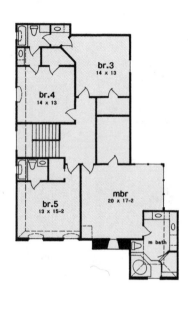

PLAN HPT750272

First Floor: 2,780 square feet
Second Floor: 878 square feet
Total: 3,658 square feet
Bonus Room: 206 square feet
Width: 68'-3" Depth: 89'-1"

The symmetrical front of this home conceals an imaginatively asymmetrical floor plan beyond. A keeping room, a sitting area in the master bedroom and a second bedroom all jut out from this home, forming interesting angles and providing extra window space. Two fireplaces, a game room, a study and His and Hers bathrooms in the master suite are interesting elements in this home. The bayed kitchen, with a walk-in pantry and a center island with room for seating, is sure to lure guests and family alike. The open floor plan and two-story ceilings in the family room add a contemporary touch.

PLAN HPT750273

First Floor: 1,909 square feet
Second Floor: 1,992 square feet
Total: 3,901 square feet
Width: 39'-9" Depth: 76'-10"

A garage-top bedroom may be the perfect place for your teenager, offering privacy, a separate bathroom, a large walk-in closet and a view out of two arched dormer windows. There are plenty of great spaces for children and adults in this elegant home. A downstairs study and an upstairs game room are two extras that set this home apart. Four bedrooms each have a private bathroom, with an additional powder room located downstairs. Notice that there are lots of extra storage space in this home and that the laundry room is conveniently located near the cluster of bedrooms.

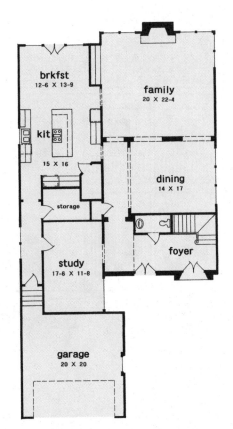

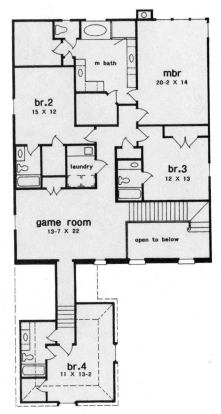

PLAN HPT750274

First Floor: 1,270 square feet
Second Floor: 630 square feet
Total: 1,900 square feet
Width: 28'-0" Depth: 76'-0"

Possessing an irresistible charm, this electric French design will elicit accolades from all who pass by. The double front porch provides a shady spot for a cool drink and a moment of relaxation. A spacious foyer, ample enough for a cherished antique, greets those who enter. Just beyond, the great room with its soaring ceiling gives additional flair to this open and inviting plan. An open-railed stairwell leads to a dramatic landing that overlooks the great room below. Access the second-floor porch easily from this landing. Two spacious bedrooms share a compartmented bath; each has a separate vanity and a walk-in closet.

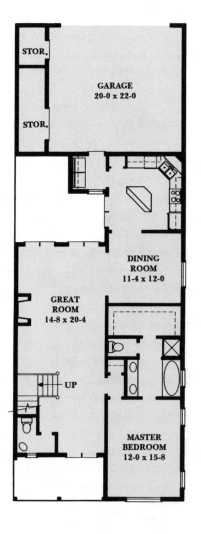

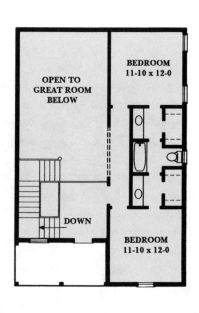

PLAN HPT750275

First Floor: 1,326 square feet
Second Floor: 1,257 square feet
Total: 2,583 square feet
Width: 30'-0" Depth: 78'-0"

The steeply pitched pavilion roof is a distinctive feature that identifies this house as a classic French design. Inside, a long foyer ushers visitors into a generous great room, which is separated from the kitchen by a wide cased opening. An L-shaped breakfast bar provides a place for a quick snack. A lavish master suite offers separate His and Hers walk-in closets and an oversized shower. Please specify basement or crawlspace foundation when ordering.

GARAGE
20-4 x 23-0

LAUN.

GREAT ROOM
17-8 x 21-10

UP

COMP./
OFFICE

DINING ROOM
11-0 x 13-0

GUEST
11-4 x 12-0

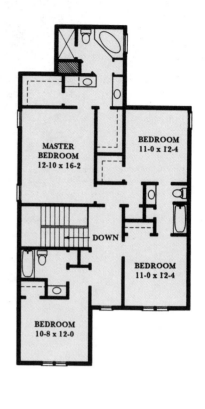

MASTER
BEDROOM
12-10 x 16-2

BEDROOM
11-0 x 12-4

DOWN

BEDROOM
11-0 x 12-4

BEDROOM
10-8 x 12-0

PLAN HPT750276

First Floor: 1,190 square feet
Second Floor: 1,220 square feet
Total: 2,410 square feet
Width: 30'-0" Depth: 72'-0"

This stately home is striking in its simplicity and grandeur. Within, the high-ceilinged rooms retain the grandeur of the original homes of the late 19th Century. An expansive great room flows into a formal dining room, separated only by elegant interior columns. Beyond, a spacious kitchen features a snack bar and breakfast area, which overlooks the secluded courtyard. A downstairs bedroom can function as an office or cozy den.

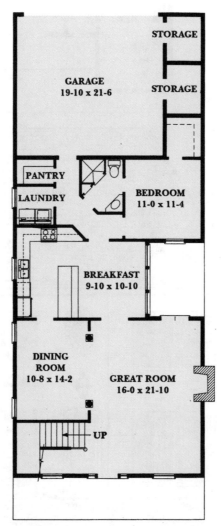

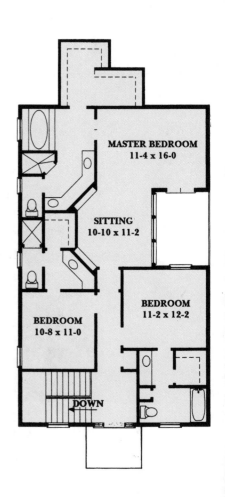

PLAN HPT750277

First Floor: 1,184 square feet
Second Floor: 1,093 square feet
Total: 2,277 square feet
Width: 28'-0" Depth: 74'-0"

The inspiration for this plan came directly from the 1878 edition of Bicknell's Victorian Buildings. Multiple windows brighten the living room, which opens to a small side porch. The kitchen boasts a walk-in pantry and adjoins a sunny breakfast area and a spacious keeping room with built-ins and a fireplace. The second floor features an inviting master suite with a relaxing bath that includes a raised corner tub. Three additional bedrooms, one with a walk-in closet, share a bath. The laundry area is conveniently close to the bedrooms.

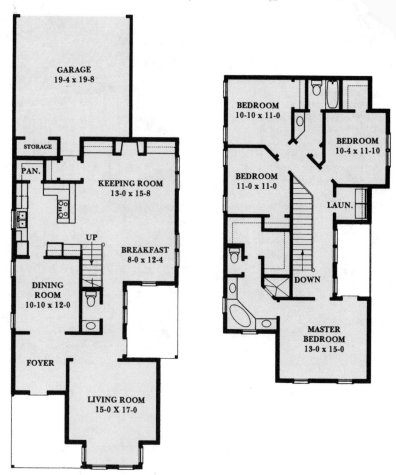

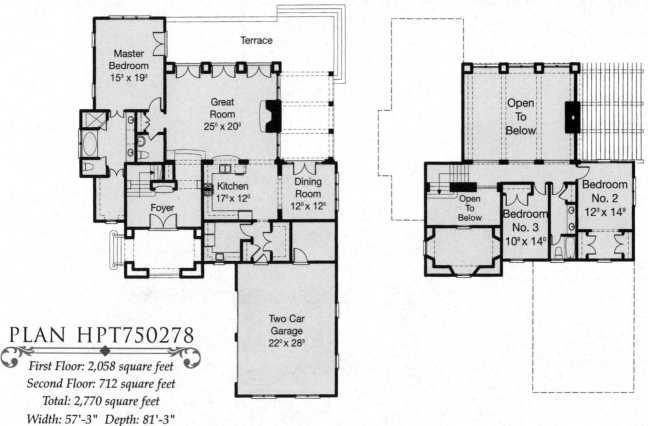

Terrace

Master Bedroom
15³ x 19³

Great Room
25⁰ x 20³

Kitchen
17⁰ x 12⁰

Dining Room
12⁰ x 12⁰

Foyer

Two Car Garage
22⁰ x 28³

Open To Below

Open To Below

Bedroom No. 3
10⁹ x 14⁰

Bedroom No. 2
12³ x 14⁹

PLAN HPT750278

First Floor: 2,058 square feet
Second Floor: 712 square feet
Total: 2,770 square feet
Width: 57'-3" Depth: 81'-3"

If you've always dreamed of owning a villa, we invite you to experience this European lifestyle—on a perfectly manageable scale. This home offers the best of traditional formality and casual elegance. The foyer leads to the great room, with a bold but stylish fireplace and three French doors to the rear terrace—sure to be left open during fair weather. The large kitchen opens gracefully to a private dining room that accesses a covered outdoor patio. The master suite combines great views and a sumptuous bath to complete this winning design. Upstairs, a balcony hall overlooking the great room leads to two family bedrooms that share a full hall bath. This home is designed with a basement foundation.

PLAN HPT750279

First Floor: 804 square feet
Second Floor: 835 square feet
Total: 1,639 square feet
Width: 18'-8" Depth: 80'-6"

This lovely design is much more than just a pretty face. A row of symmetrical exteriors creates a stunning streetscape, but the real beauty is within each home. A well-organized interior arranges the formal rooms to accommodate gatherings both grand and cozy. A centered fireplace lends warmth and a sense of comfort to the living room and shares its glow with the formal dining room. A U-shaped kitchen overlooks a breakfast bay with three windows. Upstairs, the master suite provides a covered balcony and double-bowl vanity.

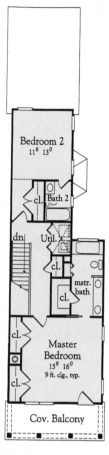

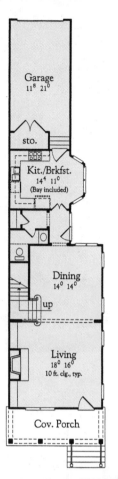

This home, as shown in the photograph, may differ from the actual blueprints.
For more detailed information, please check the floor plans carefully.

©Jeffrey Jacobs/Mims Studios

©Jeffrey Jacobs/Mims Studios

PLAN HPT750280

First Floor: 1,135 square feet
Second Floor: 1,092 square feet
Total: 2,227 square feet
Width: 28'-8" Depth: 74'-2"

Stylish square columns line the porch and balcony of this home, which has received the Builder's Choice National Design and Planning Award and the Award of Merit in Architecture. Inside, an open arrangement of the formal rooms is partially defined by a through-fireplace. Brightened by a triple window, the breakfast nook is an inviting place for family and friends to gather. A single door opens to the outside, where steps lead down to the rear property—a good place to start a walk into town. The kitchen features a food-prep island and a sizable pantry. Upstairs, the master suite offers a fireplace and access to the covered balcony.

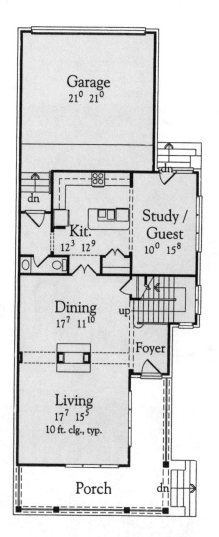

Garage
21⁰ 21⁰

Kit.
12³ 12⁹

Study /
Guest
10⁰ 15⁸

Dining
17⁷ 11¹⁰

up

Foyer

Living
17⁷ 15⁵
10 ft. clg., typ.

dn

Porch

dn

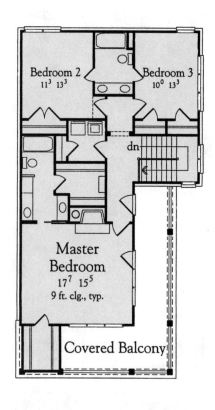

Bedroom 2
11³ 13³

Bedroom 3
10⁰ 13³

dn

Master
Bedroom
17⁷ 15⁵
9 ft. clg., typ.

Covered Balcony

PLAN HPT750281

First Floor: 1,075 square feet
Second Floor: 604 square feet
Total: 1,679 square feet
Width: 24'-2" Depth: 74'-2"

This townhouse variation has a comfortable interior, tailored for couples and families. The front porch leads to a spacious family room with a fireplace and a three-window view. A galley-style kitchen opens to casual dining space, which accesses a side porch with steps down to a courtyard. The first-floor master suite provides a walk-in closet and additional linen storage in the bath. Upstairs, each of two family bedrooms provides a set of French doors to the upper porch as well as private access to the shared bath. The plan also provides a rear-loading garage with a pedestrian entrance.

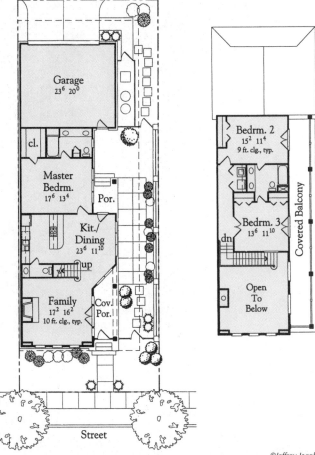

Garage
23⁶ 20⁰

cl.

Master Bedrm.
17⁶ 13⁴

Por.

Kit./Dining
23⁶ 11¹⁰

up

Family
17² 16²
10 ft. clg., typ.

Cov. Por.

Street

Bedrm. 2
15² 11⁴
9 ft. clg., typ.

Bedrm. 3
13⁶ 11¹⁰

dn

Open To Below

Covered Balcony

©Jeffrey Jacobs/Mims Studios

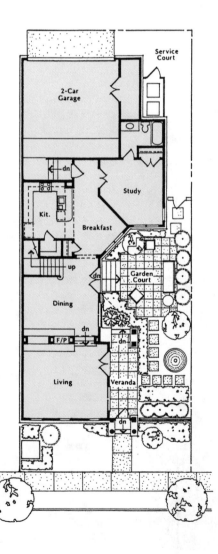

Service Court

2-Car Garage

dn

Kit.

Study

Breakfast

up

Garden Court

dn

Dining

dn

F/P

dn

Living

Veranda

dn

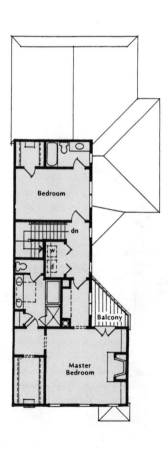

Bedroom

dn

Balcony

Master Bedroom

PLAN HPT750282

First Floor: 1,282 square feet
Second Floor: 956 square feet
Total: 2,238 square feet
Width: 30'-2" Depth: 74'-2"

There won't be any chilly mornings for the homeowner within this lovely home. The second-floor master suite boasts a massive hearth, flanked by built-in shelves. French doors open from the bedroom to a private balcony, where gentle breezes may invigorate the senses. A gallery hall leads to a secondary bedroom, which has its own bath and a walk-in closet. On the first floor, formal rooms share a through-fireplace and offer doors to the veranda and garden court. A secluded study easily converts to a guest suite or home office, and convenient storage space is available in the rear-loading garage.

PLAN HPT750283

First Floor: 781 square feet
Second Floor: 1,034 square feet
Total: 1,815 square feet
Width: 19'-9" Depth: 69'-0"

Here's a home that's both beautiful and compact. This fortunate home-owner will never feel crowded, with a well-drawn interior of spacious rooms and plenty of indoor/outdoor flow. A double portico presents a charming welcome and invites enjoyment of the outdoors. The entry leads to an open arrangement of the living and dining rooms, warmed by a fireplace. A center hall provides access to a garden court and path, where family members can linger or begin their stroll to local shops. Upstairs, the sleeping quarters include two secondary bedrooms and a master suite that opens to a covered balcony.

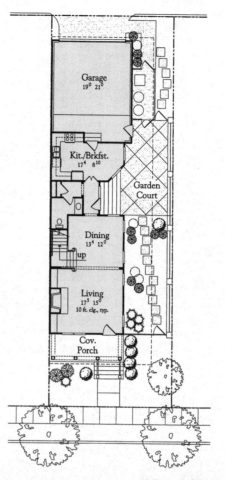

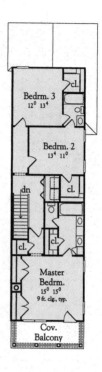

©Jeffrey Jacobs/Mims Studios

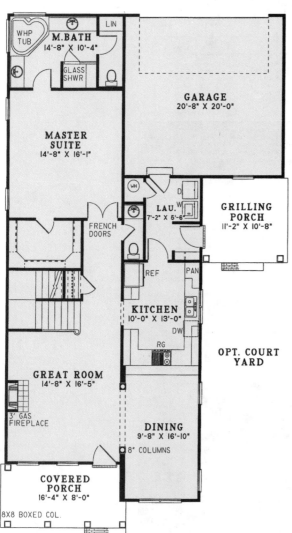

WHP TUB

M.BATH
14'-8" X 10'-4"

LIN

GLASS SHWR

GARAGE
20'-8" X 20'-0"

MASTER SUITE
14'-8" X 16'-1"

FRENCH DOORS

WH

D
W

LAU.
7'-2" X 5'-6"

GRILLING PORCH
11'-2" X 10'-8"

REF

PAN

KITCHEN
10'-0" X 13'-0"

DW

RG

OPT. COURT YARD

GREAT ROOM
14'-8" X 16'-5"

3' GAS FIREPLACE

DINING
9'-8" X 16'-10"

8" COLUMNS

COVERED PORCH
16'-4" X 8'-0"

8X8 BOXED COL.

PLAN HPT750284

First Floor: 1,298 square feet
Second Floor: 624 square feet
Total: 1,922 square feet
Width: 36'-4" Depth: 64'-10"

This design is inspired by the plantation homes of the South, with its covered porches with boxed columns, and large double-hung windows with decorative lintels. Inside, the great room is cheered by a gas fireplace, which can also be viewed from the dining room. The master suite is on the main floor to provide privacy and features French doors. Two spacious family bedrooms share a full bath and each enjoys access to the second-story porch and computer desk. Please specify crawlspace or slab foundation when ordering.

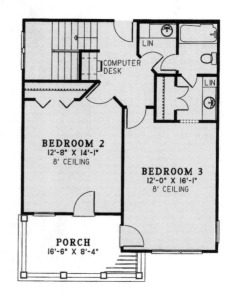

LIN

COMPUTER DESK

LIN

BEDROOM 2
12'-8" X 14'-1"
8' CEILING

BEDROOM 3
12'-0" X 16'-1"
8' CEILING

PORCH
16'-6" X 8'-4"

PLAN HPT750285

First Floor: 875 square feet
Second Floor: 814 square feet
Total: 1,689 square feet
Width: 37'-0" Depth: 51'-0"

Double gables and a covered porch give this narrow-lot home a storybook beginning. Inside, a thoughtfully arranged floor plan provides efficiency that translates into happily ever-after for the entire family. A rear deck expands outdoor living space from the great room, which is open to a center island kitchen. Formal dining is enhanced by a bay window and a columned entry that graces this room. The second floor contains a relaxing master suite that features a private bath filled with amenities and two family bedrooms that share a full bath.

DECK

GREAT RM.
19-0 x 16-6

fireplace

cl

pd. rm.

GARAGE
15-0 x 20-0

KIT.
11-8 x
11-6

UTIL.
d w   pan.

up

FOYER
7-4 x
8-2

DINING
11-4 x 12-0

PORCH

MASTER
BED RM.
13-8 x 11-8

walk-in
closet

master bath

lin.

down

railing

bath

BED RM.
11-4 x 10-0

cl

lin.

cl

BED RM.
11-4 x 11-0

B. NATHAN.

PLAN HPT750286

First Floor: 1,812 square feet
Second Floor: 1,300 square feet
Total: 3,112 square feet
Width: 35'-0" Depth: 88'-0"

Characteristics of Greek Revival architecture enliven the exterior of this four-bedroom home. A pair of square columns frames the entrance to the dining room. The foyer leads to a large great room and also to a cozy keeping room off the kitchen. The kitchen has a large walk-in pantry and a sunny breakfast area which looks out to a private courtyard. The downstairs master suite is tucked quietly away from the noise of family life. On the second level, a large sitting room and activity area overlook the kitchen below, enabling the family cook to stay involved in the family fun. Three family bedrooms and two full baths complete this floor.

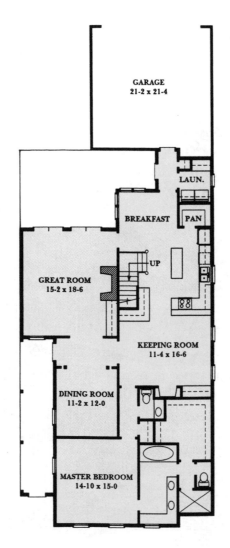

GARAGE
21-2 x 21-4

LAUN.

BREAKFAST

PAN

GREAT ROOM
15-2 x 18-6

UP

KEEPING ROOM
11-4 x 16-6

DINING ROOM
11-2 x 12-0

MASTER BEDROOM
14-10 x 15-0

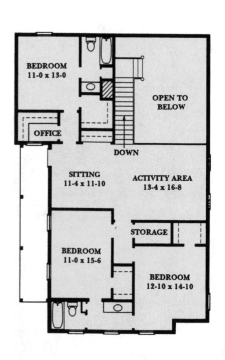

BEDROOM
11-0 x 13-0

OPEN TO BELOW

OFFICE

DOWN

SITTING
11-4 x 11-10

ACTIVITY AREA
13-4 x 16-8

STORAGE

BEDROOM
11-0 x 15-6

BEDROOM
12-10 x 14-10

PLAN HPT750287

First Floor: 1,227 square feet
Second Floor: 1,133 square feet
Total: 2,360 square feet
Bonus Space: 792 square feet
Width: 25'-0" Depth: 77'-0"

Distinctive design features of the Charleston single house make it a perfect candidate for the narrow urban lot. Since its narrow end faces the street and its two-story piazza faces the side yard, the plan affords its occupants much more privacy than a house with a front-facing porch. The street entry leads to a porch, providing a secluded, but graceful, transition from the neighborhood. A grand foyer with an open stairwell opens to a formal dining room and the great room beyond. The front study could serve as an office or guest room. Bedrooms reside on the second floor—note the sitting room in the master suite. For more space, develop the bonus space on the upper level.

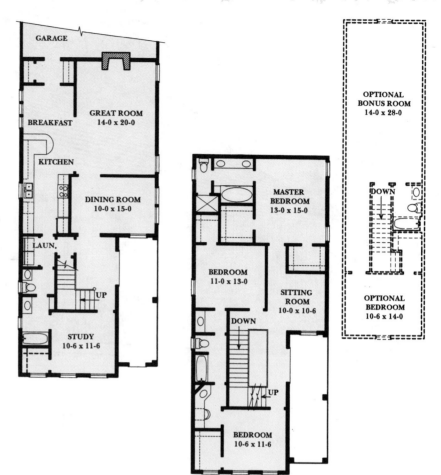

PLAN HPT750288

Square Footage: 1,700
Width: 22'-0" Depth: 77'-4"

Here is the quintessential narrow-lot house, based on the "shotgun" house, a popular style found in 19th-Century New Orleans and many other Southern towns. For the sake of contemporary planning, this version forsakes the rear door in favor of two full baths. The interior offers plenty of living space—living and family rooms, each with a fireplace, an efficient kitchen with a snack bar, and a dining room. As a starter home or a retirement home, this unique house will serve its occupants well.

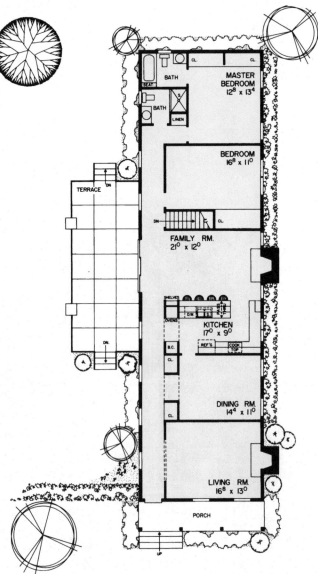

PLAN HPT750289

First Floor: 1,698 square feet
Second Floor: 533 square feet
Total: 2,231 square feet
Bonus Room: 394 square feet
Width: 35'-4" Depth: 71'-6"

A protruding porch with decorative columns and a stunning pediment complements twin dormers and shuttered windows on this home. The great room, with its cozy fireplace and wet bar, is a great place for gathering. The elaborate kitchen enjoys a double-door pantry, a snack bar and access to the side grilling porch. Tucked away to the rear of the home is the master suite featuring a bath with double doors, a glass shower and whirlpool tub. The second floor is complete with two family bedrooms—each includes a window seat—sharing a hall bath that includes dual vanities. Please specify crawlspace or slab foundation when ordering.

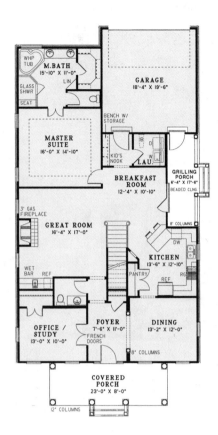

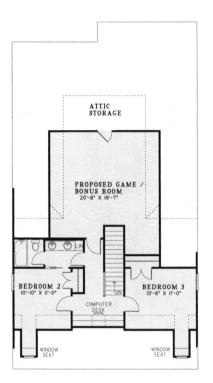

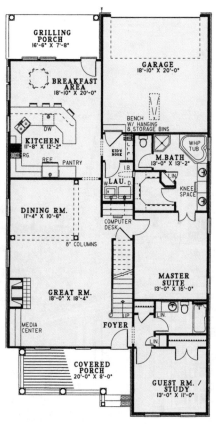

GRILLING PORCH
16'-6" X 7'-8"

GARAGE
18'-10" X 20'-0"

BREAKFAST AREA
18'-10" X 20'-0"

DW

KITCHEN
11'-8" X 12'-2"

RG.

REF. PANTRY

BENCH W/ HANGING & STORAGE BINS

KID'S NOOK

M.BATH
13'-0" X 13'-2"

WHP TUB

W.LAU.

KNEE SPACE

DINING RM.
11'-4" X 10'-6"

COMPUTER DESK

8" COLUMNS

GREAT RM.
18'-0" X 18'-4"

MASTER SUITE
13'-0" X 15'-0"

MEDIA CENTER

FOYER

COVERED PORCH
20'-0" X 8'-0"

GUEST RM. / STUDY
13'-0" X 11'-0"

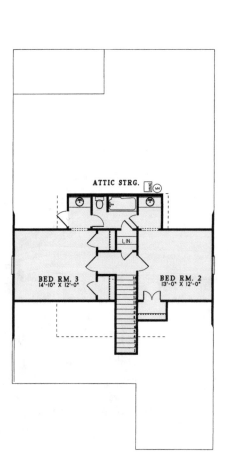

ATTIC STRG.

LIN.

BED RM. 3
14'-10" X 12'-0"

BED RM. 2
13'-0" X 12'-0"

PLAN HPT750290

First Floor: 1,694 square feet
Second Floor: 558 square feet
Total: 2,252 square feet
Width: 36'-0" Depth: 69'-0"

The front porch of this traditional design will be a
favorite spot for relaxing. The tall
shutter-clad windows enhance the
classic charm of the facade. Perfect for
a narrow lot, this home features a
front guest bedroom and built-ins
such as a media center, fireplace and
computer desk in the great room.
Don't miss the grilling porch to the
rear of the home—it is easily accessed
from the breakfast nook. Please specify
basement, crawlspace or slab foundation when ordering.

PLAN HPT750291

Square Footage: 1,915
Width: 39'-0" Depth: 72'-0"

Simple accents such as decorative columns, a gable roof and a charming dormer window give this home a straightforward, honest appeal. The great room holds a built-in media center and a focal-point fireplace. The U-shaped kitchen features a corner walk-in pantry, a snack counter and a view of three windows. The master suite offers a box ceiling, walk-in closet and heavenly private bath. Please specify crawlspace or slab foundation when ordering.

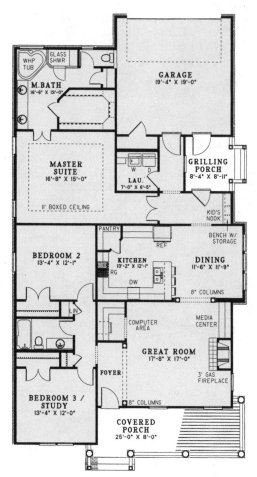

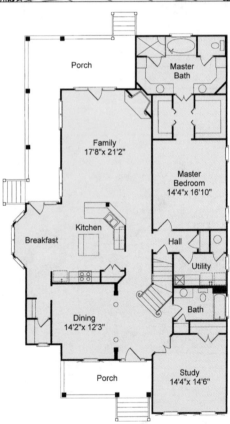

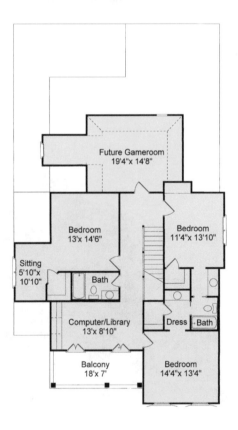

PLAN HPT750292

First Floor: 2,236 square feet

Second Floor: 1,208 square feet

Total: 3,444 square feet

Bonus Room: 318 square feet

Width: 42'-6" Depth: 71'-4"

This spacious home offers a front porch and a second-floor balcony as well as a wraparound porch in the rear. The elegant foyer, with its grand staircase, is flanked by the dining room on the left and the study on the right. The island kitchen adjoins the family room and the sunny breakfast nook. The master suite, with an elaborate private bath, is secluded in the back for privacy. Three additional bedrooms—one with a sitting room—share two full baths on the second floor.

PLAN HPT750293

First Floor: 2,578 square feet
Second Floor: 1,277 square feet
Total: 3,855 square feet
Bonus Room: 330 square feet
Width: 53'-6" Depth: 97'-0"

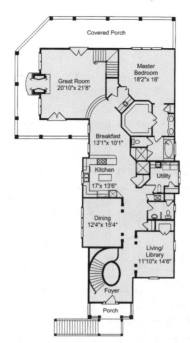

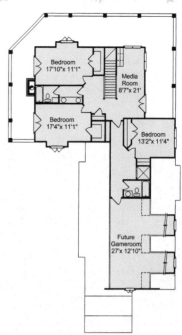

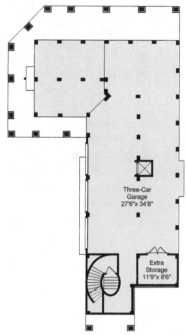

This charming Charleston design is full of surprises! Perfect for a narrow footprint, the raised foundation is ideal for a waterfront location. An entry porch introduces a winding staircase. To the right is a living room/library that functions as a formal entertaining space. A large hearth and two sets of French doors to the covered porch enhance the great room. The master suite is positioned for privacy and includes great amenities that work to relax the homeowners. Upstairs, three family bedrooms, two full baths, an open media room and a future game room create a fantastic casual family space.

Deck 25'8"x 9'

Porch 25'8"x 8'

Den 13'8"x 12'9"

Breakfast 16'6"x 10'

Living 25'4"x 18'

Kitchen 13'8"x 15'

Dining 13'8"x 12'

Porch

Bath

Bedroom 15'8"x 11'

Porch

Master Bedroom 20'x 18'

Master Bath

WIC

WIC

Utility

Bedroom 13'8"x 12'

Balcony

Bath

Bedroom 15'8"x 11'

PLAN HPT750294

First Floor: 1,742 square feet
Second Floor: 1,624 square feet
Total: 3,366 square feet
Width: 42'-10" Depth: 77'-0"

Elegant Southern living is the theme of this seaside townhouse. The narrow-lot design allows for comfortable urban living. Inside, the living room is warmed by a fireplace, while the island kitchen serves the breakfast room and casual den. A first-floor guest bedroom is located at the front of the design. The dining room is reserved for more formal occasions. Upstairs, the gracious master suite features a private second-floor porch, two walk-in closets and a private bath. Two additional bedrooms share a hall bath on this floor.

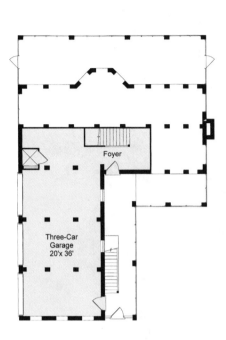

Foyer

Three-Car Garage
20'x 36'

Porch

Kitchen
14'6"x 18'11"

Breakfast
13'7"x 12'3"

Living Room
19'2"x 21'5"

Dining
16'7"x 13'1"

Porch

Util.

1/2 Ba.

Bath

Bedroom
21'5"x 12'1"

Deck
21'x 12'

Master Bath

WIC

Master Bedroom
19'1"x 21'5"

12'3"x 19'5"

Porch

Bedroom
16'7"x 12'1"

WIC

Bath

WIC

Bedroom
18'1"x 12'1"

PLAN HPT750295

First Floor: 1,901 square feet
Second Floor: 1,874 square feet
Total: 3,775 square feet
Width: 50'-0" Depth: 70'-0"

This elegant Charleston townhouse is enhanced by Southern grace and three levels of charming livability. Covered porches offer outdoor living space at every level. The first floor offers a living room warmed by a fireplace, an island kitchen serving a bayed nook, and a formal dining room. A first-floor guest bedroom is located at the front of the plan, along with a laundry and powder room. The second level offers a sumptuous master suite boasting a private balcony, a master bath and enormous walk-in closet. Two other bedrooms sharing a Jack-and-Jill bath are also on this level.

PLAN HPT750296

First Floor: 1,078 square feet
Second Floor: 921 square feet
Total: 1,999 square feet
Width: 24'-11" Depth: 73'-10"

L

This charming clapboard home is loaded with character and is perfect for a narrow lot. Columns and connecting arches separate the great room and the dining room. The efficient U-shaped kitchen features a corner sink with a window view and a bayed breakfast area with access to the rear porch. Upstairs, the master suite features a vaulted ceiling and a luxurious bath with dual vanities, a whirlpool tub and separate shower. A secondary bedroom and a full bath are also located on the second floor with a large rear balcony, completing this compact, highly livable plan. Please specify crawlspace or slab foundation when ordering.

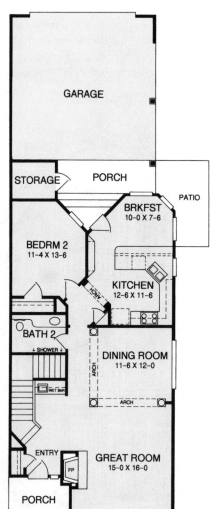

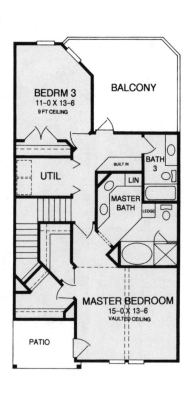

300

PLAN HPT750297

First Floor: 2,193 square feet
Second Floor: 1,136 square feet
Total: 3,329 square feet
Bonus Room: 347 square feet
Width: 41'-6" Depth: 71'-4"

This farmhouse is far from old-fashioned with a computer loft/library and future game room designed into the second floor. Two wrapping porches grace the exterior, offering expanded outdoor living spaces. The breakfast nook, dining room and family room radiate off the central island kitchen. The study/bedroom at the front is situated with an adjacent full bath, making this ideal for a guest room. Three bedrooms share two baths on the second floor while the master suite, with its elaborate private bath, finds seclusion on the first floor.

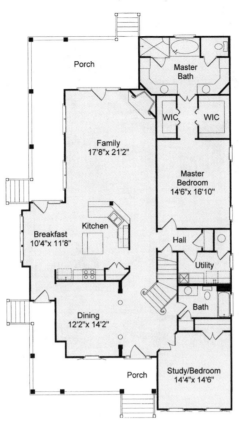

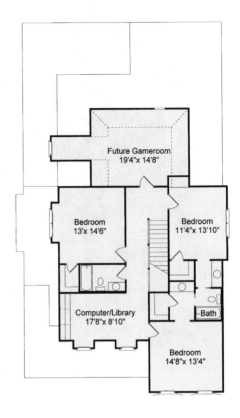

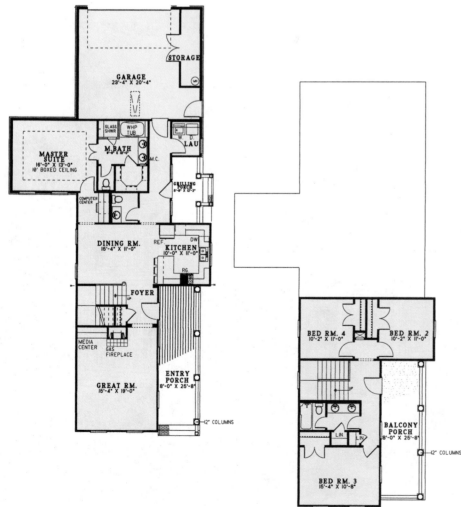

PLAN HPT750298

First Floor: 1,295 square feet
Second Floor: 664 square feet
Total: 1,959 square feet
Width: 38'-6" Depth: 78'-6"

A gracious facade of columns, shuttered windows, gabled rooflines, a long porch and a balcony make this home seem like an established landmark. The great room boasts a media center, gas fireplace and views toward the front property. A well-planned kitchen serves a snack counter and enjoys vistas through the formal dining room. A secluded master suite has a computer center, tray ceiling and a vanity with two lavatories. On the second floor, three bedrooms share access to a balcony that other family members can enjoy. Please specify basement, block, crawlspace or slab foundation when ordering.

PLAN HPT750299

First Floor: 1,558 square feet
Second Floor: 429 square feet
Total: 1,987 square feet
Width: 36'-4" Depth: 73'-6"

This two-story home is made for the narrow lot and the family who revels in luxurious escapes. Plenty of built-ins and amenities allow for the ultimate in relaxation. Keep the kids entertained in their private nook while the adults fire up the barbecue on the grilling porch. One family member can work quietly in the computer center while another reads in the window-seat loft. A media center and a gas fireplace give the great room its name, while the whirlpool tub in the master bath is always appreciated. Please specify basement, crawlspace, slab or block foundation when ordering.

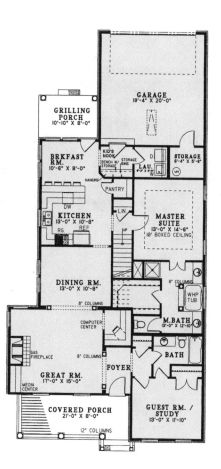

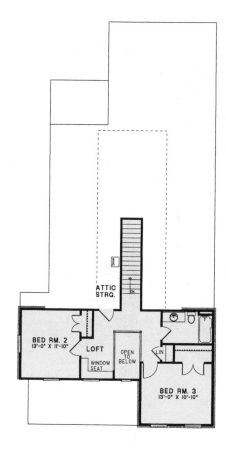

PLAN HPT750300

First Floor: 1,482 square feet
Second Floor: 631 square feet
Total: 2,113 square feet
Width: 41'-10" Depth: 56'-5"

L

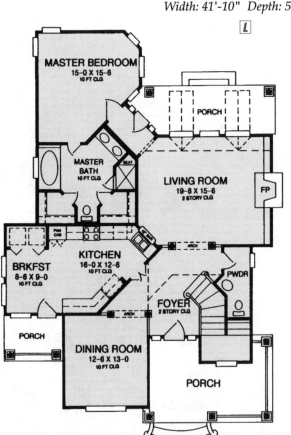

The four-square design reminiscent of the 1940s gives this home its landmark look. An inviting porch opens to a two-story foyer. Straight ahead, the living room is visible through two columns mounted on pedestals and connected by a graceful arch. A large kitchen and a sunny breakfast room invite casual conversations and lingering. The master bedroom includes a luxurious bath with His and Hers walk-in closets, a soothing whirlpool tub and a separate shower. Two additional bedrooms and a full bath share the second floor. Please specify crawlspace or slab foundation when ordering.

PLAN HPT750301

First Floor: 1,233 square feet
Second Floor: 824 square feet
Total: 2,057 square feet
Width: 31'-10" Depth: 77'-10"

Traditional styling distinguishes this narrow-lot home. As one enters the foyer, the large living room and dining room—both with volume ceilings—are visible beyond. A flex room that can be used as a guest suite or home office/study opens off the foyer. A roomy covered porch is accessed from the breakfast room and provides space for outdoor entertaining. Upstairs, the master suite has all the amenities, including access to a private second-story covered porch. Another bedroom and bath complete this efficiently designed plan.

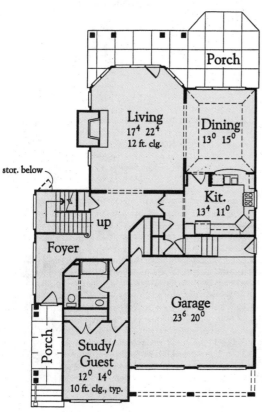

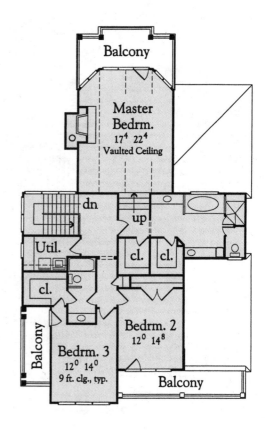

PLAN HPT750302

First Floor: 1,473 square feet
Second Floor: 1,455 square feet
Total: 2,928 square feet
Width: 41'-11" Depth: 61'-3"

Porch

Living
17⁴ 22⁴
12 ft. clg.

Dining
13⁰ 15⁰

stor. below

Kit.
13⁴ 11⁰

Foyer

up

Garage
23⁶ 20⁰

Porch

Study/
Guest
12⁰ 14⁰
10 ft. clg., typ.

Balcony

Master
Bedrm.
17⁴ 22⁴
Vaulted Ceiling

dn

up

Util.

cl.

cl.

cl.

Balcony

Bedrm. 3
12⁰ 14⁰
9 ft. clg., typ.

Bedrm. 2
12⁰ 14⁸

Balcony

Asymmetrical gables and wide muntin windows create curb appeal and more than just a little dazzle with this plan. A shallow porch leads to the foyer, while a nearby study easily converts to a secluded guest suite. The living room with a fireplace provides access to the rear porch and is convenient to the formal dining room and kitchen. Upstairs, two family bedrooms share a full bath. The master suite features vaulted ceilings, a fireplace, a private balcony, two walk-in closets and a spacious bath with a compartmented toilet.

PLAN HPT750303

First Floor: 1,267 square feet

Second Floor: 1,219 square feet

Total: 2,486 square feet

Loft: 456 square feet

Width: 44'-1" Depth: 70'-4"

The stately design of this narrow-lot townhouse is enhanced by gracious Colonial accents. The first floor offers front and rear porches, a living room warmed by a fireplace, a dining room served by the kitchen, a guest room/study, hall bath and garage with storage. The second floor holds a sumptuous master suite with a private bath, double walk-in closet and private balcony. Bedrooms 2 and 3 share a hall bath. The third level features a playroom and attic storage.

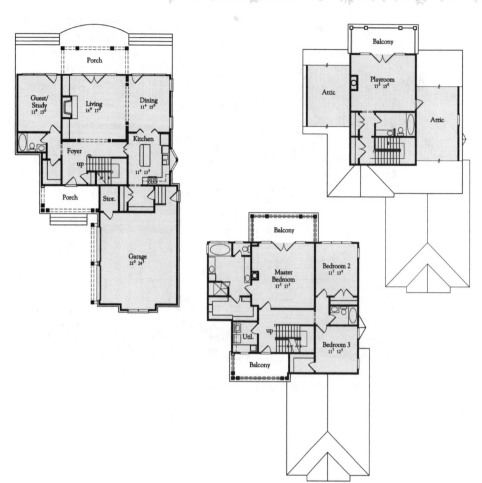

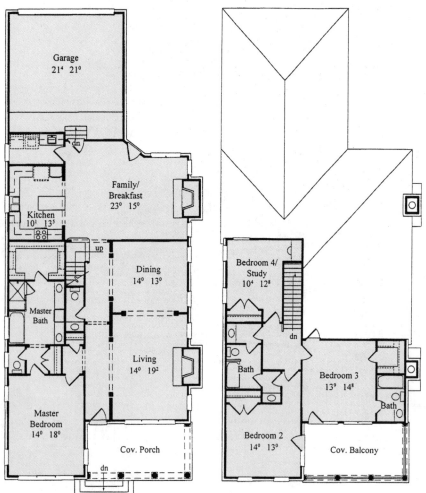

PLAN HPT750304

First Floor: 1,887 square feet
Second Floor: 899 square feet
Total: 2,786 square feet
Width: 35'-0" Depth: 85'-0"

A variety of window treatments creates a striking facade on this home. A gallery hall opens to the living room, which has a fireplace and wide views of the side property. Decorative columns help to define the spacious area between the dining and living rooms. Set to the rear of the plan, the family/breakfast area enjoys its own hearth, framed by tall windows. The master suite features a walk-in closet, two vanities, a dressing area and additional linen storage. Upstairs, three family bedrooms share two baths and a covered balcony.

LET US SHOW YOU OUR HOME BLUEPRINT PACKAGE.

BUILDING A HOME? PLANNING A HOME?

OUR BLUEPRINT PACKAGE HAS NEARLY EVERYTHING YOU NEED TO GET THE JOB DONE RIGHT,

whether you're working on your own or with help from an architect, designer, builder or subcontractors. Each Blueprint Package is the result of many hours of work by licensed architects or professional designers.

QUALITY

Hundreds of hours of painstaking effort have gone into the development of your blueprint plan. Each home has been quality-checked by professionals to insure accuracy and buildability.

VALUE

Because we sell in volume, you can buy professional quality blueprints at a fraction of their development cost. With our plans, your dream home design costs substantially less than the fees charged by architects.

SERVICE

Once you've chosen your favorite home plan, you'll receive fast, efficient service whether you choose to mail or fax your order to us or call us toll free at 1-800-521-6797. After you have received your order, call for customer service toll free 1-888-690-1116.

SATISFACTION

Over 50 years of service to satisfied home plan buyers provide us unparalleled experience and knowledge in producing quality blueprints.

ORDER TOLL FREE 1-800-521-6797

After you've looked over our Blueprint Package and Important Extras, call toll free on our Blueprint Hotline: 1-800-521-6797, for current pricing and availability prior to mailing the order form on page 317. We're ready and eager to serve you. After you have received your order, call for customer service toll free 1-888-690-1116.

Each set of blueprints is an interrelated collection of detail sheets which includes components such as floor plans, interior and exterior elevations, dimensions, cross-sections, diagrams and notations. These sheets show exactly how your house is to be built.

SETS MAY INCLUDE:

FRONTAL SHEET
This artist's sketch of the exterior of the house gives you an idea of how the house will look when built and landscaped. Large floor plans show all levels of the house and provide an overview of your new home's livability, as well as a handy reference for deciding on furniture placement.

FOUNDATION PLANS
This sheet shows the foundation layout including support walls, excavated and unexcavated areas, if any, and foundation notes. If slab construction rather than basement, the plan shows footings and details for a monolithic slab. This page, or another in the set, may include a sample plot plan for locating your house on a building site.

DETAILED FLOOR PLANS
These plans show the layout of each floor of the house. Rooms and interior spaces are carefully dimensioned and keys are given for cross-section details provided later in the plans. The positions of electrical outlets and switches are shown.

HOUSE CROSS-SECTIONS
Large-scale views show sections or cut-aways of the foundation, interior walls, exterior walls, floors, stairways and roof details. Additional cross-sections may show important changes in floor, ceiling or roof heights or the relationship of one level to another. Extremely valuable for construction, these sections show exactly how the various parts of the house fit together.

INTERIOR ELEVATIONS
Many of our drawings show the design and placement of kitchen and bathroom cabinets, laundry areas, fireplaces, bookcases and other built-ins. Little "extras," such as mantelpiece and wainscoting drawings, plus molding sections, provide details that give your home that custom touch.

EXTERIOR ELEVATIONS
These drawings show the front, rear and sides of your house and give necessary notes on exterior materials and finishes. Particular attention is given to cornice detail, brick and stone accents or other finish items that make your home unique.

IMPORTANT EXTRAS TO DO THE JOB RIGHT!

INTRODUCING IMPORTANT PLANNING AND CONSTRUCTION
AIDS DEVELOPED BY OUR PROFESSIONALS TO HELP YOU
SUCCEED IN YOUR HOME-BUILDING PROJECT

MATERIALS LIST

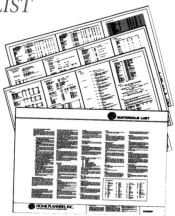

(Note: Because of the diversity of local building codes, our Materials List does not include mechanical materials.)

For many of the designs in our portfolio, we offer a customized materials take-off that is invaluable in planning and estimating the cost of your new home. This Materials List outlines the quantity, type and size of materials needed to build your house (with the exception of mechanical system items). Included are framing lumber, windows and doors, kitchen and bath cabinetry, rough and finish hardware, and much more. This handy list helps you or your builder cost out materials and serves as a reference sheet when you're compiling bids. Some Materials Lists may be ordered before blueprints are ordered, call for information.

SPECIFICATION OUTLINE

This valuable 16-page document is critical to building your house correctly. Designed to be filled in by you or your builder, this book lists 166 stages or items crucial to the building process. It provides a comprehensive review of the construction process and helps in choosing materials. When combined with the blueprints, a signed contract, and a schedule, it becomes a legal document and record for the building of your home.

QUOTE ONE®

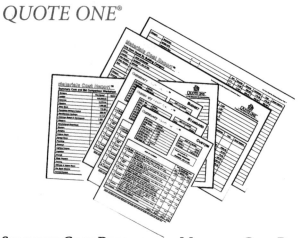

SUMMARY COST REPORT   **MATERIAL COST REPORT**

A product for estimating the cost of building select designs, the Quote One® system is available in two separate stages: The Summary Cost Report and the Material Cost Report.

The **Summary Cost Report** is the first stage in the package and shows the total cost per square foot for your chosen home in your zip-code area and then breaks that cost down into various categories showing the costs for building materials, labor and installation. The report includes three grades: Budget, Standard and Custom. These reports allow you to evaluate your building budget and compare the costs of building a variety of homes in your area.

Make even more informed decisions about your home-building project with the second phase of our package, our **Material Cost Report.** This tool is invaluable in planning and estimating the cost of your new home. The material and installation (labor and equipment) cost is shown for each of over 1,000 line items provided in the Materials List (Standard grade), which is included when you purchase this estimating tool. It allows you to determine building costs for your specific zip-code area and for your chosen home design. Space is allowed for additional estimates from contractors and subcontractors, such as for mechanical materials, which are not included in our packages. This invaluable tool includes a Materials List. A Material Cost Report cannot be ordered before blueprints are ordered. Call for details. In addition, ask about our Home Planners Estimating Package.

If you are interested in a plan that is not indicated as Quote One®, please call and ask our sales reps. They will be happy to verify the status for you. To order these invaluable reports, use the order form.

CONSTRUCTION INFORMATION

IF YOU WANT TO KNOW MORE ABOUT TECHNIQUES—
and deal more confidently with subcontractors —
we offer these useful sheets. Each set is an excellent
tool that will add to your understanding of these
technical subjects. These helpful details provide
general construction information and
are not specific to any single plan.

PLUMBING

The Blueprint Package includes locations for all the plumbing fix-
tures, including sinks, lavatories, tubs, showers, toilets, laundry
trays and water heaters. However, if you want to know more about
the complete plumbing system, these Plumbing Details will prove
very useful. Prepared to meet requirements of the National
Plumbing Code, these fact-filled sheets give general information
on pipe schedules, fittings, sump-pump details, water-softener
hookups, septic system details and much more. Sheets also include
a glossary of terms.

ELECTRICAL

The locations for every electrical switch, plug and outlet are
shown in your Blueprint Package. However, these Electrical
Details go further to take the mystery out of household electrical
systems. Prepared to meet requirements of the National
Electrical Code, these comprehensive drawings come packed
with helpful information, including wire sizing, switch-installa-
tion schematics, cable-routing details, appliance wattage, door-
bell hook-ups, typical service panel circuitry and much more. A
glossary of terms is also included.

CONSTRUCTION

The Blueprint Package contains information an experienced
builder needs to construct a particular house. However, it doesn't
show all the ways that houses can be built, nor does it explain
alternate construction methods. To help you understand how your
house will be built—and offer additional techniques—this set of
Construction Details depicts the materials and methods used to
build foundations, fireplaces, walls, floors and roofs. Where appropriate, the drawings show acceptable alternatives.

MECHANICAL

These Mechanical Details contain fundamental principles and
useful data that will help you make informed decisions and com-
municate with subcontractors about heating and cooling systems.
Drawings contain instructions and samples that allow you to
make simple load calculations, and preliminary sizing and costing
analysis. Covered are the most commonly used systems from heat
pumps to solar fuel systems. The package is filled with illustra-
tions and diagrams to help you visualize components and how
they relate to one another.

THE HANDS-ON HOME FURNITURE PLANNER

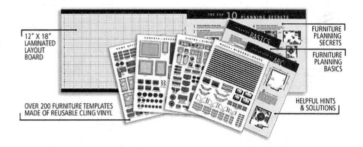

Effectively plan the space in your home using The **Hands-On
Home Furniture Planner**. It's fun and easy—no more moving
heavy pieces of furniture to see how the room will go together. And
you can try different layouts, moving furniture at a whim.

The kit includes reusable peel and stick furniture templates that fit
onto a 12" x 18" laminated layout board—space enough to layout
every room in your home.

Also included in the package are a number of helpful planning
tools. You'll receive:

- ✓ Helpful hints and solutions for
  difficult situations.
- ✓ Furniture planning basics to get
  you started.
- ✓ Furniture planning secrets that
  let you in on some of the tricks
  of professional designers.

The **Hands-On Home Furniture Planner** is the one tool that no
new homeowner or home remodeler should be without. It's also a
perfect housewarming gift!

To Order, Call Toll Free
1-800-521-6797

After you've looked over our Blueprint Package and Important
Extras on these pages, call for current pricing and availability prior
to mailing the order form. We're ready and eager to serve you.
After you have received your order, call for customer service toll
free 1-888-690-1116.

THE FINISHING TOUCHES...

THE DECK BLUEPRINT PACKAGE

Many of the homes in this book can be enhanced with a professionally designed Home Planners Deck Plan. Those homes marked with a **D** have a complementary Deck Plan, sold separately, which includes a Deck Plan Frontal Sheet, Deck Framing and Floor Plans, Deck Elevations and a Deck Materials List. A Standard Deck Details Package, also available, provides all the how-to information necessary for building *any* deck. Our Complete Deck Building Package contains one set of Custom Deck Plans of your choice, plus one set of Standard Deck Building Details, all for one low price. Our plans and details are carefully prepared in an easy-to-understand format that will guide you through every stage of your deck-building project. This page shows a sample Deck layout to match your favorite house. See Blueprint Price Schedule for ordering information.

THE LANDSCAPE BLUEPRINT PACKAGE

For the homes marked with an **L** in this book, Home Planners has created a front-yard Landscape Plan that is complementary in design to the house plan. These comprehensive blueprint packages include a Frontal Sheet, Plan View, Regionalized Plant & Materials List, a sheet on Planting and Maintaining Your Landscape, Zone Maps and Plant Size and Description Guide. These plans will help you achieve professional results, adding value and enjoyment to your property for years to come. Each set of blueprints is a full 18" x 24" in size with clear, complete instructions and easy-to-read type. A sample Landscape Plan is shown below. See Blueprint Price Schedule for ordering information.

CONTEMPORARY LEISURE DECK
Deck ODA021

CAPE COD COTTAGE
Landscape OLA003

REGIONAL ORDER MAP

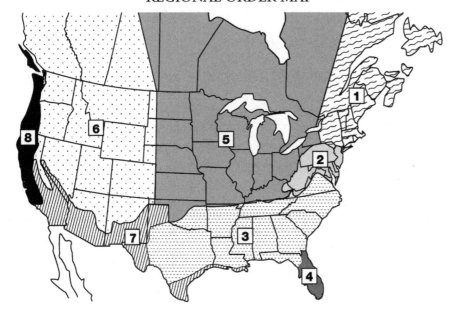

Most Landscape Plans are available with a Plant & Materials List adapted by horticultural experts to 8 different regions of the country. Please specify the Geographic Region when ordering your plan. See Blueprint Price Schedule for ordering information and regional availability.

Region	1	Northeast
Region	2	Mid-Atlantic
Region	3	Deep South
Region	4	Florida & Gulf Coast
Region	5	Midwest
Region	6	Rocky Mountains
Region	7	Southern California & Desert Southwest
Region	8	Northern California & Pacific Northwest

BLUEPRINT PRICE SCHEDULE

Prices guaranteed through December 31, 2002

TIERS	1-SET STUDY PACKAGE	4-SET BUILDING PACKAGE	8-SET BUILDING PACKAGE	1-SET REPRODUCIBLE*
P1	$20	$50	$90	$140
P2	$40	$70	$110	$160
P3	$70	$100	$140	$190
P4	$100	$130	$170	$220
P5	$140	$170	$210	$270
P6	$180	$210	$250	$310
A1	$440	$480	$520	$660
A2	$480	$520	$560	$720
A3	$520	$560	$600	$780
A4	$565	$605	$645	$850
C1	$610	$655	$700	$915
C2	$655	$700	$745	$980
C3	$700	$745	$790	$1050
C4	$750	$795	$840	$1125
L1	$825	$875	$925	$1240
L2	$900	$950	$1000	$1350
L3	$1000	$1050	$1100	$1500
L4	$1100	$1150	$1200	$1650

* Requires a fax number

OPTIONS FOR PLANS IN TIERS A1–L4

Additional Identical Blueprints
in same order for "A1–L4" price plans...$50 per set
Reverse Blueprints (mirror image)
with 4- or 8-set order for "A1–L4" plans.......................................$50 fee per order
Specification Outlines...$10 each
Materials Lists for "A1–C3" plans ....$60 each
Materials Lists for "C4–L4" plans..$70 each

OPTIONS FOR PLANS IN TIERS P1–P6

Additional Identical Blueprints
in same order for "P1–P6" price plans..$10 per set
Reverse Blueprints (mirror image) for "P1–P6" price plans ....$10 fee per order
1 Set of Deck Construction Details ....$14.95 each
Deck Construction Package ....add $10 to Building Package price
(includes 1 set of "P1–P6" plans, plus 1 set Standard Deck Construction Details)

IMPORTANT NOTES

• The 1-set study package is marked "not for construction."
• Prices for 4- or 8-set Building Packages honored only at time of original order.
• Some foundations carry a $225 surcharge.
• Right-reading reverse blueprints, if available, will incur a $165 surcharge.
• Additional identical blueprints may be purchased within 60 days of original order.

TO USE THE INDEX, refer to the design number listed in numerical order (a helpful page reference is also given). Note the price tier and refer to the Blueprint Price Schedule above for the cost of one, four or eight sets of blueprints or the cost of a reproducible drawing. Additional prices are shown for identical and reverse blueprint sets, as well as a very useful Materials List for some of the plans. Also note in the Plan Index those plans that have Deck Plans or Landscape Plans. Refer to the schedules above for prices of these plans. The letter "Y" identifies plans that are part of our Quote One® estimating service and those that offer Materials Lists.

TO ORDER, Call toll free 1-800-521-6797 for current pricing and availability prior to mailing the order form. FAX: 1-800-224-6699 or 520-544-3086.

PLAN INDEX

DESIGN	PRICE	PAGE	MATERIALS LIST	QUOTE ONE*	DECK	DECK PRICE	LANDSCAPE	LANDSCAPE PRICE	REGIONS
HPT750001	L1	5							
HPT750002	C3	6		Y					
HPT750003	C4	7							
HPT750004	C1	8	Y						
HPT750005	C4	9	Y	Y					
HPT750006	C3	10							
HPT750007	C3	11							
HPT750008	L1	12	Y	Y					
HPT750009	C4	13	Y	Y					
HPT750010	L2	14							
HPT750011	L1	15	Y	Y	ODA008	P3	OLA016	P4	1234568
HPT750012	C1	16							
HPT750013	A4	17	Y						
HPT750014	C3	18							
HPT750015	C2	19	Y						
HPT750016	C4	20	Y	Y					
HPT750017	C2	21	Y						
HPT750018	C1	22	Y	Y					
HPT750019	C1	23							
HPT750020	A3	24	Y						
HPT750021	A4	25							
HPT750022	C1	26	Y						
HPT750023	A4	27	Y						
HPT750024	A4	28							
HPT750025	A3	29	Y	Y			OLA001	P3	123568
HPT750026	A3	30							
HPT750027	A4	31							
HPT750028	C4	32					OLA004	P3	123568
HPT750029	A4	33	Y						
HPT750030	A3	34							
HPT750031	C4	35	Y	Y			OLA010	P3	1234568
HPT750032	C3	36							
HPT750033	C1	37	Y						
HPT750034	C1	38							
HPT750035	C1	39							
HPT750036	C4	40							
HPT750037	C3	41							
HPT750038	A4	42							
HPT750039	A4	43							
HPT750040	C2	44							
HPT750041	C4	45							
HPT750042	C1	46							
HPT750043	C1	47	Y						
HPT750044	C4	48							
HPT750045	C2	49							
HPT750046	C3	50	Y						
HPT750047	C2	51	Y	Y					
HPT750048	L2	52	Y						
HPT750049	L1	53							
HPT750050	L2	54	Y	Y	ODA012	P3	OLA036	P4	123568
HPT750051	C2	55	Y						
HPT750052	L2	56	Y	Y					
HPT750053	L1	57	Y	Y	ODA011	P2	OLA003	P3	123568
HPT750054	C2	58	Y	Y	ODA007	P3	OLA018	P3	12345678
HPT750055	C1	59	Y		ODA014	P2			
HPT750056	C1	60							
HPT750057	C3	61							
HPT750058	C4	62		Y			OLA015	P4	123568
HPT750059	L2	63		Y	ODA016	P2	OLA015	P4	123568
HPT750060	C2	64	Y						
HPT750061	C3	65	Y	Y	ODA016	P2			

PLAN INDEX

DESIGN	PRICE	PAGE	MATERIALS LIST	QUOTE ONE®	DECK	DECK PRICE	LANDSCAPE	LANDSCAPE PRICE	REGIONS
HPT750062	L2	66							
HPT750063	L1	67	Y						
HPT750064	C2	68	Y						
HPT750065	L1	69							
HPT750066	C3	70	Y	Y					
HPT750067	L2	71							
HPT750068	C3	72							
HPT750069	L1	73							
HPT750070	L2	74							
HPT750071	L1	75							
HPT750072	C2	76							
HPT750073	C2	77							
HPT750074	C4	78							
HPT750075	C3	79							
HPT750076	C4	80	Y						
HPT750077	A4	81							
HPT750078	C3	82							
HPT750079	L1	83	Y						
HPT750080	C1	84							
HPT750081	A4	85							
HPT750082	C1	86							
HPT750083	C1	87							
HPT750084	C2	88							
HPT750085	C1	89							
HPT750086	C1	90							
HPT750087	C2	91							
HPT750088	C4	92							
HPT750089	C4	93							
HPT750090	C2	94							
HPT750091	C1	95							
HPT750092	C2	96							
HPT750093	C1	97							
HPT750094	L1	98							
HPT750095	C3	99							
HPT750096	C2	100	Y						
HPT750097	C3	101	Y						
HPT750098	L2	102	Y						
HPT750099	C1	103							
HPT750100	C2	104					OLA017	P3	123568
HPT750101	C1	105					OLA014	P4	12345678
HPT750102	A3	106							
HPT750103	C3	107	Y						
HPT750104	C1	108							
HPT750105	C3	109							
HPT750106	L1	110	Y				OLA018	P3	12345678
HPT750107	A3	111							
HPT750108	A3	112							
HPT750109	A3	113							
HPT750110	C1	114							
HPT750111	C1	115							
HPT750112	C1	116							
HPT750113	C1	117							
HPT750114	C2	118	Y						
HPT750115	C2	119	Y						
HPT750116	A4	120	Y						
HPT750117	A4	121							
HPT750118	C1	122	Y						
HPT750119	A4	123	Y						
HPT750120	C1	124	Y	Y					
HPT750121	C1	125	Y						
HPT750122	A4	126	Y	Y					
HPT750123	C1	127	Y	Y					
HPT750124	A3	128							
HPT750125	A4	129							
HPT750126	C1	130	Y						
HPT750127	C1	131	Y	Y					
HPT750128	C2	132							
HPT750129	A3	133							
HPT750130	C2	134	Y						
HPT750131	A3	135							
HPT750132	C1	136	Y						
HPT750133	L2	137	Y	Y			OLA005	P3	123568
HPT750134	C4	138							
HPT750135	C1	139	Y						
HPT750136	A3	140	Y	Y					
HPT750137	A4	141	Y	Y					
HPT750138	A3	142	Y						
HPT750139	A4	143	Y						
HPT750140	A3	144	Y						
HPT750141	A4	145	Y	Y					
HPT750142	A3	146							
HPT750143	A4	147							
HPT750144	A3	148	Y						
HPT750145	A2	149	Y						
HPT750146	A3	150							
HPT750147	A3	151	Y						
HPT750148	A3	152	Y						
HPT750149	A3	153	Y						
HPT750150	A3	154							
HPT750151	A2	155							
HPT750152	A3	156	Y						
HPT750153	A4	157	Y						
HPT750154	A3	158							
HPT750155	A4	159							
HPT750156	C1	160	Y						
HPT750157	C3	161	Y						
HPT750158	C1	162	Y						
HPT750159	C1	163	Y						
HPT750160	A3	164							
HPT750161	C2	165	Y						
HPT750162	C2	166	Y						
HPT750163	A4	167	Y						
HPT750164	C2	168	Y						
HPT750165	A4	169	Y						
HPT750166	C2	170	Y						
HPT750167	C2	171	Y						
HPT750168	C3	172							
HPT750169	C1	173	Y						
HPT750170	A4	174	Y						
HPT750171	C1	175							
HPT750172	C1	176							
HPT750173	C1	177	Y						
HPT750174	C1	178							
HPT750175	A2	179							
HPT750176	C4	180	Y	Y	ODA012	P3	OLA016	P4	1234568
HPT750177	A4	181							
HPT750178	A4	182							
HPT750179	A4	183					OLA024	P4	123568
HPT750180	C4	184							
HPT750181	L2	185							
HPT750182	A4	186					OLA024	P4	123568
HPT750183	C4	187							

BEFORE FILLING OUT

THE ORDER FORM,

PLEASE CALL US ON

OUR TOLL-FREE

BLUEPRINT HOTLINE

1-800-521-6797.

YOU MAY WANT TO

LEARN MORE ABOUT

OUR SERVICES AND

PRODUCTS. HERE'S

SOME INFORMATION

YOU WILL FIND HELPFUL.

OUR EXCHANGE POLICY

With the exception of reproducible plan orders, we will exchange your entire first order for an equal or greater number of blueprints within our plan collection within 90 days of the original order. The entire content of your original order must be returned before an exchange will be processed. Please call our customer service department for your return authorization number and shipping instructions. If the returned blueprints look used, redlined or copied, we will not honor your exchange. Fees for exchanging your blueprints are as follows: 20% of the amount of the original order...plus the difference in cost if exchanging for a design in a higher price bracket or less the difference in cost if exchanging for a design in a lower price bracket. **(Reproducible blueprints are not exchangeable or refundable.)** Please call for current postage and handling prices. Shipping and handling charges are not refundable.

ABOUT REPRODUCIBLES

When purchasing a reproducible you may be required to furnish a fax number. The designer will fax documents that you must sign and return to them before shipping will take place.

ABOUT REVERSE BLUEPRINTS

Although lettering and dimensions will appear backward, reverses will be a useful aid if you decide to flop the plan. See Price Schedule and Plans Index for pricing.

REVISING, MODIFYING AND CUSTOMIZING PLANS

Like many homeowners who buy these plans, you and your builder, architect or engineer may want to make changes to them. We recommend purchase of a reproducible plan for any changes made by your builder, licensed architect or engineer. As set forth below, we cannot assume any responsibility for blueprints which have been changed, whether by you, your builder or by professionals selected by you or referred to you by us, because such individuals are outside our supervision and control.

ARCHITECTURAL AND ENGINEERING SEALS

Some cities and states are now requiring that a licensed architect or engineer review and "seal" a blueprint, or officially approve it, prior to construction due to concerns over energy costs, safety and other factors. Prior to application for a building permit or the start of actual construction, we strongly advise that you consult your local building official who can tell you if such a review is required.

ABOUT THE DESIGNS

The architects and designers whose work appears in this publication are among America's leading residential designers. Each plan was designed to meet the requirements of a nationally recognized model building code in effect at the time and place the plan was drawn. Because national building codes change from time to time, plans may not comply with any such code at the time they are sold to a customer. In addition, building officials may not accept these plans as final construction documents of record as the plans may need to be modified and additional drawings and details added to suit local conditions and requirements. We strongly advise that purchasers consult a licensed architect or engineer, and their local building official, before starting any construction related to these plans.

LOCAL BUILDING CODES AND ZONING REQUIREMENTS

At the time of creation, our plans are drawn to specifications published by the Building Officials and Code Administrators (BOCA) International, Inc.; the Southern Building Code Congress (SBCCI) International, Inc.; the International Conference of Building Officials (ICBO); or the Council of American Building Officials (CABO). Our plans are designed to meet or exceed national building standards. Because of the great differences in geography and climate throughout the United States and Canada, each state, county and municipality has its own building codes, zone requirements, ordinances and building regulations. Your plan may need to be modified to comply with local requirements regarding snow loads, energy codes, soil and seismic conditions and a wide range of other matters. In addition, you may need to obtain permits or inspections from local governments before and in the course of construction. Prior to using blueprints ordered from us, we strongly advise that you consult a licensed architect or engineer—and speak with your local building official—before applying for any permit or beginning construction. We authorize the use of our blueprints on the express condition that you strictly comply with all local building codes, zoning requirements and other applicable laws, regulations, ordinances and requirements. Notice: Plans for homes to be built in Nevada must be re-drawn by a Nevada-registered professional. Consult your building official for more information on this subject.

 TOLL FREE
1-800-521-6797

REGULAR OFFICE HOURS:
8:00 a.m.-9:00 p.m. EST, Monday-Friday

If we receive your order by 3:00 p.m. EST, Monday-Friday, we'll process it and ship within **two business days**. When ordering by phone, please have your credit card or check information ready. We'll also ask you for the Order Form Key Number at the bottom of the order form.

By FAX: Copy the Order Form on the next page and send it on our FAX line: 1-800-224-6699 or 520-544-3086.

Canadian Customers
Order Toll Free 1-877-223-6389

DISCLAIMER

The designers we work with have put substantial care and effort into the creation of their blueprints. However, because they cannot provide on-site consultation, supervision and control over actual construction, and because of the great variance in local building requirements, building practices and soil, seismic, weather and other conditions, WE CANNOT MAKE ANY WARRANTY, EXPRESS OR IMPLIED, WITH RESPECT TO THE CONTENT OR USE OF THE BLUEPRINTS, INCLUDING BUT NOT LIMITED TO ANY WARRANTY OF MERCHANTABILITY OR OF FITNESS FOR A PARTICULAR PURPOSE. **ITEMS, PRICES, TERMS AND CONDITIONS ARE SUBJECT TO CHANGE WITHOUT NOTICE. REPRODUCIBLE PLAN ORDERS MAY REQUIRE A CUSTOMER'S SIGNED RELEASE BEFORE SHIPPING.**

TERMS AND CONDITIONS

These designs are protected under the terms of United States Copyright Law and may not be copied or reproduced in any way, by any means, unless you have purchased Reproducibles which clearly indicate your right to copy or reproduce. We authorize the use of your chosen design as an aid in the construction of one single family home only. You may not use this design to build a second or multiple dwellings without purchasing another blueprint or blueprints or paying additional design fees.

HOW MANY BLUEPRINTS DO YOU NEED?

Although a standard building package may satisfy many states, cities and counties, some plans may require certain changes. For your convenience, we have developed a Reproducible plan which allows a local professional to modify and make up to 10 copies of your revised plan. As our plans are all copyright protected, with your purchase of the Reproducible, we will supply you with a Copyright release letter. The number of copies you may need: 1 for owner; 3 for builder; 2 for local building department and 1-3 sets for your mortgage lender.

ORDER TOLL FREE!

For information about any of our services or to order call
1-800-521-6797

Browse our website:
www.eplans.com

BLUEPRINTS ARE NOT REFUNDABLE EXCHANGES ONLY

For Customer Service, call toll free
1-888-690-1116.

HOME PLANNERS, LLC wholly owned by Hanley-Wood, LLC
3275 WEST INA ROAD, SUITE 110 • TUCSON, ARIZONA • 85741

THE BASIC BLUEPRINT PACKAGE

Rush me the following (please refer to the Plans Index and Price Schedule in this section):
___Set(s) of reproducibles*, plan number(s) _____ $_____
   indicate foundation type _____ surcharge (if applicable): $_____
___Set(s) of blueprints, plan number(s) _____
   indicate foundation type _____ surcharge (if applicable): $_____
___Additional identical blueprints (standard or reverse) in same order @ $50 per set $_____
___Reverse blueprints @ $50 fee per order. Right-reading reverse @ $165 surcharge $_____

IMPORTANT EXTRAS

Rush me the following:
___Materials List: $60 (Must be purchased with Blueprint set.) Add $10 for Schedule C4–L4 plans $_____
___**Quote One®** Summary Cost Report @ $29.95 for one, $14.95 for each additional,
   for plans _____ $_____
   Building location: City _____ Zip Code _____
___**Quote One®** Material Cost Report @ $120 Schedules P1–C3; $130 Schedules C4–L4,
   for plan_____(Must be purchased with Blueprints set.) $_____
   Building location: City _____ Zip Code _____
___Specification Outlines @ $10 each $_____
___Detail Sets @ $14.95 each; any two $22.95; any three $29.95; all four for $39.95 (save $19.85) $_____
___❏ Plumbing ❏ Electrical ❏ Construction ❏ Mechanical
___Home Furniture Planner @ $15.95 each $_____

DECK BLUEPRINTS

(Please refer to the Plans Index and Price Schedule in this section)
___Set(s) of Deck Plan _____. $_____
___Additional identical blueprints in same order @ $10 per set. $_____
___Reverse blueprints @ $10 fee per order. $_____
___Set of Standard Deck Details @ $14.95 per set. $_____
___Set of Complete Deck Construction Package (Best Buy!) Add $10 to Building Package.
   Includes Custom Deck Plan _____ Plus Standard Deck Details

LANDSCAPE BLUEPRINTS

(Please refer to the Plans Index and Price Schedule in this section.)
___Set(s) of Landscape Plan _____ $_____
___Additional identical blueprints in same order @ $10 per set $_____
___Reverse blueprints @ $10 fee per order $_____
Please indicate appropriate region of the country for Plant & Material List. Region _____

POSTAGE AND HANDLING *SIGNATURE IS REQUIRED FOR ALL DELIVERIES.*	1–3 sets	4+ sets
DELIVERY No CODs (Requires street address—No P.O. Boxes) •Regular Service (Allow 7–10 business days delivery) •Priority (Allow 4–5 business days delivery) •Express (Allow 3 business days delivery)	 ❏ $20.00 ❏ $25.00 ❏ $35.00	 ❏ $25.00 ❏ $35.00 ❏ $45.00
OVERSEAS DELIVERY	fax, phone or mail for quote	

Note: All delivery times are from date Blueprint Package is shipped.

POSTAGE (From box above) $_____
SUBTOTAL $_____
SALES TAX (AZ & MI residents, please add appropriate state and local sales tax.) $_____
TOTAL (Subtotal and tax) $_____

YOUR ADDRESS (please print legibly)

Name _____
Street _____
City _____State_____Zip _____
Daytime telephone number (required) (_____) _____
* Fax number (required for reproducible orders) _____
TeleCheck® Checks By Phone℠ available

FOR CREDIT CARD ORDERS ONLY

Credit card number _____ Exp. Date: (M/Y) _____
Check one ❏ Visa ❏ MasterCard ❏ Discover Card ❏ American Express

Order Form Key
HPT75

Signature (required) _____
Please check appropriate box: ❏ Licensed Builder-Contractor ❏ Homeowner

ORDER TOLL FREE!
1-800-521-6797

BY FAX: Copy the order form above and send it on our FAXLINE: 1-800-224-6699 OR 520-544-3086

HELPFUL BOOKS FROM HOME PLANNERS

1 BIGGEST & BEST

1001 of our best-selling plans in one volume. 1,074 to 7,275 square feet. 704 pgs $12.95 1K1

2 ONE-STORY

450 designs for all lifestyles. 800 to 4,900 square feet. 384 pgs $9.95 OS

3 MORE ONE-STORY

475 superb one-level plans from 800 to 5,000 square feet. 448 pgs $9.95 MO2

4 TWO-STORY

443 designs for one-and-a-half and two stories. 1,500 to 6,000 square feet. 448 pgs $9.95 TS

5 VACATION

430 designs for recreation, retirement and leisure. 448 pgs $9.95 VS3

6 HILLSIDE

208 designs for split-levels, bi-levels, multi-levels and walkouts. 224 pgs $9.95 HH

7 FARMHOUSE

300 Fresh Designs from Classic to Modern. 320 pgs. $10.95 FCP

8 COUNTRY HOUSES

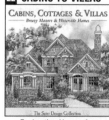

208 unique home plans that combine traditional style and modern livability. 224 pgs $9.95 CN

9 BUDGET-SMART

200 efficient plans from 7 top designers, that you can really afford to build! 224 pgs $8.95 BS

10 BARRIER-FREE

Over 1,700 products and 51 plans for accessible living. 128 pgs $15.95 UH

11 ENCYCLOPEDIA

500 exceptional plans for all styles and budgets—the best book of its kind! 528 pgs $9.95 ENC

12 ENCYCLOPEDIA II

500 completely new plans. Spacious and stylish designs for every budget and taste. 352 pgs $9.95 E2

13 AFFORDABLE

300 Modest plans for savvy homebuyers.256 pgs. $9.95 AH2

14 VICTORIAN

210 striking Victorian and Farmhouse designs from today's top designers. 224 pgs $15.95 VDH2

15 ESTATE

Dream big! Eighteen designers showcase their biggest and best plans. 224 pgs $16.95 EDH3

16 LUXURY

170 lavish designs, over 50% brand-new plans added to a most elegant collection. 192 pgs $12.95 LD3

17 EUROPEAN STYLES

200 homes with a unique flair of the Old World. 224 pgs $15.95 EURO

18 COUNTRY CLASSICS

Donald Gardner's 101 best Country and Traditional home plans. 192 pgs $17.95 DAG

19 COUNTRY

85 Charming Designs from American Home Gallery. 160 pgs. $17.95 CTY

20 TRADITIONAL

85 timeless designs from the Design Traditions Library. 160 pgs $17.95 TRA

21 COTTAGES

245 Delightful retreats from 825 to 3,500 square feet. 256 pgs. $10.95 COOL

22 CABINS TO VILLAS

Enchanting Homes for Mountain Sea or Sun, from the Sater collection. 144 pgs $19.95 CCV

23 CONTEMPORARY

The most complete and imaginative collection of contemporary designs available anywhere. 256 pgs $10.95 CM2

24 FRENCH COUNTRY

Live every day in the French countryside using these plans, landscapes and interiors. 192 pgs $14.95 PN

25 SOUTHERN

207 homes rich in Southern styling and comfort. 240 pgs $8.95 SH

26 SOUTHWESTERN

138 designs that capture the spirit of the Southwest. 144 pgs $10.95 SW

27 SHINGLE-STYLE

155 Home plans from Classic Colonials to Breezy Bungalows. 192 pgs. $12.95 SNG

28 NEIGHBORHOOD

170 designs with the feel of main street America. 192 pgs $12.95 TND

29 CRAFTSMAN

170 Home plans in the Craftsman and Bungalow style. 192 pgs $12.95 CC

30 GRAND VISTAS

200 Homes with a View. 224 pgs. $10.95 GV

Home Planners wants your building experience to be as pleasant and trouble-free as possible. That's why we've expanded our library of do-it-yourself titles to help you along.

31 DUPLEX & TOWNHOMES

115 Duplex, Multiplex & Townhome Designs. 128 pgs. $17.95 MFH

32 WATERFRONT

200 designs perfect for your waterside wonderland. 208 pgs $10.95 WF

33 NATURAL LIGHT

223 Sunny home plans for all regions. 240 pgs. $8.95 NA

34 NOSTALGIA

100 Time-Honored designs updated with today's features. 224 pgs. $14.95 NOS

35 STREET OF DREAMS

Over 300 photos showcase 54 prestigious homes. 256 pgs $19.95 SOD

36 NARROW-LOT

250 Designs for houses 17' to 50' wide. 256 pgs. $9.95 NL2

37 SMALL HOUSES

Innovative plans for sensible lifestyles. 224 pgs. $8.95 SM2

38 GARDENS & MORE

225 gardens, landscapes, decks and more to enhance every home. 320 pgs. $19.95 GLP

39 EASY-CARE

41 special landscapes designed for beauty and low maintenance. 160 pgs $14.95 ECL

40 BACKYARDS

40 designs focused solely on creating your own specially themed backyard oasis. 160 pgs $14.95 BYL

41 BEDS & BORDERS
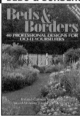
40 Professional designs for do-it-yourselfers 160 pgs. $14.95 BB

42 BUYER'S GUIDE

A comprehensive look at 2700 products for all aspects of landscaping & gardening. 128 pgs $19.95 LPBG

LANDSCAPE DESIGNS

43 OUTDOOR
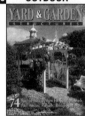
74 easy-to-build designs, lets you create and build your own backyard oasis. 128 pgs $9.95 YG2

44 GARAGES
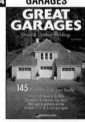
145 exciting projects from 64 to 1,900 square feet. 160 pgs. $9.95 GG2

45 DECKS

A brand new collection of 120 beautiful and practical decks. 144 pgs. $9.95 DP2

46 HOME BUILDING

Everything you need to know to work with contractors and subcontractors. 212 pgs $14.95 HBP

47 RURAL BUILDING

Everything you need to know to build your home in the country. 232 pgs. $14.95 BYC

48 VACATION HOMES

Your complete guide to building your vacation home. 224 pgs. $14.95 BYV

PROJECT GUIDES

Book Order Form

To order your books, just check the box of the book numbered below and complete the coupon. We will process your order and ship it from our office within two business days. Send coupon and check (in U.S. funds).

YES! Please send me the books I've indicated:

❑ 1:1K1 ....$12.95	❑ 17:EURO ...$15.95	❑ 33:NA $8.95
❑ 2:OS $9.95	❑ 18:DAG $17.95	❑ 34:NOS $14.95
❑ 3:MO2 ....$9.95	❑ 19:CTY $17.95	❑ 35:SOD $19.95
❑ 4:TS $9.95	❑ 20:TRA $17.95	❑ 36:NL2 ....$9.95
❑ 5:VS3 ....$9.95	❑ 21:COOL ...$10.95	❑ 37:SM2 ......$8.95
❑ 6:HH............$9.95	❑ 22:CCV $19.95	❑ 38:GLP $19.95
❑ 7:FCP $10.95	❑ 23:CM2 .....$10.95	❑ 39:ECL $14.95
❑ 8:CN............$9.95	❑ 24:PN $14.95	❑ 40:BYL $14.95
❑ 9:BS $8.95	❑ 25:SH $8.95	❑ 41:BB $14.95
❑ 10:UH $15.95	❑ 26:SW $10.95	❑ 42:LPBG ...$19.95
❑ 11:ENC $9.95	❑ 27:SNG $12.95	❑ 43:YG2 ....$9.95
❑ 12:E2 ....$9.95	❑ 28:TND $12.95	❑ 44:GG2 ......$9.95
❑ 13:AH2 ....$9.95	❑ 29:CC $12.95	❑ 45:DP2 ....$9.95
❑ 14:VDH2 ...$15.95	❑ 30:GV $10.95	❑ 46:HBP $14.95
❑ 15:EDH3 ...$16.95	❑ 31:MFH.....$17.95	❑ 47:BYC $14.95
❑ 16:LD3 .....$12.95	❑ 32:WF $10.95	❑ 48:BYV $14.95

Books Subtotal $_____
ADD Postage and Handling (allow 4–6 weeks for delivery) $ 4.00
Sales Tax: (AZ & MI residents, add state and local sales tax.) $_____
YOUR TOTAL (Subtotal, Postage/Handling, Tax) $_____

YOUR ADDRESS (PLEASE PRINT)

Name _____
Street _____
City _____ State _____ Zip _____
Phone (_____) _____—_____

YOUR PAYMENT

TeleCheck® Checks By Phone℠ available
Check one: ❑ Check ❑ Visa ❑ MasterCard ❑ Discover ❑ American Express
Required credit card information:

Credit Card Number _____
Expiration Date (Month/Year)_____/_____
Signature Required _____

Home Planners, LLC
3275 W. Ina Road, Suite 110, Dept. BK, Tucson, AZ 85741

HPT75

Canadian Customers Order Toll Free 1-877-223-6389

FOR FASTER SERVICE ORDER ONLINE AT
www.hwspecials.com

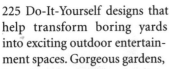